T0357462

ROMANCES
&
Practicalities

ALSO BY LINDSAY JILL ROTH

What Pretty Girls Are Made Of: A Novel

ROMANCES

& Practicalities

A Love Story
(*Maybe Yours!*)
in 250
Questions

**LINDSAY
JILL ROTH**

wm

WILLIAM MORROW

An Imprint of HarperCollins*Publishers*

Some names and identifying details have been changed to protect the privacy of the individuals involved.

ROMANCES & PRACTICALITIES. Copyright © 2025 by Lindsay Jill Roth. All rights reserved. Printed in the United States of America. No part of this book may be used or reproduced in any manner whatsoever without written permission except in the case of brief quotations embodied in critical articles and reviews. For information, address HarperCollins Publishers, 195 Broadway, New York, NY 10007.

HarperCollins books may be purchased for educational, business, or sales promotional use. For information, please email the Special Markets Department at SPsales@harpercollins.com.

FIRST EDITION

Designed by Nancy Singer
Heart icon © Kebon doodle/stock.adobe.com
Winking-face emoji © Liena10/Shutterstock

Library of Congress Cataloging-in-Publication Data has been applied for.

ISBN 978-0-06-333979-8

24 25 26 27 28 LBC 5 4 3 2 1

To the Brit:
I love you.
A lot.

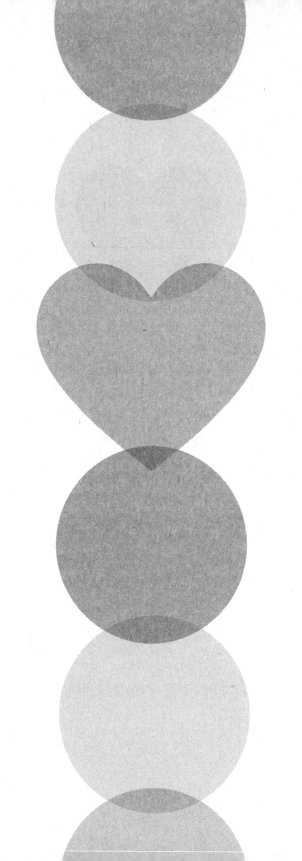

Contents

Author's Note

To write this book, I conducted interviews with more than one hundred people, including a wide range of public figures—from medical doctors and psychologists to authors, podcasters, entertainers, and financial and business experts—as well as individuals and couples from all walks of life, many of whom have utilized and/or tested the Romances & Practicalities system. Featuring a diverse array of inputs and experiences in terms of race, religion, sexuality, gender, and geographic location was important to my research and to the telling of this story.

In order to protect the privacy of the brave and generous souls who shared with me the most intimate details of their lives and relationships, I have changed some names and identifying details. In a few instances, I have attributed the stories of a single individual or couple to multiple people in order to further preserve their anonymity.

In writing about relationships generally, I most often use the neutral term *partner*, though sometimes—and certainly where specifically appropriate—opt for *husband, wife, boyfriend,* or *girlfriend*. I also sometimes use the term *marriage* interchangeably with *relationship* or *partnership*. The landscape of dating and mating has changed considerably in the last few decades; more and more people are pursuing (or are at least interested in) less traditional forms of romantic entanglement— from ethical non-monogamy to polyamory to long-term cohabitation.

The more people I spoke with, however, the more I came to believe that our wants, needs, hopes, dreams, insecurities, patterns and practices, and attempts and struggles to connect—in the context of safe, non-violent romantic pairings—are universal. My hope is that *Romances & Practicalities* is relevant for anyone seeking a long-term connection built on honesty and intimacy, whatever that might look like to them.

ROMANCES
&
Practicalities

Introduction

Thirty minutes before our second date, the Brit was called back to London.

Unlike our first magical evening together, this time his confusion about how to proceed was palpable. His lips hovered close to mine but hesitated at the point of contact. The *whens* about our future had shifted to *ifs*.

I'd been corresponding with the brown-eyed British financier for two months. What started as a setup, an innocuous email from mutual friends—*We think you two should meet!*—had quickly given way to a flurry of text messages. Like, full-on conversations, about life in the city, our jobs, our families, and when we might meet, only to discover that we had diametrically opposed work schedules. When he was in New York, I was in Los Angeles for business and visiting a friend in Toronto; when I was back in town, he was in London. Still, things soon progressed to the point where I didn't want to swipe anymore, as no chat could possibly measure up to the one I was already having—and I hadn't even heard his accent yet. When our first date finally rolled around, I realized I wanted to kiss him even before the appetizers arrived. He'd requested a second date before the evening ended. The heat between us was electric enough to make even the most jaded of internet singles wonder if there might be such a thing as "meant to be."

So when he went back to London for good, we doubled down.

I should pause here to tell you that we weren't forced apart by a global pandemic, just regular old distance: three thousand miles of ocean and five time zones. We were in a romantic lockdown. For the foreseeable future, seeing and hearing each other would have to compensate for the lack of our other three senses.

Yet somehow, there's an abundance of creative things to do when separated from those you love—or hope to love. And not just the titillating stuff, but more thoughtful ways of connecting at a distance. We started by sending each other snail-mail packages with handwritten notes to read before bed.

Then we went running together—me in Central Park, him in Hyde Park. Who needed podcasts or playlists when he was there, in my pocket and in my ears, encouraging me to push through the burn? I'd stop at the top of the reservoir to show him the view, and he'd always find some new corner of Kensington to share with me.

Years before this, my best friend and I had written notes to each other in the margins of the books we read, sharing our thoughts on the copy so we'd know what each of us had been thinking at that precise moment. As a working actress, she was often on location, and we only ever lived in the same city for a brief moment. The long-distance phase of our friendship began back in the days when text messages were ten cents a pop. But through her handwritten notes and cards, I learned how easy it was to make someone feel loved from afar. We never had a chance to miss each other.

So the Brit and I formed our own book club, reading the same titles simultaneously, discussing them chapter by chapter, spending as much time together—separately—as we could.

Through the magic of FaceTime, I watched him slather his crustless sandwiches with butter and cream cheese (trying unsuccessfully not to judge), and he watched as I blended blueberry protein smoothies. I drank tea. Surprisingly, he did not.

And then one night, I asked him something. Maybe I invited him to a family function? Or suggested taking a trip together? I honestly don't remember what we were discussing (I hadn't known I was on the cusp of a pivotal moment)—I just know that his response hit me like a gut punch:

"But I don't know you well enough yet."

I said a quick good night—and he let me. What were we doing? What was *I* doing? *I've been opening myself up to you*, I wanted to shout across the Atlantic.

The Brit and I were closer to our forties than to our teens, time not as luxurious as we'd once thought, and I was suddenly able to see that what we had may have been romantic, but it was hardly practical: Did we have a shared vision for the future? Did he want kids? In what country would we live?

The Brit was right: we didn't know each other well enough. I wondered if that was even possible from three thousand miles away. And more to the point, would knowing each other—really exposing ourselves—help or hurt? A friend had once announced that she wouldn't get serious with anyone whose parents were divorced. Another ended things because her date pronounced *nuclear* like George W. Still others had been afraid to ask the tough questions, keeping things just surface enough to land commitment. I had been there.

With the building superintendent whom I'd been seeing casually a few years prior—and let me clarify what I mean by "seeing": the sex was great, but our goals, our dreams, our plans for the weekend were worlds apart. And still I imagined a future with him. (Sex, I later learned, is easily mistaken for intimacy; just because you know someone's body doesn't mean you know their heart.)

Then there was Charlie, the forty-three-year-old silver fox with whom I'd shamelessly flirted back when our companies shared an office floor. We'd reconnected on the corner of Park and Fifty-Third on a warm and summery Saturday; before you knew it, we were midway through an impromptu two-hour lunch at P.J. Clarke's. The next night he invited me to have drinks at his favorite spot in NYC—his rooftop. Thus began (for me, anyway) a passionate affair, during which I fell for someone handsome, worldly, and completely unavailable. I'd be out to dinner getting to know someone else, thinking only of Charlie and when he would text. He'd let me leave his apartment after our evenings were finished—anywhere from eleven to two in the morning—when all I'd wanted was for him to ask me to stay. I tried to be cool with whatever this was: the last-minute plans, the conversations that stayed entirely in the present, the highs when he reached out and the lows when he didn't—a *situationship*, not a relationship.

At thirty-one, I'd been bread-crumbed, cookie-jarred, orbited, and zombied, all fancy new terms for varying iterations of noncommitment. And the longer I stayed single, the more pressure I felt, the more I started to modulate my behavior, the more wary I became of divulging too much of myself, for fear of sending someone running for the hills.

I thought I was alone in feeling this way, that there might be something wrong with me.

But of course I was far from alone.

Dating apps were supposed to make it easier to find and connect with people (and, sure, swiping from the comfort of your sofa, in sweatpants, is easy). But as they've grown in popularity, more and more research suggests this is just not the case: the addictive nature of the algorithms, the dopamine hit triggered by each new "match"—all of it is designed to encourage users to stay online and swipe without end. Multiple studies have shown that an abundance of choice—the seemingly limitless number of potential partners available online—is actually associated with an increased fear of becoming or remaining single. We've lowered our standards (the more we swipe, the more we select profiles that don't align with our preferences and values) and normalized putting people in wait-and-see mode. Whether dating online or in person, "situationships"—that is, unofficial pairings, with all the hallmarks of a relationship but no label and no formal commitment—are the new norm.

How in the world are you supposed to get to know someone like this?

Where was the guide?

I'd read *The Rules*, and tried them out on Jonas, the sandy-haired Davis Polk attorney. I set a timer and cut him off after fifteen minutes on the phone; I never accepted a Saturday-night date later than Wednesday. But it felt unnatural at best and dishonest at worst—to hide who we really were, to "sublimate our desires," as the author Taffy Brodesser-Akner wrote in an essay entitled "Stuff Your 'Rules'" for the *New York Times*. "What good is love if the person you are loved for isn't really you?"

I'd devoured *He's Just Not That Into You*, which felt revelatory at the time—a total one-eighty—although it wasn't so much a guide for getting to know someone as a list of all the reasons the man you were seeing *didn't* actually like you. (It was also a product of its time, and in retrospect comes across as overly gendered.)

In any event, I was starting to worry that perhaps the Brit wasn't that into me (at least not for anything more than short-term, New York–based fun). So on our next FaceTime, I told him exactly what I was looking for: the right partner to hopefully spend forever with, to have children and to build a home. I told him I wanted to invest all of myself, but was afraid to do so if we weren't on the same page. Somehow, the distance made it easier to put it all out there.

"You should be with a man who gives you all of himself," he said. "I'd be lucky if it was me."

I felt my stomach flip-flop, listened to him breathing on the other end of the line.

"I need some time," he said finally.

During the next three weeks, the Brit and I didn't communicate much. I made lists in my mind of things to tell him, but our texts were short. No stories, no witty repartee. I felt his absence. And I let it get to me, convincing myself that he was on a slow path toward ghosting. Years of bad dating puts you in your head about everything.

So I ended it, figuring I'd save him the trouble of ending it with me. We've had a special adventure, I typed, bleary-eyed, not brave enough to display my ugly-cry on video. And I can't thank you enough for your kindness, thoughtful gifts, and for opening up to me. I've thoroughly enjoyed it and you. But our adventure has to end here.

We were in two countries, two different places in our lives, two of too many things. It had been wonderful and bittersweet, and I would chalk it up to that.

An hour later my phone rang, his name on the screen. Apparently, my email had blindsided him; he couldn't understand where my words had come from. So we talked. About all of it. Why I'd sent the missive and why he'd needed time. He'd already come to his answer, he told me. Far from blowing me off or disappearing, he wanted to be with me. To give it a "proper go."

Forty-eight hours later, London was back in NYC.

Over the course of that quick four-day visit, we fell further in like (if not yet love), the near-breakup already a distant memory. But I didn't want to fall for a fantasy. We were still getting to know each other, after all, and there was a lot to unpack. I'd been thinking about Gwyneth Paltrow and Chris Martin's divorce, which they'd labeled "conscious uncoupling." (Bizarre, I know, to be thinking about divorce at what felt like the pinnacle of my romance.) What I wanted was *conscious coupling.* If I wanted a real partner with whom I was really compatible, I was going to have to put aside my fears and lay my cards on the table. I needed to stop letting romantic situations just "happen" to me—and get practical.

"I know this sounds a little wacky," I told him, "but why don't we make a list of all the things we want to know about each other? What are our goals? What are our dreams? What do we think about money and sex and kids and politics?" The Brit was surprisingly game, so I spearheaded our little project. I called it Romances & Practicalities— eventually hundreds of questions:

- 🖤 Are you more religious or spiritual?
- 🖤 What are your views on monogamy? Infidelity? Polyamory?
- 🖤 If you had a son, would you circumcise him? Why or why not?
- 🖤 What was the division of labor like in your home growing up?
- 🖤 Do you pay your credit card bills in full each month?
- 🖤 How do you feel about debt?

We often weren't even in the same room while attending to the list, but we didn't have to be for our conversations to be meaningful:

- 🖤 Who comes first, your spouse or your children?
- 🖤 What do you think happens to us after we die?
- 🖤 If we lost our jobs or landed in a global pandemic, what would we immediately cut from our budgets? (And yes, though it was pre-2020, that question was really in there.)

You know when you're watching House Hunters *and the couple fundamentally disagrees on the most basic decisions about where to live? My husband and I always watch with our jaws on the floor. How could they not know if they prefer the country or the city?! How could they be so far apart when it comes to the budget?! My husband and I may not agree on everything, but working through the Romances & Practicalities questions meant we'd really talked through everything. It brought us together when we were just a young, unencumbered couple and has given us a foundation that we still rely on years into marriage and parenthood.*

—RG, Port Washington, New York

The goal was to foster open communication; getting an answer "right" wasn't the aim. It was more about seeing where we differed and came together so we'd know where we stood, growing comfortable enough in the process to discuss any- and everything. In taking on the project, I found myself not hesitating to answer important questions, even before I'd heard the Brit's thoughts. I could see my younger self being so proud of this more empowered, authentic, unafraid version of me. He may like the end of the toilet paper over the roll while I like it under, but about religion—where I'd assumed we'd be worlds apart—we weren't. The Brit and I turned wonderful and bittersweet into, simply, wonderful.

And that might have been the end of our story, had I not passed the questions on to friends, and then friends of friends, and then even strangers.

Working through the list made me feel comfortable moving forward and proposing to my now-wife. I'm American and she's Canadian, and many of our friends didn't seem to know as much about their partners as we did—they after years of marriage and us after this questionnaire. I feel like we set ourselves up properly for the rest of our lives, and I'm grateful for that.

—JR, New York City

Based on the feedback I was getting, it didn't take long to realize that I was onto something, that this was *a thing*. R&P took on a life of its own. Singles told me that it helped them get clarity on their values and nonnegotiables. Couples were shocked to discover questions they'd never thought to ask, on an array of topics they'd never before addressed. Parents asked me to forward it along to their children (because honestly, who wants to take relationship advice from their parents?!), and during the height of the COVID-19 pandemic, multiple people asked to use it as a quarantine activity—couples locked down together and others apart (two of which have since married).

Then, since I'm not a relationship expert (just a hopeless romantic), I sought out advice from them: therapists, couples counselors, dating experts, grief experts, sleep experts, incredible writers and thinkers and people whose work I've long admired, who confirmed that—yes!—there was a real need for this. "I think about all those ridiculous rules," sexologist Dr. Logan Levkoff told me. "Don't talk about finances, don't talk about politics, don't talk about religion. It doesn't make a difference how great your sex life is or how much you love someone. Relationships implode pretty quickly if your core values aren't aligned. Communication is critically important."

Psychotherapist Lori Gottlieb, cohost of the popular *Dear Therapists* podcast and author of the mega-bestseller *Maybe You Should Talk to Someone*, shared with me a secret of the trade: "I do so much work with people who are happy. Their friends are like, 'You're going to couples therapy before you're even married? That's a really bad sign.' So they explain, 'No, we're going *because* we're happy. We want to have tools so that when things inevitably come up, we're not blindsided.' It's kind of the secret of couples therapists: we see many very happy people who are not yet married—not because they have doubts, but because they want to talk things through first. That's why I like your questions."

Communication is key, but I think it's tough to ask for what you want—or even truly know what you want—from life or a relationship. A list of questions is such a great idea to help guide those conversations, because it takes the pressure off.
—JB, Miami, Florida

It's also why I'm passionate about getting *Romances & Practicalities* into as many hands as possible. I know those who read it will be inspired, empowered, and ready to take their relationships by the balls. Er, *reins.*

After ten years and 250 questions, the Brit and I have been engaged and married, traveled to countries I'd only dreamed of seeing, set up homes in London and New York, and have two children.

We were a logistical nightmare, an easy breakup statistic, yet we made our relationship work in spite of the very issues that were destined to derail us. And I've since learned that for me—and the other couples who've used R&P—the sexiest kind of romance is also the most practical.

How It Works

· · · · ·

THE R&P SYSTEM

Q: So . . . I just ask my partner the questions? Do we have to go in order? Do we have to finish within a certain timeframe? How does this work?

A: *Romances & Practicalities*—the *book*—is meant to be read straight through; along the way, you'll see how the Brit and I (and dozens of other couples) navigated tricky topics and difficult conversations, and you'll receive loads of expert advice. But how you choose to navigate Romances & Practicalities—the *questionnaire*—is entirely up to you.

You can skip around, tackle different chapters at different times, and pass over questions that aren't applicable or that you don't quite have the courage to ask (yet). The important thing is to take it at your own pace. The Brit and I certainly didn't get through the entire list in one go; it's not like we banged through 250 questions to see if we'd "make it" or if our relationship would go the distance. You could spend a week (or weeks) talking just about money or sex or kids or politics.

As you look over the list, you may come across a question or two that you already know the answer to; I'd suggest not skipping over those entirely. Ever heard the saying that couples rarely fight about what they're fighting about? (In other words, an argument about emptying the dishwasher might really be about the fact that they forgot your anniversary.) In a similar sense, you may find that the R&P questions aren't always what the questions are about. A simple question about pet ownership or household chores might lead you to an entirely new topic—a discussion about finances or a story about your childhood home or upbringing. If that's the case, then by all means, go with it!

And remember, the goal isn't necessarily to arrive at the "right" answer, but to grow comfortable enough to discuss anything and everything. The ability to communicate effectively is what moves a relationship from merely romantic to romantic *and* practical.

Q: Do I have to get my partner on board?

A: Not necessarily. Couples on their second or third date probably aren't ready to discuss long-term financial planning or describe their ideal wedding venue. If your partner is still a *prospective* partner, consider peppering in some of the lighter questions over drinks, to test the waters. If you're comfortable, you might actually suggest R&P as a getting-to-know-you activity. Or, when there's a lag in the conversation, toss out one of your favorite questions to give the evening new energy. It's confidence in your pocket, structure to rely on when there isn't any. This is a tool that's meant to be flexible.

Or—like the Brit and I did—you can absolutely take this on as a couples project. Part of me was surprised that he agreed (and readily!), but his willingness to put himself out there suggested that he was already invested in the idea of an "us." Keep in mind, too, that while R&P may be about practicality, it's meant to be fun. I know a couple who turned the questionnaire into a weekend ritual; every Friday night they'd try a new restaurant and pick a new topic.

Q: What if I'm single?

A: Think R&P seems kind of pointless without a partner? Perish the thought! I firmly believe that taking the time to consider your red flags, your nonnegotiables, and your values sets you up for a more successful relationship when you do meet someone. And because I'm not a psychologist or a couples counselor, I asked some experts about it:

"I think the reason communication can be difficult, generally speaking, is because sometimes we've never given ourselves the freedom to think about what it is we truly want," sexologist Dr. Logan Levkoff told me. "Knowing what your goals are—not just in a partnership, but for who you want to be in life, who you want to be as a human, a parent, a friend, a partner—requires some self-reflection, and we often don't do that work. It's not that we can't, but we've been taught that it's sort of decadent to think about our own needs."

I also spoke to Dr. Alexandra H. Solomon, a clinical psychologist and professor who teaches the most popular class at Northwestern University, "Building Loving and Lasting Relationships: Marriage 101" (the wait list routinely fills up on the first day of registration). "The way that many people look for love on their phones these days, it's very externally focused," she cautions. "You know, *I'm looking for a partner who ticks all the boxes.* We're very focused on what the *other* person is bringing to the table. But our best and bravest work is to look at the pair of glasses that *we* wear, the lens through which we experience relationships, and how our pasts and our cultural contexts and our network of wounds and sensitivities affect those dynamics. The heart of my work has become helping people understand themselves better."

And that's the beauty of R&P: working through the questions is an opportunity for self-discovery, and that's just as important as getting to know a potential partner.

Q: What if my partner gives me a "wrong" answer?

A: Years ago, a friend of mine started dating a new guy she was really excited about. A few weeks later, I sat next to her at dinner, mouth agape, as she explained why she had suddenly ended it: "I mean, he lives in a *walk-up*."

We all have deal-breakers.

Some are questionable at best. Others are legitimate complaints having to do with mismatched values or fundamental incompatibility, and it can be good to address that right up front. That was the case with author and actress Jill Kargman. She's as famous for her wicked sense of humor and razor-sharp social commentary as for her Bravo hit *Odd Mom Out,* which is exactly why I wanted to talk to her.

"There was something about our lives," she told me about a man she once dated. "There was a weird parallel—even though he was from Boston and I was from New York. We both had grandmothers in Florida. We're both Jewish. We're both ambitious. Education is important to us. And then on our second date, he said, 'I love being in New York right now, but I'm just passing through. I could never raise a family here.' And I was like, *Let's get the check.* Because I am never leaving. I would wither on the vine and die; my entire soul is rooted in New York. And if he thought this was just a phase, rather than a destination, this was never going to work out."

Had she always been so . . . *ballsy*? I asked.

"No. I definitely was in situations as a young person where I didn't want to rock the boat. I went along with shit that I would never put up with now. But by then I just had really clear boundaries. And that was actually great, because it moved our relationship forward faster."

Indeed. Jill's date that night, the entrepreneur Harry Kargman, had immediately backpedaled, she told me. "He was like, 'Wait, no. Like, I just mean, like, in *theory*.'" They've been married since 2002 and reside (happily) in NYC.

And then there are times when something you thought was a hard line or a nonnegotiable turns out not to be. That was the case with the Brit and me. I was raised Jewish, and he's Church of England. I thought the difference in our religious backgrounds would be a major issue, especially when it came to circumcision. (I actually know a couple who broke up—for good—on what was supposed to be the day of their son's bris.) So I had a choice: I could pray for daughters, or we could talk it through. And what I eventually came to realize (and let me stress: what *I* came to realize—someone else's conclusion may be entirely different) was that if my future sons had to look at their genitals to understand their culture and heritage, then I wasn't doing my job as a mother and educator; I hadn't instilled in them a strong enough sense of who they are and where they come from. It wasn't until the Brit and I talked it out—and I thought it out, and thought it out some more—that I gained that clarity.

I realized something else, too: had I been with someone who shared my faith, I would have performed all the ceremonies and rituals I'd grown up with without ever really interrogating why I was doing them. In order to ask the Brit to participate, I needed to understand what those traditions really meant, why I wanted to continue them, and why they were important to me.

"It's crucial to understand each other's 'why,'" Eve Rodsky tells me. She's the author of the brilliant book *Fair Play*, which helps couples rebalance their domestic workload. "For example, you might think sending out holiday cards is a complete waste of time and money, but your partner might think they're a necessity. Why? What would happen if you stopped sending them? What value do they bring? You might find that the only reason you send out holiday cards is because you feel like you *have* to, or maybe you have family all over the country and cards are easier than having hour-long phone calls with every single second cousin. What's important is that you're willing to listen and willing to have hard conversations with your partner. You'll learn a lot about each other and what you truly value."

Q: What if I'm . . . afraid?

A: I'll let you in on a little secret: I may have written R&P—the religion questions and the financial questions and the communication questions—knowing the Brit and I would have to contend with the answers, but that doesn't mean I wasn't afraid. I had so much fear. I had so much to lose; I'd been burned so many times before. But I'd also been afraid to be authentically me, and I knew I had to change those patterns. Romances & Practicalities wasn't born from a place of strength, but from the hope that if *I* loved myself, someone else would too.

Of course, that fear is totally normal. "At a very basic level, there's such a rush around falling in love," says Dr. Solomon. "It's exciting, and the neurochemistry of attraction is so compelling. There's this collective experience of knowing what that rush feels like, and a collective idealization of that feeling. But the actual process of falling in love and getting to know someone is about peeling back the layers and stepping into vulnerability. That's the part that tends to scare and confuse us. I think most people would prefer to stay focused on the 'sparkly' part."

So what can we do?

"I think the most important thing is not to bring this up as an apology," advises Dr. Solomon. "I have this saying: WWBD? What Would Beyoncé Do? Beyoncé probably wouldn't say, 'Um, I kind of, sort of, would love to maybe ask you, like, two or three questions? And we'll just see? We'll see what happens?' She wouldn't do that. She'd be like, 'Listen, this is a wonderful tool. I believe deeply in it. And I am really excited to have this conversation with you.' So it's about approaching your partner from a place of grounded leadership."

One of the reasons I knew the Brit was for me was that I never felt the need to run his texts (or my responses) by any of my friends. There was a sense of safety with him, and that allowed me to go to this place of authenticity. How novel!

"Communication is only valuable if you're going to be honest, right?" adds Dr. Levkoff. "You have to be forthcoming and candid. And it's a great litmus test for whether or not someone is a worthy partner for you."

CAUTION AHEAD!

Years ago, a good friend of mine, Cleo, called me up to tell me about some drama concerning the guy she'd been dating, on and off, for the better part of a year. Supposedly they had great chemistry, but to be honest, I wasn't a fan: he was wishy-washy and non-committal. So imagine my surprise when she said he'd apparently had a change of heart and was suddenly ready to settle down. He'd even shown up to their last date with a list of questions (which she suspected had come from his therapist).

Just one problem: at no point did he initiate an actual *conversation*.

"He was going down this list of questions," Cleo said, "but he wasn't actually discussing anything with me—he just gave me his prepared answers. He was like, 'How important is religion to you? Because I'm not going to services.' Then he'd switch to an entirely new topic: 'I'm not having children. I'm just letting you know that.' There was absolutely no discussion, no compromise, which is never a great way to start a relationship."

And, of course, she was right: that is a terrible way to start a relationship.

So, before we get started, a quick word of warning:

R&P is not a job interview. It's not a score-keeping exercise. It's not a test you administer to a partner (prospective or otherwise) to determine if they've passed or failed. The goal here is to share with each other, to be open with each other, to let your guard down, not put your walls up.

"My worst-case scenario," Dr. Solomon told me, "is someone brings their little, like, binder to the table and crosses their arms, and asks, 'Well, what do you think about blah, blah, blah?' and then just sort of sits back and assesses. The questions have to be paired with relationality. They are a gateway to mutual exploration. I would never want anyone to use your questions—or any questions—as a defense against vulnerability, right?"

Right, indeed.

1

Animals & Pets

> You enter into a certain amount of madness
> when you marry a person with pets.
> —*Nora Ephron*

Okay, rewind.

I started this story by describing a first date so good it sparked a transatlantic relationship—so I might as well tell you about it.

Especially since it almost didn't happen. In fact, after two months of correspondence, after repeatedly trying (and failing) to coordinate schedules, my girlfriends had warned me: perhaps the Brit was just one of those guys who liked to text, but never really planned to take me out. I had a feeling they were wrong. I *hoped* they were wrong. And finally, the stars aligned: the Brit was due back in New York when I was actually going to be in town. Plans shaped up quickly, and before long I was fantasizing that our Friday-night dinner date would extend through the weekend, naturally unfolding into a whirlwind forty-eight hours.

The first hiccup came a week later, when he had to postpone his flight from Thursday to Monday. (Something about a last-minute meeting.) But any concerns I might have had about him backing out or making excuses or otherwise flaking were quickly alleviated. I don't think I can wait until Tuesday, he'd typed out, the triple periods pulsing, the message revealing itself in all its flirtatious glory. Instead, he suggested we meet for drinks shortly after he landed. At midnight. At the bar in his hotel. On Monday.

What a way to start the week.

I floated through that day, and then whiled away the evening hours, catching up on work, doing the dishes, reorganizing my bookshelf—it was a little like being back in college, actually, killing time before heading out at the ungodly hour of eleven thirty. At nine I stepped in the shower and started the intentionally long process of getting ready. By ten thirty I was triple-dipping my mascara wand and searching for an episode of something—anything, a rerun of *The Office*—to keep my mind occupied. Then finally, I stepped into the perfect outfit: a fitted white dress and nude heels, which ratcheted me up three inches and gave me the confidence to move mountains.

At ten forty-five I heard the *ping!* of his incoming text and practically leapt for the phone, my stomach already tied in nervous knots, bubbling with delicious anticipation. He'd landed.

A half hour later, another ping: a taxicab emoji.

The texts came in rapid succession after that, each one winding me up further: a photo of the glittering Eiffel Tower replica near LeFrak City, just off the Expressway in Queens. The Manhattan lights in the distance. A street sign as he entered the Midtown Tunnel. And then . . .

Nothing.

At eleven forty-five, still nothing.

Near midnight, I entertained a fleeting thought: that there'd been an accident, or some problem with his cab. But by twelve fifteen, when I *still* hadn't heard anything, I felt myself slipping, sinking into that sad, kind of pathetic place you never want to tell eligible men about:

I felt sorry for myself.

Sorry for—once again—letting myself get excited about something that was clearly less real than I'd thought. Sorry (and a bit embarrassed) that my friends were seemingly right: maybe the Brit really didn't want to meet up? Maybe he really was one of those guys whose needs were met by witty text banter? Or maybe he was just a player. Or not that interested. Or an *asshole*. I sponged off my makeup, peeled off my dress, and changed into the rattiest pair of sweatpants I could find, all the while promising myself that I'd stop checking the phone—though, of course, the sound was on. *At full volume.* Finally, after deciding not to become a total cliché and eat my weight in ice cream, I switched my cell to silent, tucked myself in, and turned out the light.

Just then, a +44 number flashed on my screen.

"It's London calling my phone," I answered, my tone unintentionally cold. Protecting myself. "Are you okay?"

"I'm not good. Not good at all," he responded, hurried and anxious. "My phone suddenly shut off in the tunnel, and when I arrived at the Standard, the only block of rooms they had available was flooded—they've had to transfer me to a hotel across town. And I couldn't get my phone turned back on until just now, so I couldn't even call you."

It was the first time we'd ever actually heard each other's voices.

"I'm so sorry, but I'm glad you're okay." I waited a beat, not quite sure how to play it. "I'm sure you're exhausted."

"I am. I'm going to get into bed, and I'll text you tomorrow, okay?"

"Yup, okay. Sounds good. Sleep well."

And that was it.

We had decided early on, probably around the time our texts had shifted from staid getting-to-know you small talk to double entendres and suggestive banter, not to "ruin it" by FaceTiming, or even talking on the phone—we didn't want to officially "meet" over our devices. All that effort not to kill the vibe, to avoid any undue awkwardness . . .

I went to bed hoping he'd text in the morning.

And, of course, he did.

Impossibly romantic evening—hopefully?—*take two.*

This time the Brit was, to my delight (and relief), already at the restaurant when I arrived. Gray suit, no tie, shirt unbuttoned at the collar. More handsome than his photos. He stood. I smiled and slid into the corner booth.

"Welcome," the waitress said, appearing out of nowhere and placing menus in front of us. "Have you been here before?"

"He has, but I haven't," I said, smiling at him as I spoke. "Though I'm very excited to be."

"Wonderful. And are you celebrating anything special tonight?"

It was obvious why she'd asked. It was the type of restaurant I might've reserved for a birthday or some other special occasion. And we *were* sort of celebrating, in the sense that we were finally meeting in person. "Yes," I said. "Yes, we are."

I could feel her urging me on with her eyes. Meanwhile, the Brit shot me a nervous glance, clearly no idea what I was going to say next.

"Moments," I answered, though even I didn't know where *that* had come from.

"Moments? Wha—"

"Just . . . *moments.*" I cut her off. "We're having a moment."

She smiled, gave an abrupt nod, and promised to return for our drink order. The second she left, the Brit burst out laughing. "I didn't know where you were going with that, but . . . okay. Moments."

He kept the bubbly flowing over dinner, and though I'm more of a one-glass girl, I was grateful. Not that we needed it—the conversation flowed as easily as it had over text. (Thank God this wasn't one of those scenarios where the chemistry didn't translate.) We talked some about London, as I hadn't been back to visit in years, and we laughed a lot, punctuating the meal with a running joke about our inquisitive waitress, hoping aloud that she wouldn't appear with a candle shoved into dessert to mark our "celebration." Before I knew it, he'd paid the check and was asking if he could walk me home.

It was a peaceful evening in the city, the summer sky still streaked with blue, and I was happy for more time with him. We strolled along Central Park South, the weather on our side, warm but not hot—the gooseflesh on my arms thanks entirely to the company. As we rounded the corner, the Brit reached into his jacket pocket. "I don't often shop at the airport, but I wanted to bring you a little gift, and this made me laugh. I'm not sure if you remember—"

He pulled out a porcelain pillbox, a red, white, and blue Union Jack painted on the lid. "We talked about things people collect, how we both know people who collect little boxes. Tons of little boxes that fit nothing inside, taking up space in people's homes."

"Of course I remember." I laughed, taking the pillbox and turning it over in my hands. "And clearly this is my very own box, the first of my new collection."

He took my hand as I thanked him. There was electricity there. I believed he felt it too, and hoped the evening would end with the kiss I'd been craving since the caramelized sea scallops.

We crossed into the median at Park Avenue, promptly got stuck there waiting for the light to change, and found ourselves standing in front of a metal sculpture amid the tulips, a public art installation— steel cube stacked upon steel cube, each one curved and dimpled, flowing one atop the other, like water. It was uncharacteristically quiet on Park, and with the seconds ticking by, we both looked down at the placard, then back up at each other.

Moments, the exhibit was called.

Moments.

We were clearly having another one right there in the middle of the street. The Brit squeezed my hand, just as the little man popped on to the traffic light, signaling us to walk.

The nearer we got to my apartment building, the slower we seemed to stroll. When my front door came into view, he asked me to dinner again, for the very next evening.

"I'll be there," I said, already looking forward to it.

"I really enjoyed our time together." He took my face in his hands. I tipped back my chin and closed my eyes and, just as he brought his lips to mine, heard the sharp squeal of tires and two quick blasts of a car horn. *Awwww, yeah. Get in there, buddy!*

To my immediate right, stopped at the streetlight in front of us, a pile of young men was spilling out the open top of a red convertible. With my face still in his hands, we burst out laughing.

"Woooooo!"

"Kiss that girrrllll!"

"Get a room!"

I gave him a quick peck on the lips. "See you tomorrow," I said cheekily, then turned and sauntered inside, putting perhaps just a little extra sway in my hips, willing myself not to trip.

Four minutes later, my phone lit up:

> > I had high hopes, but you were better company (and more stunning in that dress) than I could have expected. See you tomorrow.

So you see, after all the preliminary drama, that first date was *good*. Kind of magical, in fact. Which is partly why it was such a gut punch when the Brit eventually told me, after months of long-distance courtship, after FaceTiming and sending each other snail-mail packages and reading the same books together and going on runs together, that he still didn't know me "well enough."

You already know what happened next: I broke up with him. But then he called, insisted that he really did want to give things a "proper go," and booked that last-minute flight to NYC.

It was nearly Christmastime by then, cold and dreary, and I'd been shut up for weeks scrambling to meet an important deadline. I'd also agreed, as I was essentially housebound, to watch my parents' dog, an eight-pound brown-and-white Havanese named Latte. By then I knew the Brit wasn't much of a dog person, but his arrival—after our near breakup, after weeks of not really talking and of working myself to the bone—promised to be just the reprieve I needed.

Chalk it up to British manners, or the impending holiday, but even last minute he managed to toss into his luggage a few small gifts for me, including a very fancy, very decadent chocolate bar, almost Neapolitan-style, in the sense that it had three distinct flavors: milk, dark, and white chocolate. (Irony of ironies, we both secretly prefer the mass-produced, inexpensive stuff. Give me Cadbury any day of the week!) The rest of that evening is hazy now. I know there was a fair bit of cuddling on the couch, but I also know we didn't waste much time before calling it a night. Getting reacquainted, so to speak.

I woke around five thirty the next morning—early, still dark—to an odd sound. Kind of like . . . *rustling*. Kind of like *plastic rustling*. I threw off the covers and crept into the living room, and sure enough, the dog had worked her way through most of my gift, which I'd foolishly left out on the coffee table. Chocolate is toxic for dogs, of course. But this was an eight-pound dog. And a massive freaking chocolate bar.

Oh my God, I thought, alone in the darkness, *we have killed Latte.*

I didn't wait around to see if she was actually already sick. I threw on some sweatpants and Uggs—I don't think I even brushed my teeth or washed my face—and sidled up next to the Brit, still sound asleep in the bed. "So, listen, Latte ate some chocolate. I need to take her to the vet—"

He sat up with a start. "That's bad, right? Of course it is. Just let me—"

"No, no, no. It's fine. I'll go." The man had just crossed an ocean, it was five thirty in the morning. I didn't want to put that on him, so I didn't bother waiting for a response, just scooped up the dog and headed out into the cold. Mercifully, the animal hospital was mere blocks away. I settled in for a long wait, fearing the worst.

He started texting me almost immediately, and I set about giving him updates: They were running tests. They had induced vomiting. They'd likely give her charcoal (to absorb the dreaded chocolate). And then, rather abruptly, the Brit's tone changed: This is ridiculous, he typed. I do not want you there by yourself. I want to sit with you. I'll be there in ten.

I was glad to see him. Even if the sight of him, in jeans and a fitted sweater, seemingly fresh as a daisy, made me briefly rethink my Uggs-and-sweats ensemble.

Soon enough, one of the vet techs made her way into the waiting room. Latte was fine, she assured us, but still needed quite a bit of monitoring. "It's going to be a while."

I thanked her, sank back into my chair, and reached for a shockingly old magazine. But the Brit gently took my hands in his. "Lindsay?" he said. "We're going to leave now. I'm going to take you to the diner for breakfast. And we are going to start our day."

"But—"

"We will call," he continued. "We will come back. We will do whatever it is that we need to do. But there's no point in sitting here. You can't even be with her, so there's nothing for you to do."

I'd kept it together until that point, burying the guilt and the fear behind a stoic sense of *doing what needed to be done*—but that's when the tears came, hot and fast. I remember nodding and crying, letting out a kind of pathetic and whiny *okkkaaayyy*. And though it's been years now, I still have this vision of us walking across a New York City street that morning: I'm in just a hoodie, too rushed to have bothered with a coat, my hair in a messy topknot, not a stitch of makeup on my face—to be abundantly clear, I looked like *shit*—and the Brit's arms around me, telling me that everything would be okay.

● ● ●

I hadn't yet come up with Romances & Practicalities—it would be weeks before I got the idea to make a literal list of everything we still wanted to learn and didn't yet know about each other—but that weekend made something clear: just how much someone's attitudes about pets communicate about them as a person. Which is *not* to say that good partners must be animal lovers—as I mentioned, the Brit really isn't into dogs; he actually has a mild fear of them. And yet when Latte came home from the hospital, her face stained black from the charcoal, after she'd adopted that sad tail-between-the-legs posture that all dogs get after having endured a "procedure," he was so attentive. Latte spent the better part of the next few days perched right on his lap. I'd also appreciated the way the Brit hadn't added to my emotional burden, hadn't peppered me with questions: *What should we do? Are you hungry? Should we eat?* On the contrary, and in the best sense possible, he'd taken charge while I'd been a wreck. I started to see what he might be like as a true partner, how dependable he was, how kind . . .

"You're totally right," Dr. Evan Antin said, after I told him my theory that questions about pets are useful to get to a person's essence. "Their sensitivity level, their empathy level. You can learn a lot about someone very quickly."

I'd sought him out for the simple fact that I am not an animal expert. In addition to his post at the Conejo Valley Veterinary Hospital, Dr. Antin is a wildlife advocate and passionate conservationist—but you may know him as simply "the hot vet." (He's twice been named "Sexiest Veterinarian Alive" by *People* magazine, and though it feels odd to so completely objectify someone in this way, let me just confirm: *the nickname is apt.*) I'd breathed a sigh of relief when he signed on to our Zoom session petting a cat (one of five cats he owns, incidentally) and not his snake, since just typing the word *s-n-a-k-e* gives me the willies.

"Do you see many similarities between how animals and humans behave in terms of . . . courting?" I asked.

"A lot," he said, raising his eyebrows and dropping his chin for emphasis. "*A lot.* We're all animals at the end of the day, and there are a ton of parallels. I mean, you go out to a bar or a club, and it's a bit like being in the wild, right? You see all these guys flexing, trying to look good. And if an attractive woman walks in the room, you see how they start behaving with each other. They might be a little more showy. They might stick out their chest a bit more. If they're an alpha type, they might become a bit more assertive. It's not that different from, say, gorillas or lions. Once a female enters the picture, things change. Lions might fight. Gorillas might beat up on each other. It's more exaggerated. More—"

"Primal?" I offered.

"Yeah, but it's the same kind of thing. And a lot of it comes down to competition."

I was thinking about how fascinating the psychology of courtship is, how hardwired we are—humans and animals—to behave in certain, predictable ways, when Dr. Antin admitted, rather sheepishly, "I think that's why I like dating shows so much. Even the trashy ones. It's like, I'm ashamed of it? But also . . . I just find them so interesting."

Agreed, which is why we spent the next few minutes discussing my current binge: *Love Island.*

R&P QUESTION #9   **If we were to have a pet, what would the division of labor look like? Who would be responsible for walking/ feeding/cleanup/vet visits, and so on?**

In the world of R&P—whether I'm sharing the questionnaire with friends, or friends of friends, or even strangers, or interviewing couples (and singles) who've used it, or consulting with experts about the most common pitfalls of dating and mating—one question seems to come up more than any other: *How is it possible we've never talked about this?!* (Or the subtle variant: How could *they* have never talked about this?!) From the seemingly insignificant to the positively monumental—where to live, whether or not (and when) to have kids—it is astounding how often couples fail to really talk, and how often they fail to talk before committing.

Lacy Elliot and her husband, Aaron, are not those people.

Though they married young (at just twenty-three), they dated for a full five years before they got engaged—all through college. And they talked about *everything*: their educations and career paths and job expectations, their future earning potential and budgetary concerns, their religious beliefs and household chores and plans for travel and thoughts about children, even their love languages. "His are touch and words of affirmation, and those are literally my bottoms. Mine are acts of service and *maybe* quality time—but even that we talked through," she'd told me confidently. More than just their willingness to communicate, the intent and care with which they spoke struck me: they'd made it a practice to check in each evening, thanked each other often, and placed a premium on kindness. In fact, the more I listened to her—*politically we're not 100 percent on the same page, but it's almost like that doesn't really matter because respect is so important*—the more I couldn't help but feel impressed. So at first I was a little confused when something about their dog kept coming up: an issue Lacy kept circling around, kept sort of hinting at.

"Total pandemic puppy," she'd said of their micro-mini Goldendoodle, Rory. "I didn't grow up with animals—my dad has really bad asthma—but it's always something I really wanted. I love dogs. My husband actually proposed in a pet shop. And I think when the world shut down and we realized, well, we're not traveling anywhere for a while . . ."

I totally understood the sentiment. And, of course, Lacy and her husband are far from alone; a quick Google search confirmed that nearly one in five American households (some twenty-three million people) adopted a pet in just the first year or so after the onset of COVID-19, between March 2020 and May 2021.

"But you don't really know what it's like until you do it," she continued. "The responsibility side of it, I mean. You have to walk the dog every morning, you have to walk the dog every night. I think that was a really big learning curve that was hard on Aaron."

I paused just long enough to wonder why this might've been hard, specifically, on her husband. "And you don't live in a place where you can just open the door and let her out," I offered. "That's what I find the hardest about living in a city with a dog. You have to dress for the weather. Put your baby in a stroller if there's only one adult at home . . ."

"It's a whole thing," she agreed. "It's packing everyone up. Piling into the elevator. It's training your dog to hold it until they *get* to the park—that took, what, a year and a half? But also, I mean, this is New York City, so we've met such a wonderful dog community. And sometimes we talk about the fact that, you know, it's actually good that it forces you to get outside. Even if it's seven degrees, or it's raining . . ."

"Uh-huh," I said, getting the sense that a bomb was about to drop.

"But you know, my husband works a lot. He's tired. And I think sometimes taking care of Rory just feels like extra. 'Cause, like, I'm not comfortable taking her out at night by myself. So no matter what's going on, *he* has to do it."

"Well, surely you talked about what pet ownership would look like?" I asked. "I mean, you must have talked about pets—he proposed in a pet shop."

"Yeah, not really," she said, and the *ding, ding, ding* of recognition immediately rang in my head. "We didn't even—we literally walked into the pet store. And Aaron was like, 'It'd be so classic *us* to see a dog, fall in love, and literally walk out with it.' And then he said, 'We're not doing that. We're talking this through first. We're doing all the things.'"

"You walked out with the dog, didn't you?" I asked, though I already knew the answer.

"We walked out with the dog," she said, nodding. "And now Aaron is becoming resentful."

•   •   •

"Yeah, that would've been nice to know getting into it," Dr. Antin said when I later described Lacy's predicament. "Just in fairness to both parties. I mean, maybe a cat would've been a better fit for them?"

I knew that wasn't the case. Lacy's love for dogs, and for Rory in particular (who at one point she'd described as "my shadow, my *soul dog*") was pretty all-encompassing. But it did get me thinking. "When a couple comes in with their pet, can you tell whether or not they've properly talked about—"

Dr. Antin started laughing before I could even get the sentence out. "All the time."

"And what do you see?"

"I follow some veterinary pages on social media," he continued, "and there are actually a lot of memes about this: a boyfriend or husband has brought the dog in, the vet's trying to ascertain—you know, what seems to be the problem?—and the boyfriend or husband is like, 'I don't know. *She* said the dog's not well.' And it comes down to that, basically. In my experience, it's more often the woman who wanted the pet and the guy who resisted—it's too expensive, it's too much work, it's this or it's that. I'm not saying all men are like that, by the way, or that men don't care about animals, just that I see this particular dynamic all the time. It's very common. So, yeah, it's clear when couples haven't talked or worked things out, and it's important they get on the same page."

I'd known, even before the start of our conversation, that I intended to ask exactly what sorts of things couples should discuss before acquiring a pet. The preferred division of labor, certainly (R&P Question #9). I figured we'd talk, too, about the financial implications of pet ownership, as well as the time required and the emotional commitment—and we did. (For the record, Dr. Antin's advice for anyone contemplating an animal adoption boils down to this: do your research first.) But as he was describing various dietary needs and space requirements, I was reminded of something Lacy had said: *You don't know what you don't know.* "Even if you've never been a dog owner before," she explained, "you know you'll have to walk the dog, feed the dog, but you don't really internalize what that means until you're the one actually doing it."

That suddenly struck me as profoundly true. After all, Lacy hadn't twisted her husband's arm; despite an initial reluctance, Aaron had been totally game to adopt Rory. And while they definitely should've discussed things first, Aaron might not have realized that walking the dog every night, without fail, would turn out to be a giant pain in the ass; that, in fact, it *wasn't* something he wanted to do.

As often as I've heard the question *How could we have never talked about this?!* (usually delivered in an exasperated tone), I'm reminding couples of the true goal of R&P—that it's not about delivering or seeking the "right" answers. Too much emphasis on a "right" answer implies the existence of a wrong one. Being "right" gets conflated with winning, and in order for someone to win, somebody else has to lose. The exercise devolves into competition and gamesmanship. The goal of R&P, on the other hand, is to start a communication that never actually ends. Because the truth is, most conversations aren't one and done. Circumstances change. People's minds change. As a woman I later interviewed explained (rather poetically), *So much is going to happen. You're going to lose your mother, and your father will have to move in with us. We'll try for just one more child but end up with twins. We'll swear never to leave the city, visit the country, and realize we never want to go back. Human beings are by nature changing and evolving.*

So why talk? Because it's generally easier to *revisit* a subject than to broach it for the very first time, especially if the first time is months or years into a relationship. Talking early, and often—even in theoretical terms—helps establish a level of comfort and familiarity, a baseline. As time passes and circumstances evolve, it won't be so difficult to address whatever needs to be addressed.

In the last few minutes of our conversation, one of Dr. Antin's new kittens appeared on my screen. I'd already met Henry and Willy, the old-timers of the crew, ages fifteen and sixteen, respectively. I thought about what it must have been like when he brought his new kittens home, whether they'd gotten along with the older cats or if there'd been tension. "What do you do when two people start dating," I asked, "and they both have pets, and those pets don't vibe?"

"Yeah, so this is another common problem."

"It is?" I asked, genuinely surprised. I'd tossed the question out off the top of my head.

"A lot of people—they're not trying to do anything wrong, they just honestly don't know how you should approach that kind of thing. And this is really important—this can change the dynamic of how animals engage with each other for potentially the rest of their lives. You need to be really strategic."

Well, *now* he had my attention.

"Ideally," he began, "you want to introduce them in a neutral space." In other words, neither of your apartments or homes. You also want to introduce pets gradually, and in stages. If you're at the park, Dr. Antin explained, it might be enough to let them see each other just from a distance. If you're indoors, you should keep them in separate rooms—though they'll still be able to hear and to smell each other. When he's introducing his own animals, he keeps them on either side of a closed door.

The next step is to provide lots of positive reinforcement—snacks, treats, praise. "This is something I've done with all of my cat introductions," he told me. "Once they start to see each other, just a peek, I'll throw some catnip on the ground. So there's a positive association with this new thing, this new cat on the other side of the door. *Every time this new cat's here, I get something I like.*"

The third step is to play it by ear and to gauge the situation: Is there playful interest? Are there signs of aggression? Is it safe to progress to the next stage? And if so, then perhaps you put a time limit on that interaction. Fifteen or twenty minutes before you separate them, re-commence with the positive reinforcement, and then try again.

"Long story short," Dr. Antin continued, "most people don't realize that. They say, 'Oh yeah, bring your dog over.' And then the dog that lives in that house is like, 'Who the hell are you?'"

"You're playing with my toys," I added, nodding.

"Yeah, you're playing with my toys, and you're in my space. Versus having met somewhere else and cultivated a friendship on some level. It's sad when you hear about households where the cats can never be in the same room. Or where, every year or so, the dogs get into a fight and I have to stitch them up.

"Anyway," he said, suddenly backpedaling, "I'm sure you're not trying to get into *that* in the book."

"No, no, no!" I insisted. And I meant it, because I'd never thought about it that way before, but why wouldn't you do this with animals? *The practicality before the romance.* To me, it made perfect sense.

R&P QUESTION #4   **What pet(s) would you be absolutely unwilling to own?**

"I don't know if I would have dated a dog person," Jim said, holding his wife's hand with his left, making air quotes with his right. "Dogs are, like, a whole other realm."

Not long after I'd decided to turn R&P (the questionnaire) into *R&P* (the book), a friend mentioned a couple she knew with a profound love of cats, and insisted that I simply had to talk with them. And for Jim and his wife, Carey, a handsome couple in their early fifties, it turned out that a mutual love of cats had indeed been somewhat foundational to their relationship.

"We met on Match.com," Jim explained. "I'd actually gotten bored with it, but right before I disabled my account, she sent me a message.

And I don't know why, but for some reason I felt compelled to find out, okay, what did this person say? We started talking, and I guess"—his eyes shifted to his now-wife—"because you had your problem-child cat, Petunia, and I had a cat with a lot of medical needs, we ended up having these long conversations about the care we had to provide. And then we branched out to other stuff."

They were also charmingly hilarious. Just behind them was what Carey had referred to as their "cat cremation graveyard."

"It's not a graveyard!" Jim interjected. "It's just little boxes up on the shelf."

We addressed the profound truth that animals always seem to warm (or not) to the right people: "His cat pushed one of his old girlfriends out of bed once," Carey deadpanned.

The corner of Jim's lip turned up ever so slightly. "*That* was funny."

But just as quickly as we'd dived into pet ownership, we'd moved on to other things. The fact that dogs (unlike cats) require so much care and attention—which can make travel difficult—led to a conversation about a long-ago trip Jim had planned to visit his brother, who'd been attending grad school in Germany (and how he'd invited Carey, though at the time they'd only been dating for a couple months). We spoke about how one of their cats developed pancreatitis and needed an expensive procedure, which led to the revelation that Carey, then a fledgling financial planner, had turned Jim on to Suze Orman's old Sunday-night show. "I'd never seen anything like that before," he said, before sharing that he'd come from a blue-collar background, that growing up, his family never much emphasized or talked about money. "The only importance was that we never had enough of it."

That's the thing about pets: as a topic of conversation, the subject is utterly innocuous. And yet it provides this unique window into someone's life, their history, even their soul. One minute you're talking about litter boxes, the next you're learning about someone's hobbies, or their childhood, their parents, and how they were raised. When I spoke with younger men and women, especially, in the course of my research—most of them navigating swipe culture, enduring first date after first date after first date—I found myself suggesting they try peppering in some pet-related questions, because *nobody* will freak out or feel like you're invading their privacy if you ask how they feel about animals. And yet the potential exists to learn so much.

"We met when we were twenty-one, started dating when we were twenty-two," Dr. Antin told me of his now-wife, Nathalie, who on their very first date, dressed to the nines, decided that she simply *had* to save all the earthworms splayed on the sidewalk outside the restaurant, stranded there after a heavy rain. "She's picking up all these earthworms and putting them back in the planter boxes and the gardens, and I was like, that's pretty awesome. I was able to see early on that we could be compatible, because I mean, a lot of people wouldn't do that. It said a lot."

I hope you'll approach these questions in that same spirit, that you'll stay open and keep it fun. And if you've got no idea where or how to begin, just start here:

R&P QUESTION #1   **Did you have pets growing up? How does that color your perception about having pets now?**

2

Communication

Communication is not about saying
what we think. Communication is about
ensuring others hear what we mean.
—*Simon Sinek*

I landed in London at 6:25 a.m. and headed straight for the restrooms at Heathrow. I wasn't going to bother changing clothes, but I needed at least a few minutes to freshen up and throw some makeup on my face. The Brit was to meet me at street level of the London Bridge Tube station. I had fantasies of reenacting the famous escalator scene in *Cruel Intentions*, that haunting piano melody from "Colorblind" by the Counting Crows providing the soundtrack, the sight of my lover's face slowly coming into view as he waited for me at the top.

"I'm impressed," Reese Witherspoon says in the film, a half grin on her face.

"Well, I'm in love," answers Ryan Phillippe, before leaning in to kiss her, right there in the middle of the train station. The camera circles around them while the lyrics "I am ready" repeat over and over again.

That's how I felt—*ready.*

I hadn't been back to London in years, but as I made my way through the terminal, I already felt right at home. I'd been a theater kid growing up. I loved English playwrights, the witty aphorisms and that dry British humor. I loved the lilt and sway of the accent, the smell of malt vinegar wafting from the chip shops, and imagining who lived in those ornate brownstones lining the squares about town. I'd visited as a girl, and my mother had taken me to tea. I loved the ritual and the decadence of it, the crustless sandwiches cut just so. When I'd spent a semester studying abroad in London, I'd been charmed to discover that we'd be served tea and biscuits every afternoon at four o'clock, no matter the schedule.

I only wished *this* trip—and my time with the Brit—was to last more than a week.

"What's wrong with you?" he'd asked not twelve hours earlier, just before I'd left for the airport. He'd asked many times—I knew he was teasing—but I hadn't been in the mood to play.

"What do you mean, what's wrong with me?" I teased back anyway, keeping the mood light.

"You're pretty much perfect. You're smart, beautiful, funny, seemingly *normal*, not at all dramatic—"

"I'm just me, babe. If you want drama, I'm not your girl."

"I'm done with dramatic dating," he'd said with an exasperated smile. "It's just refreshing, that's all. I honestly don't know how no one has snatched you up yet."

And there it was. I hated when he brought up the fact that I was still single. It was like he was waiting for the other shoe to drop, waiting for me to turn possessive or crazy. To prove that I was, in fact, too good to be true. He often alluded to things not being what they seemed. But we'd made a deal with each other: no games. Just the straight, honest truth. And as far as I could tell, he was holding up his end of the bargain.

So was I.

I headed underground and felt my phone buzz. A text from the Brit:

> So sorry. At home but stuck on this work call.
>
> Think you can manage from the Tube to my place?

So much for my *Cruel Intentions* fantasy. He explained that his flat was a short walk from the station, that I should hop in a cab if it started to rain or my bags were difficult to maneuver, and apologized profusely for not being there to meet me—but he'd watch out the window for my arrival while he was stuck on the phone.

I sighed, tapped out a quick response: No problem xx

London proper welcomed me with a downpour. The second I spotted a black cab—mercifully only a block or two along my trek—I hailed it and hopped in. We passed a Victorian-era hospital straight out of *Call the Midwife*, Tower Bridge, and the Tower of London before finally turning onto a quiet cobblestone street. The Brit's building was tucked away at the end of a cul-de-sac, mere meters from the edge of the Thames.

I heard my name and spotted him waving in the window, the phone still pressed to his ear. "Fourth floor!"

Any lingering worries about the previous night's conversation were gone. Now I was just a bundle of nerves, the excitement suddenly so intense I was practically shaking with adrenaline. I took a few deep breaths in the lift, wheeled my luggage through the door to his flat (which he'd left open), and studied him as I waited for his call to end—the deep-set brown eyes, the constellation of freckles on his cheek, the strong hands and what I knew he could do with them. *Hang up the phone!* I shouted in my head. When he finally did, he took three quick paces in my direction and ripped the damp clothes from my body.

God, this was so much better than phone sex.

I knew I'd be on my own for a portion of the day; the Brit had a midday meeting he couldn't move. As he got dressed for the office, he told me to make myself at home—unpack my bags, use the closets and drawers in the second bedroom if I "fancied." He left me with a kiss and a promise to return in the early evening before we went for dinner. I was thrilled.

I flopped my arms down at my sides, let them sink deep into the comforter. It was still pouring outside, so I had two options: sleep off the jet lag (bad idea) or take the Brit's advice and unpack. I took a quick turn around the apartment first—it was funny to see it this way, in person, after all those hours on FaceTime—and finally rolled my bags into the second bedroom. It was well-appointed, if a little bland: bed, dresser, nightstands. I crossed the room and carefully slid open the doors to the wardrobe when something toppled out and hit me directly in the chest before falling face down on the floor. A picture frame. One of those wooden Pottery Barn triple frames, long and rectangular. I bent down to pick it up and stopped cold.

The closet was packed—*to the rafters*—with women's clothes.

I backed up and sat on the bed. The Brit did not have a roommate. He did not have another girlfriend—*that I knew of*. He had a sister and a mum, but I couldn't for the life of me figure out why he'd be storing an entire women's wardrobe (not to mention shoes and bags and boxes and accessories). It was still too early to call either of my besties back in the States, so I sat staring at that closet, motionless, for a good five minutes, until finally reaching forward for the frame. I flipped it over. Staring back up at me was the Brit, smiling, happy, handsome—

And a woman. A pretty brunette. Whom I'd never seen before. This was definitely not his mother or sister.

Well, *now* I had some fucking questions.

R&P QUESTION #10   **How do you fight? How do I fight? How do we fight, and how does that feel?**

Communication is key—an idea so common and so widely agreed upon as to practically be a cliché. Seriously, find me a couples counselor or a marriage therapist—a random person off the street even—who doesn't believe that listening to your partner's wants and needs and having your own wants and needs heard is the linchpin of a healthy relationship. And yet practicing healthy communication, well, it's easier said than done (no pun intended). According to a YourTango.com survey of mental health professionals, for example, 65 percent cited communication problems as the most common reason for divorce. A study by the American Academy of Matrimonial Lawyers produced near identical results—67.5 percent of marriages that break up dissolve thanks to a breakdown in communication. As if that weren't enough, here's what Laura Wasser, arguably the most famous divorce lawyer in the country (who's represented everyone from Kim Kardashian to Britney Spears to Jennifer Garner) recently told *The New Yorker*: "Even if you don't have a prenup, have the conversations that you would have if you were having the prenup, because communication is the reason most marriages break down, more than anything else."

Stars, they're just like us.

Why is it that this thing that seems so normal and natural, such a foundational and obvious part of everyday life, is actually so difficult? Why is it so hard to communicate without getting defensive?

I asked *everyone*. Every therapist, every relationship expert and sexologist and researcher and professor I spoke with in search of some kind of definitive answer, and it turns out that even communicating about communication is tricky—because I received a slew of answers, all of which had merit:

We interpret everything through our own unique lens

Rebekah Rosler is someone Malcolm Gladwell would have labeled a "connector," one of three archetypes in his bestselling book *The Tipping Point*, someone with "an extraordinary knack for making friends and acquaintances." In other words, she's the type of person who seems to know everyone. Among other endeavors, she has launched and manages something like thirty different private Facebook groups—a network of many, many thousands of members. She's a licensed clinical social worker, a postpartum doula, for years ran the New York wing of a major political lobbying organization, and has become a rather keen observer of people's mannerisms and tendencies and habits. She also happens to be funny as hell.

"Until I was, like, thirty years old," she told me, "I just assumed everybody thought the exact same way that I do. So if I communicate something to you, you're going to think about it, internalize it, and eventually come to the same conclusion or idea, or go through the same thought process that I did."

Here she paused for dramatic effect, the corner of her mouth turning up ever so slightly. "Not true. Not even remotely true! Instead, you're going to take all of your history, your baggage, your past relationships, your past . . . whatever, project all that onto what I said, and then decide, 'Okay, here's how I'm going to respond.' And then I'm going to be like, 'What in the *fuck* are you talking about? That is not at all where I was going with this?'"

She acted out the rest of the imaginary conversation, her head swiveling from right to left: "*But that's what you said! That is* not *what I said.* Listen, I took my husband to therapy the second after we got married. He was like, 'But we have no problems?' And I said, '*Exactly.* Now is the time to make sure that what I'm saying is what you're hearing.'"

Incidentally, we so often feel misunderstood by our partners that "reflective listening" is indeed a common exercise in therapy. One person might start by stating how they feel, and the other is meant to repeat or paraphrase the thought (e.g., "What I heard you say was . . .") until they've correctly understood and acknowledged their partner's perspective.

We think we shouldn't *have to* communicate

Among the PhDs I spoke with, the therapists and academics who study couples day in and day out, virtually all of them brought up the impact of social conditioning. "Here's the thing," sexologist Dr. Logan Levkoff told me. "We grew up our entire lives with this sort of fairy-tale imagery—everything we watch, everything we see, shows us these aspirational love stories that deal with conflict very neatly and tie it up into a bow at the end. So oftentimes we don't really have any models for how to communicate, how to negotiate, how to have tough conversations. Instead, there's this fantasy that the best relationships are those where you don't have to talk about anything. You just magically know what the other person is thinking, feeling, doing, like it shouldn't have to be work. And that's really unfortunate, because no one is a mind reader."

You can say that again. I thought back to that fateful FaceTime, when the Brit declared that we "didn't know each other well enough yet." In hindsight, he'd meant it both literally and logically—we really *didn't* know each other that well—and yet I'd imagined all these ulterior motives, wondered if "we don't know each other well enough" was code for "I don't actually like you that much."

We get emotionally triggered

Just as the nervous system is activated when falling in love flooding our bodies with dopamine and oxytocin, sparking the sweaty palms and the butterflies and the sudden penchant for firing off whole strings of overwrought, emoji-laden, hyperemotional text messages (just me?)—it gets activated when we're in conflict, too. To talk about that, I reached out to Dr. Nicole LePera, better known as "the holistic psychologist." If you're at all familiar with her work, then you've almost certainly engaged with her content on Instagram, where she has developed an absolutely massive following. "We're going to feel threatened when we hear a different perspective, especially from those closest to us," she explained. "We go back to that emotionally driven kind of 'lizard brain' that everyone talks about. Our focus becomes *us*. Preservation becomes our sole priority. We can't hold space because that person actually feels like a threat, so we do get combative."

Part of Dr. LePera's appeal lies in her ability to talk about mental health and trauma in a way that feels familiar and instantly relatable, but also—I think—in her vulnerability. I probably share her posts more than most people's, so was delighted to discover that she was just as willing to share when we spoke one-on-one.

"Just yesterday, my partner simply asked—it wasn't even an argument! She simply said, 'Hey, can we cuddle in the morning before we get up for work?' And instead of just saying yes, my response was 'I'm always open to cuddle.' So she says to me, 'I just made a request. You don't have to win.' And I realized, oh my God, she is so right. That was not even in conflict! She simply stated what she wanted, but I had to one-up her, immediately. *Oh, you want to cuddle tomorrow? Well, I'm* always *open to cuddle.* As if she was accusing me of something! I had to swoop in with some defense."

And sometimes, we really *can't* communicate

"I talk about the nervous system a lot," Dr. LePera continued. (Indeed, as a "holistic" psychologist, she incorporates a range of therapies and modalities into treatment, placing a particular emphasis on the mind-body connection.) "A lot of us aren't equipped—in our bodies—to navigate how it feels to hear something upsetting. So first and foremost, we avoid. We don't bring up the things that are uncomfortable, or that could cause imagined conflict. We'd rather just sweep it under the rug. But for some of us, the way that our nervous system has habituated to protect ourselves is to go into that literal dorsal vagal state of shutdown."

In other words, rather than responding with "fight" or "flight," we "freeze."

"I remember at the beginning of my relationship with Lolly," she said of her wife, "she'd ask, 'Are you here? Where are you?' I was physically present, but she could see that I was completely shut down. I would get quiet, give one-word answers, that type of thing. So it's about recognizing that that's a state of overwhelm. It doesn't mean we won't communicate, or don't want to, even. It's actually very frustrating to be the person who's shut down, because there's often a lot happening inside that you can't verbally get out and release."

• • •

"Oh, man. I knew this was going to be like a therapy session."

I was talking with a woman named Julia Baldwin about how she and her husband argue when she made the crack about therapy. It was a joke I heard a lot in the course of researching and refining R&P. Opening up about communication challenges with a loved one—really, any challenges—even to a layperson probably isn't all that different from a counseling session. In fact, I was stunned at how often my interviews with these generous people who'd graciously donated their time and perspective ended with *them* thanking *me*.

"I'm passive," she continued. "My husband is much more up-front about confrontation, and I very much shy away from it, especially if we're having an argument. I'll just shut down and say, *Okay, you think your thing. I'll think my thing.* I think part of it is a game. Like, secretly I'll win if I just don't say anything at all. It's a very passive-aggressive mentality."

She had a point. Trying to covertly win an argument without even telling your partner that's what you're doing *is* rather passive-aggressive. But that wasn't at all what I'd been thinking in the moment. Instead, I felt oddly proud of her. "I love that you know that about yourself!" I said.

Plenty of people don't. We don't all have that kind of self-awareness, which is something I'd chatted about earlier with Alexandra Solomon, professor of the "Marriage 101" course at Northwestern. "A lot of people can't tell you how they argue," she'd said. "Sometimes they don't even see that they have been arguing. They just tell you what other people have done to them that made them mad or made them leave."

"They're not able to say, for example, 'I'm passive-aggressive,'" I'd ventured.

"That's right. This is actually what we're working on in class this week. We're talking about conflict, but the goal is for each and every student to notice: Okay, over time, the kinds of arguments I've gotten into—what's the theme? What's the common denominator? What is your pattern? Do you tend to get loud? Do you tend to pull away? Do you get passive-aggressive? Do you freeze? Does your mind go blank?"

By the way, if you're thinking it sounds strange that the most popular class at a major research university is one on marriage, you wouldn't be alone. The course launched in 2000—Dr. Solomon, then a grad student and teaching assistant, took the reins roughly a decade ago—with the aim of imparting a countercultural message: successful partnerships are less about *finding* the one than *being* the one. The bulk of coursework focuses on self-exploration, as a means to more effectively communicate and weather conflict. For a culture obsessed with love and sex, Dr. Solomon has pointed out, we don't place much value on relationship *education*.

That's why I'd felt proud of Julia, and why I told her so.

"Oh, yeah. I mean, I married my mother," she continued. "I say it all the time: I married my mom, which is so weird because my husband, how he handles things? The one person who I would clash with is, of course, the person I'm married to."

One of the most fascinating parts of hearing people's stories is seeing the patterns emerge, the ways they were shaped and molded by their childhoods. Equally fascinating is the fact that two people can be raised in the same household and yet have vastly different experiences, with vastly different outcomes. "It's funny, because my sister went through Pre-Cana with her husband, too," Julia said, referring to the marriage prep course that's typically required of anyone planning to wed in a Catholic church. "She came home—I love this story, because it's just so her—and she goes, 'The priest said I'm a hailstorm. I'll just keep attacking. And Doug's like a turtle. He'll go into his shell.'"

"So she's like your mom?"

"Totally."

"And you're more like Doug."

"My husband and I aren't that extreme. I don't think he's an attacker, per se. But what a great visual—just to have the words, the analogy, to help you process what's happening in the moment. I think that's such a great tool. *I* didn't get a tool. I wish I'd had one."

If there was anyone I knew who could help with tools, it had to be Dr. LePera. Part of her draw is in her promotion of what she calls "self-healing," a belief that all of us are intrinsically capable of resolving and healing from whatever traumas or hardships we've endured. "I think a lot of communication issues, shutdowns, breakdowns, are actually because there's a lack of safety," she said. "I could want to say something, but maybe I had a reactive parent or I have a reactive partner, and every time I go to share myself, I'm overpowered, overwhelmed, yelled at, right?"

I nodded. Sounded a lot like a hailstorm, actually.

"The first step is an awareness, a *consciousness*, as I would call it. For example, if I have a partner who shuts down or flees any hard conversation, that can feel really invalidating. And in the past I might have taken that personally: *Oh, you're leaving because you don't care. This conversation is not important to you.* But if we have a different language—they're leaving because they're having a physiological response, because this is too emotionally overwhelming or stressful for them—now we can shift to possibly being more compassionate. *They're detaching right now because they're overwhelmed and stressed.* For a lot of us, that's a huge shift.

"Then that awareness leads to new choices we can make," she said. "So, if I understand that your shutting down or fleeing isn't about me or our relationship, I might not get activated, right? I can stay calm and grounded. Or, if I continue to become activated—because again, all of this is wired into our subconscious—I can maybe make the choice to self-regulate: by paying attention to how my body is feeling, by tuning in to my body rather than spiraling in my mind, by doing some deep belly breathing, the somatic work to calm myself down. The calmer I am, the safer my partner is going to feel.

"That doesn't mean we continue to sweep conversations under the rug. At a later time, when we're both calm—when I'm not activated and they're not in flight mode—we can reengage. You might even be able to co-regulate together. But I think a big shift happens when you have that awareness. It's about creating the safety."

Her comment about "co-regulating" reminded me of something a friend of mine had said. Melanie Rud is an editor and beauty writer who's also written fairly extensively about the breakdown of her first marriage. Divorced at thirty-two—an age when many of her friends were just starting to contemplate walking down the aisle—she felt isolated and alone, albeit no less a believer in love. Then she remarried at thirty-four and wrote, too, of that whiplash-inducing experience.

"In my first marriage," she told me, "conflict was always very bad. It was something I was always trying to avoid; it never felt like we were on the same team. So when my now-husband and I had our first fight, I remember innately wanting to revert back to that old version of me—and then very quickly realizing, no. I don't have to do that. This is different. Yeah, we disagree. But we love and care about each other. The relationship is the priority. He's also just way more chill than I am. And so now we have this rule: if we're having a heightened conversation, a contentious conversation, we have to sit right next to each other, and we have to be touching. We don't sit on opposite sides of the room."

"How did you come up with that?" I asked.

"That was my husband. One time I was really pissy about something, and he said, 'Why are you, like, really far away? Why don't you just come over and give me a hug for a minute?' And that closeness—it can very quickly defuse a situation."

Safety is something the Brit and I would also have to learn. Very early on, I noticed that his tendency was to shut down, to get quiet, to disengage, whereas mine is to talk. I think out loud. I want to talk through everything, work through everything, get everything out in the open, rapid-fire. That awareness led to a conversation, and ultimately an agreement: I would work to pull myself back a little, to honor his need for time and space, if he could allow me a few minutes to talk, to get it out, before we took that break.

"Yes, that's incredibly important, what you're talking about," said Dr. LePera. "What do you do when you're feeling unsafe? What is your active protection? Yours is to seek understanding, to have your train of thought seen and heard and reflected back to you. Whereas I'm more like him. I need a minute to process, otherwise I say things off the cuff that I don't mean. And that's beautiful what you were able to do, to meet in the middle. It wasn't that he had to be immediately available. It wasn't that you had to stop getting your needs met. And it's back to this idea of understanding yourself, being an observer of how you navigate conflict. All that comes with awareness."

You wouldn't think the topic of fighting makes for particularly enjoyable conversation, and yet "how do you fight?" is one of the most popular questions in the world of R&P, in the sense that it generates the most feedback. We typically focus on the *what*—the substance of an argument—without ever bothering to consider the ways in which our patterns and triggers play off or mesh with a partner. Over and over, I heard variations on the same theme: I never even thought to ask.

"'How do you argue?' is such a beautiful question," Dr. Solomon told me. "Because it's not pathologizing." In other words, it's not about right or wrong. "It's open. It's curious. It's asking, 'What will our stance be?'"

**R&P
QUESTION
#19** **Do you feel you can communicate with me about any
subject and under any circumstance?**

Over the last few years, there's another response I've grown accustomed to hearing when explaining my story of meeting the Brit and the resulting questionnaire and the basic concept of R&P: "Oh, that reminds me of the thirty-something questions that lead to love!"

I get it. Back in 2015, the writer Mandy Len Catron penned an essay for the *New York Times*, "To Fall in Love with Anyone, Do This," that described her attempt to re-create a 1990s-era experiment supposedly designed to spark romance between strangers. The "most tantalizing detail" of the study, she had written, was that two of the original participants later married. But the real kicker came at the end of the piece, when Catron revealed that after giving it a whirl, she and her date, a university acquaintance, had also fallen in love. The essay went viral, and the "36 questions" were suddenly everywhere, usually framed as a kind of love hack or cheat code. Finally, here was a tool backed by science!

But here's the thing: *falling* in love isn't the same thing as *staying* in love.

And, in fact, the experiment on which the article was based wasn't actually designed to make anyone fall in "love" at all; the goal of psychologist Arthur Aron and his colleagues was merely to "induce closeness"—a short-term sense of familiarity—for future research purposes. Which, when you think about it, makes much more sense. Questions like "Given the choice of anyone in the world, whom would you want as a dinner guest?" or "Tell your partner something you like about them" don't help anyone ascertain whether or not they're compatible long term. They don't account for physical attraction, the alignment of goals or values, or the intricacies of building a life together. I happen to think the "36 questions" are a wonderful exercise (and that Catron's essay is beautifully written); the Brit and I have done them, and enjoyed doing them. They're just not especially practical.

And yet, I was struck at how often couples who tried R&P also reported feeling a sudden and intense connection. Over and over, I heard feedback about feeling or rediscovering that "spark" or chemistry, even about the questions triggering spontaneous make-out sessions. Communication can be tricky, and full of potential land mines, but it can also generate a profound sense of intimacy. For no one was that more true than my friend Tara. She had recently divorced, and we met up for dinner after she told me that she'd met a new man—and decided to try R&P after only two dates.

"When you're younger," she said, tucking into an entirely-too-expensive plate of truffle mac 'n' cheese, "you don't think there'll ever be issues that come up between you. You're kind of on a hope and a prayer. You think, long term, everything will sort of . . . work itself out. It's a fantasy. So now I'm being very deterministic about what I want. If someone isn't willing to meet me halfway, I'm okay walking away from them."

"So tell me about this new guy."

"James," she said with a smile.

"James," I echoed. "And you've been on two dates. What did you say to him? I mean, how did you bring up R&P?"

Tara set down her fork and tucked a lock of brown hair behind her ear. "Well, I met him online, as you know," she said. "And even though we'd had two really good dates, I realized I had absolutely no context for this person. You're getting to know someone in the span of a few hours once or twice a week, but you don't really know anything about their life. So it might seem kind of—I don't know, mundane—to have these serious conversations so early on, but at the same time, it felt really important. I don't want to be back in that space of trying to guess what someone really thinks or feels. I don't want to get to the point where we're loved up and super close, and suddenly it's been a year and I'm just now asking the questions. So I just brought it up to him. I said, 'Look, I really feel like we need to understand some things about each other.'"

"And was he on board?"

"Not totally. Not at first," she said. "I think he felt like it was going to be some production. But I explained that it was important to me, that it should be important to him too, and then he came around. I thought that was a good sign."

I nodded. It was a good sign; I'd felt the same way when the Brit had agreed. "How did you get started?"

"He was already coming over for dinner that weekend. We were sitting at the kitchen table, we'd just finished eating, and he was actually the one to say, 'Let's go. Let's start the questions.' So I took out the list. And let me tell you, this was beautiful."

Tara scooted forward in her chair and leaned in conspiratorially. "One of the first questions we tackled was 'How do you fight? How do I fight? How do we fight, and how does that feel?' And even though we haven't really fought yet, this ended up being my favorite question of the night."

I suppressed a smile; it wasn't anywhere close to the first time I'd heard that. "Had you ever thought about how you argue? Was that something you were able to talk about?"

"Well, he answered first," she said, lifting an eyebrow and pursing her lips as if to say, *And the answer was not good.*

"Uh-oh. What did he say?"

"He said, 'I don't argue.'"

"Avoidance?"

"Exactly, right? I'm thinking to myself, *Oh God, here we go again.* So I ask him, 'What does that mean? You just avoid arguing? Are you telling me that you just, like, walk away?' And he says, 'No, no, no. Let me give you an example.'"

Tara explained that James had made up a scenario wherein she suggested they go out for dinner and dancing—a night on the town—while he preferred to stay home. (Apparently her new beau worked "crazy long hours," so I suspected the argument he'd dreamed up was far from hypothetical.) "But then he said that if I just explained to him why it was important to me," she continued, "if I explained that going out makes me feel good or it connects us as a couple or whatever the case may be, then he would say, 'Okay great, hon. How 'bout we go out tomorrow night?'"

At this, Tara raised her eyebrows and pushed herself back from the table for emphasis. "I was like, 'You just *compromise*?!'" she said, incredulous.

I couldn't help but laugh a little. "Those are like magic words for you," I conceded.

"Right? Because that's the thing that held us back the most in my marriage, not being able to compromise, not being able to find middle ground. And the crazy thing is, all the signs were there from the beginning! Looking back, I really think my ex put his cards on the table, he was clear about who he was all along. And I just . . . accepted it. I'd been trying to make it work and thinking I was being a good person by going along with his wants and needs and subverting my own. Because I thought that's what you were *supposed* to do! I thought that made me a good partner! But in reality, I was just making it easy for him, by not putting my cards on the table, by not being clear about what I needed. That's why I won't be with someone who ignores my asks anymore. I'll never make that mistake again."

She paused for a moment, just as our waitress dropped a piece of molten chocolate cake on the table. "It's funny," she continued, picking up a spoon, "because the questions triggered a lot of memories. Memories of how I dealt with things in the past, or how my ex dealt with things. And now, in contrast, I can look at James and be far more appreciative of the characteristics that make him a good partner for me, or that have the potential to make him a good partner for me. You wouldn't think that just asking each other questions would be so revealing, right? I mean, it sounds so simple. Boring, even."

I'd heard that concern before, too. In fact, I'd heard it from almost everyone who'd tried R&P—that asking a series of questions or initiating "serious" talks with their partner might seem like a drag, or would possibly crush the flirtation and fun of a new romance.

We dipped our spoons into the cake, watched the chocolate pool on the bottom of the plate.

"So the reason we didn't get through the questions—"

"Is because you started making out," I interjected.

Tara smiled, one of those big ear-to-ear grins you can't stifle no matter how hard you try. "This had been going on for maybe thirty minutes at this point," she said, "and I can't even remember what question we were on, but I literally stood up and said, 'That's such a good answer,' and I went and kissed him. The whole thing was such an incredible turn-on. And eventually I felt comfortable enough suggesting that we, you know, take it upstairs."

"Oh my God, it happened," I said, suddenly a giddy schoolgirl. "Tell me everything!"

Tara held her napkin up to her face, playfully covering her eyes and feigning embarrassment. "And you know what's crazy?" she said, once the redness had faded from her cheeks. "We didn't even drink the entire bottle of wine at dinner. I had, what? Half a glass? It was like I didn't need it. There's this, I don't know, psychological safety that happens when someone's sharing such deep and intimate thoughts and ideas with you, so I didn't need the alcohol to feel comfortable with him. And that made me feel like such a grown-up. Instead of a teenager or someone who's on a date and all nervous and not sure what to do? I felt like a total adult. I just had this sense of assuredness. So, yeah, we went upstairs. And it was *amazing*."

"Of course they did," Dr. Solomon said, laughing, when I told her about my conversation with Tara several days later. "Of course it was a literal turn-on. It's the oldest heterosexual stereotype, but very often for men, sex is a gateway to emotional intimacy. And for women, emotional intimacy is a gateway for sex, right? That's a very sweeping generalization, but it's one that I see all the time in my practice."

As Tara and I were finishing up dessert and grabbing the check, she quickly scrolled through her phone. "Oh, that reminds me," she said. "James wanted me to tell you that the questions worked."

"What do you mean, 'worked'?"

"He said that if he'd known that it would turn me on—and turn him on—just to answer some questions . . ."

She trailed off for a moment, lost in thought. "It's so funny," she continued, "because I thought the process was going to rule things out."

"And maybe it will rule things out," I told her. "Maybe you'll discover something that James won't be willing to compromise on. Or you'll come up against some kind of deal-breaker. But talking about things . . . I mean, communication is beautiful."

"Oh my God. It's so horny. Communication is so horny."

"Oh, no," I said, laughing. "You just said, 'Communication is so horny.'"

"*So* horny. Who knew?" she said, pushing herself up from the table. "And by the way, you can quote me on that."

3

Relationships, Sex & Sexuality

Third base ain't what it used to be.
—*Logan Levkoff*

In the immortal words of my friend Tara, communication may be "horny," but as I sat staring up at that closet full of clothes, the person I most wanted to speak with was not my boyfriend but rather my bestie. Unfortunately, I was on London time, and she definitely wasn't awake yet. I paced the flat aimlessly, suitcases still full, periodically returning to the second bedroom to make sure I hadn't been imagining things.

Nope, still packed.

But doing laps around the same couple hundred square feet wasn't doing me any good, so when the rain mercifully let up, I went for a walk. And as I strolled along the cobblestones, I mentally ticked through every possible reason a spare wardrobe in the Brit's apartment might be filled with . . . an entire women's wardrobe.

He did have a roommate but had neglected to tell me.

His sister kept her stuff at his place. *All* of her stuff.

He was renting a room in someone else's flat.

He liked to dress in women's clothing? But in a corporate, LK Bennett sort of way?

Yet none of that made any sense to me based on the man I was getting to know. The room certainly didn't look lived in: there was nothing atop the nightstands (not even lamps); the bed was sparsely made, not a decorative pillow in sight. I knew we'd talk about it—surely the Brit had some perfectly reasonable explanation?—but this was uncharted territory, and bringing up uncomfortable subject matter had never been my strong suit.

I walked along the river, past converted warehouses still bearing the names of various teas, spices, and grains, which lifted me out of my funk. In Victorian times, the area would've bustled with the business of trade. I took a deep breath, imagined the air thick with the scents of goods now immortalized on each of the buildings: Cinnamon Wharf, Vanilla & Sesame Court, Spice Quay. What it wouldn't have been bustling with nearly two hundred years ago was women's clothes, nor closets full of them.

Okay, definitely not over it yet.

When it was just shy of an acceptable time to rouse your best friend from slumber (though totally still dark in her part of the world), I rang.

"Show me," she said over FaceTime, groggily.

A moment later: "Yes, that's a full closet," she confirmed.

And while we couldn't solve the mystery—only one person could do that for us—I eventually hung up feeling more confused than discouraged. All I knew for sure was that I didn't want to set a bad precedent. Growing up, the vibe in our home would get tense; eventually my parents would utter the four words my brother and I had come to dread, but knew were coming—*we have to talk*—but the black cloud of energy would hit you as soon as you walked through the door. I knew there was a different way to handle this, some way to make the Brit feel safe, some way to communicate that I was open to discussion, that I genuinely wanted to hear him out, no matter what the consequences or his answers might be. I just had to figure out when and how to do it.

He was exuberant when he got home, so happy to have me in his space that I forgot all about the closet for a while, swept up in his excitement as we headed to dinner. The Wolseley was an old 1920s auto showroom turned café on Piccadilly, with domed ceilings and black-and-white marble floors, and waitstaff outfitted in knee-length aprons and gray vests. It all felt very proper and very British, a perfect first outing in London. I didn't want to dwell on what had happened earlier, wanted to preserve these special first moments we were having in *his* city. Afterward, we crossed through Green Park on the way to the Mall and Buckingham Palace. It was quiet, surprisingly so, just the sound of my heels clicking along the pavement. The time felt right.

"Something interesting happened to me today," I said casually. We were hand in hand, walking at the pace of two people who didn't have anywhere else in the world to be.

"Oh?"

"Mm-hmm. When I opened the closet in the second bedroom, a picture frame fell out. Because the closet was literally jam-packed with women's clothes."

His hand closed just a bit tighter around mine. Then he stopped and turned to face me. "What do you mean, the closet was full?"

"I mean, someone's entire wardrobe is packed into that closet, so I didn't have anywhere to put my stuff," I replied calmly, almost smiling. "I didn't want to jump to any conclusions, which is why I'm only bringing it up now. But I wasn't expecting a triptych of photos to fall out on me, especially not of you and another woman."

"You didn't get hurt, did you?" he asked, almost tripping over the words. "I mean, the frame didn't hurt you when it fell, did it?"

"No, I'm okay."

"Sorry," he said, shaking his head. "Wow. I'm really sorry. That must have been a shock!"

"Not sure yet." We'd started walking again, and I kept the tone conversational. My heart wasn't beating as fast as I thought it would be, and I was sort of proud to be having what felt like a very adult interaction.

For a moment or two, the Brit was silent—and it was okay. It actually surprised me how okay it was to wait together in that silence. The iron gates outside the palace loomed large, the path ahead illuminated by amber circles of lamplight.

"Do you remember the woman I told you about, who I dated for a number of years?"

I nodded, realizing that I now had a face to go with the name.

"Those are her clothes."

"Oh?"

"But we've been over for years, as you know. Ages."

"Then why are her clothes still in your flat?"

"I didn't realize they were," he said with a bit of a sigh, and I braced myself for whatever he was about to say next. "She moved back to France when we ended things—that's where she's from. The bed set is hers, too. That room has literally, obviously, been her storage unit. But I haven't seen her since she moved out, and I never even go in the second bedroom. And because I travel so much for work, and was living in New York for so long . . . I really am just as surprised as you are. Again, I'm so sorry. God, that must've been weird."

He was still holding my hand when he stopped and turned to face me once more. "Okay, how many of your girlfriends have been placed on high alert about this? How many do I need to call and reassure that everything's okay and that you're my one and only?"

He had such an easy way of making me laugh, of lightening the mood. "Just two," I said. "Just two friends."

It wasn't ideal. *Closetgate* was unexpected and strange—but then again, it dredged up some stuff we needed to work through in order to take the next step in our relationship. It opened the door for us to really talk about why the Brit had dated a woman for years, lived with her, and yet it hadn't worked out. It opened the door for me to talk about my past relationships, too, and why none of those had gone the distance.

Broaching the subject of ex-lovers is never easy. And yet—as Dr. Levkoff assured me—"We are who we are based on all the experiences we've had leading up to this moment." On the topic of sex and intimacy, there was no one I wanted to speak with more. Dr. Levkoff is a renowned author, speaker, certified sex educator, and—fun fact—an expert on the first three seasons of the mega-hit *Married at First Sight.* (Full disclosure, we also attended the same all-girls summer camp as kids. Even then, as we put toothpaste on our pimples and pined over boys, she was the resident love expert.)

"I feel like this topic often comes up around the whole idea of people having a 'number,'" she said, "and how people feel about sharing that number. Or oftentimes people assume, particularly if a past relationship was close in time to the current one—that's when it feels a bit more competitive. But we're in relationships for however long, typically because at some point they were successful. So I think it can be helpful to know *what* was successful. What were those key learnings? Not about the person you were with, but about your experience of being a partner."

For all my insecurities, jealousy was never one of them. I haven't really been threatened by other people. Curious, of course. Motivated by? Definitely. But mostly I've wanted to learn from patterns and tendencies. I saw that information as a great tool, and it was in that spirit that the Brit and I forged ahead. We delved deeper into our pasts, but always with the goal of clarifying our future. And from that vantage point, it was a joy to discover that there was so much to discuss.

R&P QUESTION #38   **Do we have good sex? Is there anything you'd like me to do differently?**

In the course of my research, I was stunned by how often people described difficulty communicating with their partner and yet opened right up to me: about failed marriages, childhood trauma, financial catastrophe, fears and insecurities, and, yes, sex. One young woman I spoke with had been raised in a Catholic home and received a Catholic education before attending a large public university; she was so uncomfortable speaking up that she'd faked an orgasm during essentially every sexual encounter she'd had. (It wasn't until after college that she grew comfortable even with the idea of masturbation, after confirming that she "wouldn't go blind from doing it, like the nuns said.") Another, also raised in a conservative Christian household, was cohabitating with her fiancé—but hadn't told her parents yet. The sex-related prompts on the R&P questionnaire had been particularly helpful, she explained, "because that's the kind of stuff we don't exactly talk about just . . . outright."

On the flip side of that coin is my friend Emmanuelle, who is this gregarious, wildly generous, earth-mother type: full of love, extremely sensual, the sort of woman for whom nothing is too personal and nothing is off-limits.

"Scott and I had chemistry the instant we met," she said. I'd caught her in the middle of a workday; we were chatting on Zoom while she fielded calls from clients and other attorneys. "He had these beautiful lips. The kissing was so intense. And I have to say, nobody has ever sucked on my nipples the way he did. I remember looking down and watching what he was doing, trying to figure out why it was so incredible."

Seriously, nothing is off-limits.

"That probably made you think the sex would be uh-may-zing," I said.

Emmanuelle scrunched up her nose and shook her head. "We weren't having a lot of sex yet because I was studying for the bar exam—and really, I'd just been looking for a distraction. I was not thinking this was going to turn into anything serious. But I have this vivid memory: We'd gone for a hike. We had both taken a shower. Scott was naked on my bed, and we started to make love—but it was so hard and fast, and it was over in four minutes. And then it was done. I was like, *What is happening? What is this?!*"

Emmanuelle is a decade older than me; I'd met her not long before she embarked on a midlife career change and became a criminal defense lawyer. Scott was also in his early forties when they'd started to date. And it was around that time that she'd taken me to lunch, when I'd been visiting Los Angeles for business. We had barely tucked into our fish tacos when she dropped her voice and leaned in: "*I can't believe he's gotten to this age and doesn't know how to have sex. What would you do? Cut and run? Or should I say something?*"

Ultimately, she did say something—I knew how the story ended—but I was more curious now about what she had said back then, and how Scott responded. "I want to talk about it with you," I explained, "because you talked about it with him. So take me through it. I mean, sex is such a touchy subject for most people. No pun intended."

She finished straightening the papers on her desk and shot a quick glance in the direction of her office door, just outside my field of vision. "It had happened a couple of times by then—what I used to call the 'pump and dump,'" she said. "So I finally asked him, 'Can we talk about making love? Can we talk about, like, what your experience has been? Because it feels like you're in a rush.' And he said to me, 'I *am* in a rush. I'm trying to come as quickly as possible.'"

The word practically flew out of my mouth before she'd even finished her sentence: "*Why?*"

"Well, that's what I asked him: Why? And he said, 'Isn't that the goal for both of us?'"

Emmanuelle dramatically lifted her eyebrows, as if to say, *Can you believe that?!* "I said to him, 'For me, sexual contact, making love, is another kind of conversation. When we make love, we're having a conversation with our partners.' I tried to explain that just lying next to each other, just touching, just like, luxuriating in each other's skin . . . That there was pleasure in taking your time, in delaying gratification."

"And did he have any idea what you were talking about?"

"Not really, no," Emmanuelle said, laughing. "But he was so sweet. He basically told me that he liked what I was describing, and that he was willing to learn. And he had absolutely no ego. Because he knew I wasn't coming from a place of criticism, but from a place of love. I didn't say to him, 'What are you doing?!' I was like, 'Let's talk about what your experience has been.'"

"Why did you decide to say something?" I asked. "Because back then, you weren't sure it would be worth it."

"Yeah, because I hadn't been looking for anything serious. I didn't want to risk hurting this guy's feelings for what I was sure would be a short-term thing. But I knew there was something there—we had that connection. And ultimately, we were together for ten years."

"Which is amazing, because that was such a hurdle at the beginning of your relationship."

"It was the Empire State Building of hurdles!" Emmanuelle exclaimed. "Let me tell you: I was expecting moderate improvement, but Scott became a fantastic lover. So for people who are wondering: Should I say something? Uh, yes. You should. Because not only could it get better, but how that conversation goes can tell you a lot about the kind of person you're with."

| R&P QUESTION #41 | What are your views on monogamy/infidelity/polyamory? |

Not everyone is as open and uninhibited about sex as my friend Emmanuelle. (She once told me that she googled vaginas and explained the intricacies of female engorgement after learning that an older friend—a woman in her sixties—merely "thought" that she had "probably" experienced an orgasm before. Spoiler alert: she had not.) But talking with her partner, Scott, didn't just lead to better *sex*, it had an enormous impact on their entire relationship. In fact, she made it clear that had things not improved in the bedroom, their relationship never could have lasted as long as it did. And that got me thinking: Is there such a thing as true sexual incompatibility? Are there intimacy issues that can't be solved by talking?

"I would say that if someone is unwilling to learn, to share, to be vulnerable, to talk about their expectations, their needs, what feels good, what doesn't feel good, what their boundaries are, then yes, people can be sexually incompatible," Dr. Levkoff said. "But it's not because, like, their bodies don't work well together. It's that you have not developed, or you've chosen not to develop, the skills needed in order to enhance that intimate part of your life."

"Okay, but surely we can acknowledge that for a lot of people, talking about sex isn't easy."

Dr. Levkoff smiled knowingly and nodded her head. "One of the questions I get a lot," she began, "particularly from middle schoolers and high schoolers, is, How do I [fill in the blank] without it being awkward? How do I ask for consent without being awkward? How do I say 'This doesn't feel good' without being awkward? And my response, which is not meant to be callous, is, Who in the hell told you talking about sex wasn't awkward? Who told all these people it was easy to talk about sex and bodies and feelings? I don't know when *awkward* became such a bad word. It assumes vulnerability, and a little humanity, right? If you're truly awkward, you're being authentically *you*. If you can't be awkward with someone, then they are not the right partner. I don't know any relationship—whether it lasts for a month, a year, or a lifetime—that is successful if you cannot be vulnerable in some way with that other person."

If talking about sex demonstrates a willingness to be vulnerable (or at least awkward), as Dr. Levkoff suggests, then it would stand to reason that couples who *frequently* talk about sex might have more intimate and fulfilling relationships—and it turns out, that is exactly what research tells us. In study after study, the ability to talk about sex is strongly correlated with overall relationship satisfaction. According to the Gottman Institute, the research and training platform run by renowned psychologists Drs. John and Julie Gottman, virtually every cultural subgroup in the United States struggles when discussing sex and intimacy—except Latinos and Hispanics, and gay and lesbian couples, who tend to talk about sex more candidly, have sex more often, and report greater sexual satisfaction. Those same findings were replicated in a seminal study known as the Normal Bar, a survey of more than seventy thousand individuals across more than twenty countries, which likewise found that talking about sex is a "vital form of foreplay" and that Latin couples and gay couples, in particular gay men, communicate more directly and frequently about sex. (Perhaps because sex in general is not as "taboo" in those cultures.)

The inverse of this holds true, too, by the way: among couples who don't talk about sex, only 9 percent are satisfied with their relationships. And when you reflect on the strength of that correlation, when you consider that talking about sex requires vulnerability, that it demonstrates a curiosity and an openness and a desire to explore with and to better understand your partner, you naturally start to wonder: What happens when that communication breaks down completely? To talk about that, I phoned up Jo Piazza.

Jo and I had something of a meet-cute years ago, the circumstances of which are straight out of a rom-com. I was waiting for a table at some hot new restaurant with a friend, in line behind Jo and her friend, and the four of us got on so well that we ended up dining together. Jo also happens to be an award-winning journalist, a bestselling novelist, and the author of *How to Be Married*, a memoir/travelogue about life as a newlywed. After that she launched a podcast, *Committed*, in which she interviewed couples about staying together against the odds. After that—in an unexpected and sort of hilarious pivot—she launched a podcast about extramarital affairs called *She Wants More*. "It just felt like a natural progression," she explained. "I had heard about the ups and downs of marriage, and I was seeing a lot of women I knew—in particular, one of my closest friends—starting to step out on their marriages. I really wanted to understand why. I wanted to understand what the inflection point was. And it sounds so cliché, but clichés are clichés for a reason: it's almost always the communication breakdown. I've now interviewed hundreds of women for the affairs podcast, and all of them said the communication was failing."

For Jo, the focus on *wifely* infidelity was purposeful. Cheating by men has historically been downplayed and even normalized—think of the sportscar and the hot young girlfriend, a classic midlife crisis trope—whereas cheating by women has been viewed as much more scandalous. (In popular culture, men might get a red Ferrari, but women wind up with a scarlet letter.) We still live in a world that sublimates female desire. And yet research suggests that female infidelity has risen sharply since the 1990s, as Jo discovered when she started putting her podcast together.

"I think you start looking for something else when you're not talking to your spouse about all the things you should be talking to your spouse about," she said. "Communication equals intimacy, right?" (I couldn't help but think of Tara's maxim—communication is horny—and all the couples who told me they'd wound up in bed after experimenting a little with R&P.)

"And a lot of the women I interviewed—they want good tie-me-up sex. They want threesomes, all that stuff. But they've never talked about it. They never talked with their partners about what they want, or what they like to do. I spoke to so many women who said, 'I could *never* tell my husband that.'"

Research about infidelity is hard to quantify, for an obvious reason: most people don't want to admit when they've been unfaithful. Even Jo asks in the first episode: "Are women really cheating more than they used to? Or are they finally just talking about it more?" But I was fixated on the cultural implications, in particular what she'd said about "tie-me-up sex." According to the Normal Bar survey, for example, nearly 80 percent of women admit to being at least intrigued by "kinky" sex (whatever their personal definition of *kinky*). And yet Jo was describing women who seemed embarrassed by their desires. I wondered: How much of the breakdown in communication might be attributable to outdated ideas about what we're "supposed" to want?

"Sexual compatibility is a communication issue, yes," Dr. Levkoff told me. "But it's also a vulnerability issue, and it's very much a societal issue. Think about the rise in people speaking publicly about ethical non-monogamy, for example. Those are conversations that are critically important to have, but we often don't have them—for fear of judgment, maybe—until we're all in. And then it's like, 'So, by the way . . .'"

I realized I was already nodding. "Imagine how difficult it is, for a lot of people, to talk about sex at the beginning of a relationship," I said. "It's only going to get harder if your needs change, or your desires change, and you haven't even had those ground-level conversations."

"Right, and I think I can be so bold as to say this as a definitive: *needs change*. People's needs in the middle chapter of their lives tend to be very different. Maybe the best example is after having carried your own biological children. All of a sudden, there's a reset on what feels good. If you're nursing, your breasts might not be erotic places for you for a while. That doesn't mean that your partner can't grow with you, that you can't work through those changes together—"

"But if you've never talked about it . . ."

"You know," Dr. Levkoff began, "in a world where women, in particular, are taught that we're not supposed to want sex for the sake of sex—I think when things inevitably change, there's so much guilt and shame around it. And then all of a sudden, you feel this overwhelming sense of dread. Like you have a secret. You're not fulfilled, so now what do you do? If you can't have that conversation with someone, that's a miserable, isolating position in which to find yourself."

I wondered if anything had changed for Jo after listening to so many women describe a breakdown in communication. Was anything different now about the way she approached talking and sharing with her husband?

She laughed. "Nick and I had gotten into a bottle of wine right after the podcast came out. And he asked me, 'Does this make you want to have an affair?'"

"And?"

Jo shook her head. "I got all my ya-yas out. So many of the women I interviewed—they're having affairs because they got married really young, and they never got all their ya-yas out. But I dated all of the weird dudes, and I drank all of the vodka at Bungalow 8. I don't think I missed out on anything. I think that's why it's easier for me to be a mom now, too. Because I can very happily settle into a certain kind of domesticity. I actually really crave and embrace stability. A lot of people feel smothered by that stability and those routines—and again, it's a lack of communication. They never talked with their spouse and said, like, 'I crave adventure. How can we make sure to keep having adventure in our lives?' But Nick and I do."

I thought about how often I've reminded people that most conversations aren't "one and done," how important it is to establish a baseline of comfort.

"That's why I think your questions are also really good for married couples," Jo said. "I think you need that spark sometimes—it's like, what's the continuing education? You have to take continuing education for almost any trade you practice, and yet we don't have continuing education for marriage—and that may be the most important business partnership that we undertake."

The "Sexual State of the Union":
A Conversation with Dr. Emily Morse

Clearly, communication is key to a fulfilling sex life and a healthy relationship—but the ability to talk about doin' the deed is so important that sex educator Dr. Emily Morse, author of *Smart Sex* and host of the top-rated podcast *Sex with Emily*, thinks you should ideally be checking in with your partner at least once a month, a practice she calls the "sexual state of the union."

So tell me, why the need to "formalize" our communication around sex?

Emily: Because good sex doesn't just happen. Everything in our lives that we deem important, whether it's being a good parent, being a healthy person or having a really strong workout routine, being good at our jobs or great in the workplace, we prioritize, we take steps toward. Couples who are sexually compatible likewise understand that if you don't prioritize your sex life, if you put it on the back burner, you're going to feel less connected, more resentful, and a lot more like roommates than romantic partners.

R&P
QUESTION
#39

How often should
we have sex?

And by "prioritizing sex," you don't actually mean just doing it more.

Emily: Right. I've had people tell me they've *never* had a partner bring up sex before. We're talking about full-on adults with children and families who've been married for twenty years, and this is the one area of life they don't discuss. So it really does become the elephant in the room. Most of the sexual problems in our relationships have nothing to do with sex and everything to do with communication. And I want to clarify that talking about sex doesn't rob it of its magic. There are so many couples who think, *Well, if we talk about it, we're not going to have that spontaneity.* But for many of them, they're *already* missing that spontaneity. They're not having sex that feels authentic and real, and they're silently suffering.

How might couples get started?

Emily: Know that it's probably going to be awkward or clumsy at first. If the conversation feels *un*sexy at the start because you're nervous, that's okay. This isn't foreplay. To get things going, you might ask, "What would you like to see more of in our sex life?" Or, "How can I make it more satisfying for you?" I generally encourage people to keep it brief—ten minutes is enough time to check in about what's working, what's not, and what you might like to change going forward. You're basically planting the seeds for the sex life to come. I also always say to pay attention to timing, tone, and turf. The timing, for example, is when you're hanging out on date night—not smack-dab in the middle of a million other things. The tone is curious and casual. The turf is outside the bedroom. Sometimes we have these conversations, and because they're so heightened, we get defensive. It can really help to talk when you're taking a walk outside, or you're on a road trip; you and your partner can take a few breaths, and you don't necessarily have to make eye contact, so it's a little less awkward. Finally, I ask people to remember that this isn't criticism but something you're working on together. You don't want to initiate a state of the union when you're Hungry, Angry, Lonely, or Tired (HALT).

And what if you're single?

Emily: Good sex starts with healthy communication, and that includes conversations you have with yourself. You have to ask yourself: What are my beliefs around sex? What are my values? Do I have any lingering shame? Trauma from my upbringing? Am I silently judging myself—

or others—around sex? Because all of these deeply held beliefs, which we're not necessarily aware of and which are often subconscious, will impact your ability to be satisfied sexually. Conversations around sex are not normalized; there's a lot of shame around it. We don't have a lot of healthy examples of talking about sex. But when we start to prioritize our pleasure, it's going to have a positive impact on every area of our lives.

●   ●   ●

One of Dr. Levkoff's earliest books, published almost two decades ago now, was a parents' guide to talking about sex with their kids and teens entitled *Third Base Ain't What It Used to Be*. The title was an obvious reference to the old baseball metaphor—"first base" is making out; intercourse is a "home run." But it also spoke to the fact that attitudes around sex are always changing, and I was curious why she'd chosen it.

"It was a nod to a particular moment in time," she confirmed.

The time was the early 2000s, and the *New York Times* Style section had just published a rather panicky article about seventh and eighth graders engaging in oral sex. Five months later, *Sex and the City* featured a subplot in which Samantha is hired to plan a million-dollar bat mitzvah for a wealthy thirteen-year-old client, Jenny. The precocious teen and her friends (in dress and speech not so different from Carrie and *her* friends) alarmingly insist that blow jobs are no big deal, as well as "the only way guys will like you." (*Sex and the City*: always topical!) It was the era of sensationalized reporting about "rainbow parties" and moral panic about explicit lyrics in popular music. "It was an acknowledgment that what counted as sex or the order in which you're 'supposed' to go didn't really apply anymore," Dr. Levkoff said. "I'm not sure it ever did, but it was calling out that old model."

So what does *sex* mean today? Is there a new way we should be thinking about it? A new model?

"That word brings up so many things for people, right? If you grew up in a fairly traditional, puritanical way, *sex* is someone's penis and someone's vulva and vagina—that's sex. That's the top of the pyramid, the pinnacle of what you're 'supposed' to be doing. But obviously, that is chock full of heterosexism. The definition doesn't really work for me.

"For me—and what I tell my students—sex is a series of things that we do to share our bodies intimately with another person. There's no hierarchy; one thing doesn't count more or less. All have the capacity for pleasure. All come with responsibilities. Everything counts. I think defining sex this way also alleviates some of the pressure to define ourselves by what someone else may be doing. For example, 'Do we have sex more or less than everyone else?' Well, who cares? Are you experiencing intimacy and pleasure? Are you feeling connected? Then it shouldn't make a difference if you're having more or less than the person next to you."

In the course of researching R&P, it was brought home for me again and again how much our attitudes about sex—about what we want, what we're comfortable asking for, what we think exists within the bounds of "normal"—are influenced by how we were raised. I spoke to a group of young women—former sorority sisters—whose experiences were as diverse as if they'd been plucked at random. Some were now married and contemplating children; one had not yet had an actual boyfriend. For perhaps the first time, I really understood that two people could be the same age, live in the same town, indeed exist within the same social circle, and have wildly divergent needs and wants and expectations. Which is, of course, why talking about it—no matter how awkward and uncomfortable—is so vital.

"At every parent workshop I give," Dr. Levkoff told me, "I ask everyone to think back to their own upbringing. To ask themselves, had I gotten different messages about sex or sexuality, how would the choices I made be different? How would my life be different? I want them to sit with that. Because oftentimes, we wind up parroting what was communicated to us. We don't realize, for instance, that had I been taught to feel empowered by my body, I might not have relied on other people to love me or 'fix me.' Maybe I would have had more experiences had I known that I could advocate for myself. Maybe I wouldn't have stayed with the emotionally abusive boyfriend had my parents not taught me that dating around would make me seem like a slut. I think framing it that way changes how people see raising children in the sexualities space. They realize that had they been given different tools, they might have made different choices. And that's really what's at stake."

●　●　●

As for me and the Brit, Closetgate came up just once more. I was back in town and asked him to please find a way of returning this woman's clothes to her. They'd been hanging in his closet for years; either she wanted them back or she didn't, but—truth be told—I wanted them out of the flat.

At first, he didn't understand the urgency; it wasn't like he and his ex were in touch. But I ardently believed that if the Brit and I were going for it, truly, then a former lover's clothing no longer had any business taking up space. When he understood why it was important to me, he promised to take care of it. I even helped pack some of her belongings into airtight storage bags in order to make room in the closet for some of my things. And the next time I visited, the wardrobe was all clear.

. . . Except for one coat that I liked and had secretly stashed in the front hall closet. Sophie, if you're reading this now: I'm sorry, and thanks!

4

In-Laws & Families of Origin

Families are like fudge—mostly
sweet, with a few nuts.
—*Anonymous*

Here's a little something you should know about me: I have what you might call the gift of gab. Which is to say, I could talk to a wall. Make friends with a doorknob. I don't really get nervous when it comes time to meet new people. Besides, I'd already met the Brit's father, a warm and witty man, a retired school administrator with kind eyes and a close-cropped silver beard, and we'd gotten along swimmingly. But now I was meeting the Brit's mum, and let's not bullshit: meeting the woman who could one day become your mother-in-law is always more fraught.

It was April, and I was back in London. The Brit's mum was about to ring in a big birthday at a small celebratory dinner with close friends and family. I was the Brit's plus-one.

The night before, we arranged to tour an exhibit at the National Portrait Gallery—the three of us, plus the Brit's sister—so that we'd have a chance to officially meet before the party. I figured, at the very least, we could talk about the art.

Just shy of five, I was standing in the Brit's bathroom, giving my hair and my dress a final fluff, when he appeared in the doorway, arms crossed, casually leaning back against the frame. We locked eyes in the mirror, and he smiled. "You're beautiful," he said.

I felt beautiful with him admiring me like that. But then, with a little shake of his head, he asked, "Seriously, how are you still single?"

And just like that, my confidence plummeted. Again.

I'd always envisioned pushing baby carriages down the streets of New York City with my girlfriends—we'd be on maternity leave together, naturally, after having gotten married around the same time. Instead, I'd plastered a smile on my face for the bouquet toss at wedding after wedding, played the role of exuberant "aunt" at shower after shower. And I had grown so self-conscious about not having yet found my partner, my person, that even a cheeky comment from the Brit—"What's wrong with you?"—sent me reeling: *I was too fat. I was too skinny. I was too needy. I was too independent. I was trying too hard. I wasn't trying enough.* I, I, I, I, I . . . Down the rabbit hole I went, consumed with worry about all the things that must have been wrong with me.

In the past, I had tried responding to those questions with an assertive "I just haven't found my person yet," or the more coquettish "I've been waiting for you." Deep down, I knew he meant them as compliments. But I just couldn't take them that way, and standing in that bathroom, I decided that I had had enough.

"Listen," I said, setting down the hairbrush and keeping my tone even. "I'm not going to deflect comments like that anymore. I know you don't mean to, but it hurts my feelings when you ask why I'm still single. It makes me feel bad about myself, no matter your intention. Okay?"

The Brit's face fell. He stepped forward and placed his arms around me. "I never want to hurt you," he said softly. "I'm grateful that you're not taken!"

I hadn't yet shared with him that all my life I'd been told I was too sensitive, that I took things too personally (now was perhaps not the time to delve into our respective childhoods). But if he could really hear me, if he could stop lacing otherwise sweet interactions with that twinge of suspicion—*When are you going to change? When are you going to show me who you* really *are?*—I'd be able to open my heart to him that much more in the coming weeks.

And anyway, we were late.

By the time the Brit and I made it through the exhibit (his mum and sister had gone ahead, so as not to lose our group's reserved time slot), they were waiting for us at the end. We said a polite hello—double kiss!—and made our way to the rooftop restaurant, a modern space with plate-glass windows offering commanding views of the London Eye and Trafalgar Square. We found a spot at the corner of the bar, and the Brit's mum and I positioned ourselves across from each other, so that rather than being side by side, we could chat face-to-face.

I loved her. She was worldly and whip-smart, with a long-standing and deep-seated love of language. (She'd been a professor of French and German.) She had the same coffee-brown eyes as the Brit, too, which I suppose made her somehow seem familiar.

At the end of the night, I presented her and the Brit's sister with small nice-to-meet-you gifts. (Classic overzealous New Yorker, eager to make a good impression.) They were both unfailingly gracious, even if I could see that the gifts made them a tad uncomfortable. Then again, perhaps the problem wasn't that I'd brought something but rather what I'd brought: tea. My favorite brand of American tea, a little touch of home.

I didn't yet know that, like my boyfriend, neither of them drank tea. But more to the point, what was I actually thinking? Who brings tea to London?!

The next night, near the end of her birthday dinner, the Brit stood and gave a lovely toast to his mum. I was glad that the evening—both evenings—had gone well. And I spent the better part of the next few days thinking about them both, about the Brit's family, about his parents. Wonderful people, albeit very different people. I could see that now that I'd met them.

Their divorce was a bit of a mystery at that point. I knew only that it had happened not long after the Brit left for university, and that for him it had been a shock. But the few times the subject had come up, he hadn't offered much in the way of details, and I hadn't pushed.

One afternoon I was headed back from Borough Market, the famous indoor-outdoor food market just south of the river, with a loaf of bread, some cheese, and the gourmet gingerbread men I knew the Brit liked. I loved being able to pop in, partly for the convenience and partly because the market reminded me of quaint Locust Valley, Long Island, where I'd grown up. I was walking along the banks of the Thames, the sack of groceries slung over my shoulder, thoughts of his parents, the divorce, the birthday dinner, the dreaded gifts (tea to London!) all swirling around in my head . . .

And then it hit me.

It was like that moment in *Clueless*: trumpets crescendo, fountain illuminates, and Cher says aloud, "I love Josh!" For the first time, I was able to see that all those questions, all those comments—*What's wrong with you? How has no one snatched you up yet? When are you going to show me who you* really *are?*—did not, in fact, have anything to do with me.

The Brit had perceived his life and his family as one thing, packed up for college, returned home for a visit, and everything had changed. A shoe had dropped. A massive rug had been pulled out from under him. More than that, he was cerebral; I knew him well enough by then to know that as this new family dynamic took shape, he would have been replaying certain moments in his mind, searching for clues that he must have missed.

This had always been about the Brit and *his* insecurity.

Well, that was my theory, at least.

R&P
QUESTION
#52 **What is your relationship like with your father (or father figure, if that's what you have)? With your mother (or mother figure)?**

"I don't know if you've talked to people who are products of divorce, or whose parents divorced a couple of times, and now they're afraid to get married? I'm the opposite," Gina said. "My parents met, three weeks later got engaged, and they've been happily married for forty-five years. So if I didn't have that instant connection with someone—if I didn't know within three weeks that I was going to marry them—then that person wasn't for me."

It was not the first time I'd heard this. In fact, by the time I'd started chatting with Gina Navarro, a former cosmetics executive turned stay-at-home mother of two, I'd interviewed at least three other people with near identical stories: their parents had married within weeks of meeting, and as a result, they had internalized the idea that "true love" is magic, instant. That you don't even have to choose your partner in life; you'll just know.

"You were trying to emulate your parents and their love-at-first-sight experience?" I asked, though of course I knew that's exactly what she was doing.

"Right. Love at first sight. *This is it.* And everybody in between is just a really good time—because when I meet my person, I'm going to look at them and know right away. It's going to be this fairy tale. That's what I thought a normal, healthy relationship was supposed to look like."

"Did you ever talk with anyone about this?"

"You mean like a therapist?"

"I mean like your girlfriends." Given how rarely love-at-first-sight relationships actually go the distance (previous interviews notwithstanding), I wondered if Gina had ever gotten any pushback about her convictions.

"My friends knew I was extremely picky. I've had girlfriends be like, 'Gina, he's a great guy. He brings everything to the table.' But—I'm a visual person, right? Like, if I decide to host a party, I know exactly the tablecloth I'm going to use, the candlesticks. If it's not what I envisioned, then it's wrong. That's how it was with my future romantic partner: he's going to be this, this, this, this, and this."

The only difference between Gina and the others like her I'd spoken with was how militant she was, how many relationships she'd broken off at the smallest sign of friction. I liked her straight off; she was bubbly and loquacious and incredibly generous with her time (and her insights). But she'd been brutal in her romantic life, convinced that something better was almost certainly just around the corner. Talking with her reminded me of the conversation I'd had with therapist and author Lori Gottlieb; in particular, the notion that you can learn a lot about yourself by understanding what irritates you about a partner.

"I think sometimes what annoys us about another person," Lori had said, "is actually something that annoys us about ourselves. So let's say you're at a party with your partner and he or she is dominating the conversation or trying to be funny—and it really annoys you. It might be that you're sort of that person, too. Or maybe it's that you want to *be* that person. So sometimes things that annoy you are things you need to look at in yourself. Because it's partly about the annoying thing that they're doing, but it's also partly about you. It's triggering something in you."

I'd told Lori that I interviewed a woman who couldn't for the life of her figure out why her husband not taking out the trash was such a big deal, until she realized that her dad had taken out the trash every night, thereby relieving her mom of the duty. She'd fully expected the same—even though she'd never actually told her husband that.

"Yeah. We have a saying in therapy: If it's *hysterical*, it's *historical*. That means that if you're having a huge reaction to something that's maybe a four or five for the average person—and by the way, I don't mean hysterical in an antifeminist way; I mean this for men, too—if it's hysterical, if you're having this really big reaction, it means something is happening inside of you. You've got to figure out what that is, and what it means. Why does it bother you so much? What is this stirring up? Anger, sadness, frustration, feeling unseen, feeling misunderstood? How much of that is about what's actually going on, and how much is because it mirrors some experience from the past? Not the actual content of what's happening, but the emotional resonance?"

Not long after our chat, Gina sent me a follow-up email—she'd had an aha moment while emptying the dishwasher. I mentioned that I was adopted, she wrote. And she had; we'd spoken briefly about her father's first marriage, which produced two sons, twelve and fourteen years older than Gina. After his first wife passed from cancer, he eventually remarried, and with his second wife—Gina's mother—adopted two more children: Gina's elder sister and, six years later, Gina herself. Even though I won the adoptive family lottery, and was raised by the most loving and supportive parents, they do say you can experience adoption-related trauma, even as a newborn. And I genuinely believe I experienced some level of trauma related to abandonment at a very young age.

For her, that trauma broke down into a simple formula, which she'd helpfully written out:

Abandonment = A subconscious fear of rejection = A need to be perfect

We'd talked about her perfectionism, too. Gina had told me that as a child, she'd never once been grounded, never been put in "time-out," because she'd never given her parents a reason to discipline her. On the contrary, she'd grown up hearing a constant refrain: *You were the best baby. You were the best two-year-old.* "I think I was so good because, in a weird way, I was grateful to them," she'd said.

It was clear how that perfectionism had played out in her romantic relationships. If she wasn't living the fairy tale—if she wasn't prepared to marry someone within weeks—she moved on. (Translation: she broke up with partners before they could reject or abandon *her.*) What I'd wanted to know was: What changed? When I'd asked what was different about her husband, Neil—a man she made clear was in no way perfect!—she'd listed a litany of great qualities, all the reasons she loved him, but she couldn't really articulate why she'd been ready to commit.

Now, in her email, she was telling me that she hadn't been ready to commit at all. That, in fact, they had broken up a year or so into the relationship. It literally took a national disaster—Hurricane Sandy—for me to agree to go out with him again, she wrote. And I made him "date" me all over. I can't believe this didn't come up in our conversation. He was persistent!

By then, Gina had realized that her parents' relationship, which she'd always idealized, was not actually perfect. My parents never fought because my dad is the most easygoing person ever, whereas what my mom says goes. They don't really communicate.

Meanwhile, something about Neil's persistence broke the spell. Gina was able to see that things could be imperfect—but still extraordinary. Talk about a lightbulb moment, she wrote. I mean, deep.

R&P QUESTION #53   Do you want to emulate your parents' marriage or relationship? Why or why not?

R&P QUESTION #54   Is there a couple other than your parents whose relationship you respect or whose relationship has served as a guide for you?

It's not exactly a secret that we're shaped by our families of origin and the circumstances in which we were raised. The normalization of therapy, rising interest in pop psychology and trends like "attachment theory" and "gentle parenting," a growing emphasis on the importance of prioritizing mental health—all of it suggests that we're perhaps more aware of our interiors than ever before. And yet no matter how self-aware we are, so much of our day-to-day behavior remains predicated on the past. Without even realizing it, we're often operating on autopilot.

I spoke with one woman, Isabelle, whose mother had a tendency to infantilize her father—by telling him to sit up straight at the dinner table, or tutting if he reached for another chicken wing, or chiding him about his weight. It wasn't mean-spirited, Isabelle explained, and by all accounts her parents had a wonderful marriage. But then Isabelle told me a story about how she'd unwittingly started to parrot that behavior—specifically, when her then-boyfriend, now-husband left a dirty cup in the sink. "We had just moved in together," she'd said. "He was in the shower, and I was already so sick of picking up his shit." So she marched into the bathroom, ripped back the shower curtain, and practically screamed at him, "IS THIS YOUR CUP?" She broke into laughter as she described the scene: her poor boyfriend standing there, naked, utterly flummoxed—all this over a coffee mug?—and Isabelle reading him the riot act and swearing up and down that she was *not* a maid and shouting that he could put his own damn cup in the dishwasher. "I really needed to learn how to, like, cool out," she said. *Is this your cup?!* is now a long-running in-joke in their relationship.

I spoke with another woman, Grace, who thought she was living the exact life she wanted. She moved to New York City at seventeen to study at the Fashion Institute of Technology, met her future husband, Josh, got engaged, got married, had a baby, and settled into a charming apartment on the Upper East Side. And since it was everything she'd ever wanted—the family and the nice home in the historic neighborhood—she ignored some signs that had been there from the beginning: like the fact that Josh was difficult to pin down about anything pertaining to the future, that he was a bit of a partier, that he never wanted to talk about anything "serious." When he later started displaying signs of alcohol dependency, she ignored that, too. "I was like, 'If I leave him, I'd be doing the same thing my mom did,'" she told me. So she stayed. Had another baby. And eventually, when his drinking worsened and money started disappearing from their joint account, she realized she had to leave, and headed back home to Georgia to start over. "The irony of it all is that I ended up basically replicating my mother's life," she said. "My dad was an addict. My parents separated when I was a kid. I was so afraid to be like her, but my mom and I actually joke about it now: I basically re-created her exact life."

And then I spoke with Alina. She was an Eastern European immigrant who dated a slew of men who'd reminded her of the guys back home, not to mention her father: chauvinistic, possessive (her words). "My father was macho," she told me. "And my mother was very easygoing. You know, weak. He took advantage of her." Not all that long after arriving in the States, Alina had fallen deeply in love with a man four years her junior, an immigrant like her, tall and apparently so painfully handsome he could have been—and often did pass for—a model. Their relationship was wildly passionate but volatile. And, like all the others, he was controlling. "All he was doing was bossing me around," she said. "'Don't go there, don't do this.' Like, trying to prove that he was the boss. I was like, 'Can I live with this for the rest of my life? Could he be a good father, a role model for my children?' I was tired of men telling me what to do. So what that I love him?"

She ended it—despite how painful the breakup was, how often she thought about calling. But the very next man she met was the man she later married, her husband, Steven.

"I knew I had to find someone who was nice to his mother," she told me. And she studied Steven and his family, the deep respect they had for each other, the way they joked and laughed, but also the way Steven held the door for his mother and took her coat whenever they went out. The way he doted on her. "I saw something special between the two of them, a very tight relationship."

In the run-up to their wedding, Alina told their officiant how fond she was of Steven's parents' marriage, how much she admired that after years and years together, they still held hands, still expressed such sweet and obvious affection. During the ceremony, he had woven those hopes and wishes into his official remarks, had shared that Alina looked to her future in-laws as an example she intended to replicate.

"With Steven, everything was quiet," Alina told me. "We didn't have that kind of adrenaline-fueled relationship." By which she meant, they didn't have the ups and downs she had experienced before, the high highs but also the low lows, largely born of insecurity and immaturity and a fair bit of drama. Steven, by contrast, was calm and steady. She talked about how much pleasure she took even from the tone of his voice, how he liked to begin each morning by insisting that it was going to be a wonderful day. "I found a guy who was the opposite of my father," she said. "Easygoing, levelheaded. And when I saw his family, it was like, *Oh, this is where that's coming from*. It was *smart* love."

We don't always think about our potential or future in-laws when we're falling in love. But it's true what they say: when you marry someone, you marry their family. And the "wisest" among us, according to Geoffrey Greif, PhD, a professor at the University of Maryland School of Social Work, "will have given thought to the family they're marrying into."

It was that quote, which I'd come across while perusing the Goop website, that prompted me to reach out to him. Well, that, and the fact that Dr. Greif literally wrote the book on in-laws. (Seriously, it's called *In-Law Relationships: Mothers, Daughters, Fathers, and Sons*, coauthored with colleague Michael Woolley.) It was also the very first question I had for him: Why is learning about your partner's family so important? Why is it "wise" to seek a better understanding of where your partner comes from?

"Because you're marrying into a whole family tree. The guy you see sitting here," he told me, gesturing to himself, "is the product of my mother and father's family trees, my observations of their relationships with siblings, spouses, with their parents and their children, cousins. You're not just seeing me sitting here, in and of myself. I'm the product of a lot of . . . stuff. And that stuff—positive and negative—helps me interact or doesn't help me interact with my wife, who has her whole family tree."

In other words, just as we're shaped by our own families, our partners are of course shaped by theirs. As part of his research, Dr. Greif interviewed more than 1,500 in-laws in order to further investigate the complexities of those relationships. *I* was most interested in the clues that his research might provide, the unexpected ways in which a partner's familial background might play out in a romantic pairing.

"One of the things we found, for example, is that people who grew up observing their father close to his siblings will more likely be close to their own siblings." (Interestingly, a mother's closeness to her siblings had no measurable impact.) Dr. Greif posits that a father's closeness to his brothers and sisters might indicate his adoption of a particularly warm and loving and somewhat nontraditional role, "which makes you more loving and emotionally expressive with your siblings." I thought of my own brother, to whom I've always been extremely close. In fact, several of the women he dated over the years were notably threatened by the nature of our relationship. And though I hadn't planned to ask about it, I wondered what Dr. Greif might say to others who are likewise close to their siblings and might experience the same kind of friction while dating.

"I would say that [being close to a sibling] is a great thing," he told me. "It shows an ability to be intimate, and that's a great springboard for intimacy into adulthood. If I grew up close to my siblings, that would tend to predispose me to be capable of having an intimate relationship with an adult. Whereas if I grow up and everything is estranged, in theory that could potentially set me up for having trouble establishing an intimate relationship. So I'm all for that kind of intimacy. The more intimate relationships one has in life, the better. And I would have to say that your brother was dating the wrong people."

I happened to agree—and shout-out to my sister-in-law, who warmly embraced our tight bond.

We also talked about the ways family routines and traditions can sometimes impinge on a couple's relationship. Nearly 20 percent of new marriages in the United States are interracial or interethnic, while one in three is interfaith. "If I'm a Eurocentric white male," he said, by way of example, "and I've grown up in a culture that values independence from families, and I marry a Latina, who comes from a very family-based community—if she's on the phone with them all the time or her family comes over all the time, and I'm used to having space, how do we negotiate those kinds of things?"

We tend to operate under the belief that our relationships are about only the two of us, when really they're the product of many, many people's stories and histories and desires and opinions. Those histories don't always magically mesh or *click*; in fact, it's often the process of partnering that tends to dredge up old wounds or bring conflict to the surface. "The kind of attachment that we had in our family of origin is only replicated or approximated in romantic relationships," Dr. Solomon told me. "When we fall in love, all that old stuff is going to get activated, all of our attachment patterns or fears. We're going to be at risk of taking on really similar roles in our romantic relationships that we took on in our family of origin."

Unless, of course, we're willing to talk about it. Dr. Levkoff weighed in here, too. "I think knowing what someone's relationship models are gives us some inclination of how they might act in our relationship. People will often make it clear that what they saw in their own home was something that they admire, or something that they absolutely detest, right? Even that conversation brings up some stories about someone's family, and how they navigated conflict, what they saw working, what they didn't, what they would have changed, and then you have an opportunity to say, What do you want to do differently? How do you see that playing out?"

How often do you speak with your family? How often do you visit?

"I don't know how much you know about my family," Dr. LePera said. One of the things I most admire about the holistic psychologist is her willingness to share her own life and her own struggles—via social media, certainly, but, in particular, in her book *How to Do the Work*, in which she revealed that she'd grown up as part of a first-generation Italian family in Philly, the "picture of middle-class normalcy and happiness." Under that facade, she writes, "we were a sick family." She goes on to describe unhealthy coping mechanisms, codependency, and emotional enmeshment; since I'm a fan of her work, I knew quite a bit of that background.

"Here's how this played out with my wife and me in the beginning of our relationship," she said. "Whenever I would go to my parents' house, there was a lot of resentment. There was a lot of stress around my home visits. I would get agitated days in advance. I would be snippy when I was there. I was drinking a lot when I was at home. So there came a time when Lolly was like, 'I actually don't enjoy time with your family anymore. I love your family. I love you. I want to support you. But you're mean to me when we're there.' So her choice was to limit the amount of time she spent with them."

"But wasn't that hard on you?" I asked, the pitch of my voice rising. I grew up in a happy home, but I'm a Jewish girl from Long Island—my family and I don't know any other way than to be in each other's business.

"Yeah, my family is wondering, 'Where's Lolly?' And I'm making excuses: 'Oh, she's watching the dog.' Talk about being pulled between! But the reality of it was, if I dropped into my heart, I didn't want to go, either. It was stressful to be relied on in the way that I'd been relied on for decades. And that frustration that I was feeling was really about my inability to have boundaries with my family. So at first it was lies; then I got more comfortable saying, 'Oh, she's just taking some time for herself today.' And then I finally got to a place where I was like, *I need to stop.* I started to come less frequently. And eventually I cut off contact for the better part of eighteen months, to give myself some time and space to discover myself. And that ended up being one of the greatest gifts—to me, first and foremost, and then to all of my relationships: with Lolly, with my family. Now, on the other side, we have boundaries. We have limits."

For better or worse, a side effect of the normalization of therapy is that terms like *boundary* and *toxic* and *triggered* have entered the popular lexicon. "Therapy-speak," as it's known, gets bandied about constantly online, but it's frequently misused—sometimes to "diagnose" a person, or to reject accountability, or to sit in judgment. (In just the last few years, a number of high-profile celebrity spats over the use—or misuse—of the term *boundaries* have played out on social media, further popularizing the term and lighting up internet discourse.) "Just for the record," I asked Dr. LePera, "tell me, what is a boundary?"

"I think this is the confusion: a boundary isn't an act of coercion, an act of control, or an ultimatum. It's really focused on *me.* What am I going to do differently? How can I show up differently? What limit can I place on myself? So here's kind of a silly example: You're sliding into my DMs and saying mean things. Do I tell you to stop? Or do I keep myself safe by not looking at it or hitting block? That's a boundary. You can keep pinging me all you want. But I'm not going to respond, I'm not going to engage in that stress. People often misinterpret boundaries and use them to control: *I don't like this, and now you need to stop.*"

Given the confusion, and, given the fact that our patterns and behaviors are so deeply ingrained and require a certain amount of awareness to recognize, I wondered about Dr. LePera's ability even to see—before her wife chose to take a step back—that she perhaps needed some limits.

"Do you think that if, at the very beginning, you and your wife had asked each other, 'What boundaries do you have with your family?' you would've had the wherewithal back then to say, 'We don't have any boundaries,' or, 'This is something I struggle with'? Because sometimes I think it takes another person to point out what might be problematic dynamics that you can't yet see."

"I didn't know what boundaries were," she said, shaking her head. "I wouldn't have said anything was wrong. And yes, to your very wise point, this happens in childhood. When we're in our childhood home, we imagine every home on the block looks and operates the same. And then we have friends, and we go over to their homes. And we're like, 'Oh, this home looks different.' Right? They're acting different. Things are different. The closer we get with friends and romantic partners, the more we get an outsider's perspective, the more those blinders come off."

I nodded. "What happens if you get hit with a question—if you're reading this book and working through the R&P questions—or your partner makes an observation, and you realize you don't know how to answer? Or you think, 'Gosh, I'm not ready for this. It's not that I don't want to have these conversations. I'm just not equipped to have them yet. This is bringing up some stuff from my past that I haven't worked through or even thought about yet.'"

"Yeah. It's communication, right?" Dr. LePera said. "Even if it's *I don't know how I feel.* There's a scenario where you have these conversations, you read this book, you know the questions are important, but you don't yet know the answers. For a lot of us, just the sheer practice of asking ourselves questions is new. And I think what you said was actually beautiful: These are really important questions, and I need a little more time myself, just to see how I feel. Or, this is bringing up a lot for me right now, let me make some sense of it. And we can engage in this conversation later. That way you're honoring your truth, and you're also giving your potential partner the opportunity to respond in a way that works for them."

* * *

Later in the evening, on the same day I'd had my *Clueless* epiphany, the Brit listened quietly as I strung my theory together—that perhaps his parents' divorce had made him wary about our future, or even about me. That perhaps I really *was* hiding something, that I wasn't quite who I portrayed myself to be. I waited patiently as he slathered a slice of baguette with butter. He took a bite, reached for another—bread, butter, cheese—and soon enough started to open up. He told me that he didn't remember a lot from that time—the divorce and the immediate aftermath, all these years later, were still fuzzy—but he did recall seeking out an old friend whose parents were also divorced, trying to glean a sense of what it all meant and what he might expect next. He'd never thought about it before but admitted that he likely did have a fear of finding something beautiful only for it to fall apart.

After that talk, I was able to let a comment like "I still can't find anything wrong with you" go—because I knew it was his way of saying, *I love you, and I'm scared, but so happy you're mine.* Those comments were a reflection of how he grew up, the circumstances and experiences unique to him, not a criticism of where *I* was in life.

As I've gotten older, I've learned to take a step back, to be less reactive and emotional about things that would have hurt my heart immensely in the past. I try to see people as real people, because we all have flaws and a past that makes us who we are. It's so easy to make absolutely everything about ourselves, to refuse to look at a conversation from all angles; it's what we're conditioned to do from childhood. But putting yourself in someone else's shoes, I've so often found, can give you clarity, and a sense of empathy, and peace.

5

Chores, Domestic Duties
& Building a Home

Putting a garbage liner back in
the pail is my love language.

—*Eve Rodsky*

I've always found it funny how often professionals—of all stripes, no matter their particular field or specialty—wind up diagnosing the health of their clients' relationships. Carey, the financial planner (and cat lover) from chapter one, told me right off the bat, "I can tell within the first five minutes whether a couple has issues: a wince here, a lack of engagement in the conversation, the use of accusatory language. I see it all." In late 2023, HuffPost ran an entire article about all the things your housekeeper picks up on. ("We can always tell when a couple is having relationship trouble," claimed one cleaning service CEO.) Same goes for the queen of New York real estate, Barbara Corcoran, founder of the eponymous Corcoran Group and, since 2009, one of the savviest investors on ABC's *Shark Tank*. "It was the most interesting part of the business," she told me. "So often my first thought when meeting a couple wasn't *What are they looking for?* or *What will they buy?* My first thought was *This marriage won't last."*

How could she tell?

"The dead giveaway was using the words *I* or *me*. You know, 'The view is very important to *me*.' Well, what about the person sitting next to you? Someone who told you what *they* wanted, who did all the talking and answered all your questions, while the other person sat quietly in the background? That thing ain't gonna work. Nobody's a sheep. In better partnerships, you hear 'The view is very important to *us*.'"

Whether you're cohabitating, thinking about moving in with your significant other, or just occasionally spending the night with someone, a home says so much about a person: Are they slovenly or tidy? An avid reader, or is nary a book in sight? Ultra-luxe aesthete with a taste for Thom Browne sweats and high-end cutlery? Or high-energy extrovert, with a gym bag positioned by the front door and a fridge covered in holiday cards, photos, and invites? Clues are everywhere. Had I been paying attention—back in the days when I was pining for the silver fox, hoping to turn our very one-sided situationship into something more serious—I would have seen that there was no room in his apartment, *or* his life, for a permanent partner, as evidenced by the tiny dining table with the lone chair tucked beneath it, the single nightstand with the sole lamp, or the fact that he never, and I mean *never*, had toilet paper.

The rhythm of home life came up early on in my relationship with the Brit, too, albeit in an altogether different context. We hadn't been dating very long when he said to me, as we were side by side in the bathroom one day, moving through the steps of our morning routines, "Would you please, *please* try and remember to put the toilet lid down?"

"What do you mean?" I asked, genuinely confused. "I always leave the seat down."

"Not the seat. The *lid*. The lid of the toilet."

It was pretty clear from his tone that this was not the first time that he'd had that thought—and far from feeling offended, I was fascinated. It hadn't occurred to me to put the lid down. That wasn't something we did in my home growing up. So had he never said anything, I likely never would've closed it, never would've realized how much that bothered him—and how annoying would that have been? (Incidentally, and after reading up on the subject, we should all be putting our toilet lids down. Closing the lid before flushing, and keeping it closed, apparently helps to mitigate the spread of, ahem, *particles*.) In any event, I was glad he spoke up; shutting the lid was a small gesture, a tiny change I could make to demonstrate that I loved him and that his comfort mattered.

Feeling comfortable expressing a domestic niggle?

Check.

R&P QUESTION #74   **What is the ideal division of domestic labor?**

"I don't think people realize how *much* that matters," Willa told me. We were talking about the idea that people are generally happier in their relationship when their home is in order. The forty-one-year-old married mother of two, a former magazine editor turned university administrator, had already told me about her jam-packed schedule. "I have friends whose husbands *do* clean up after themselves, or take out the trash without being asked," she continued. "My husband is not that person. And that's okay. But if I'm asking him to do it, I need him to do it. And it infuriates me when he doesn't."

"Did you have discussions about the division of household labor and how that would look in your relationship before you took the plunge?" I asked.

"Honestly, no. And I think one of the reasons my husband is the way he is is that when we first got married, I didn't want him to do anything. I *liked* doing all the food shopping. I liked doing the cooking. I liked doing the laundry. And it's because I saw my mom doing that. My mom was a stay-at-home mom, and I really looked up to her. I wanted to be her. But I'm very different now from when I first got married. I'm more exhausted now, with kids. I work full-time. I'll pass out in one of the kids' beds and wake up at two in the morning—haven't brushed my teeth, haven't washed my face. And I'm like, *Ugh, I have to go downstairs and run the dishwasher.* If I go downstairs and the dishwasher is already running? I love my husband so much. I'm so happy. But when he doesn't help, or he doesn't listen, that's when I get frustrated."

In this day and age, most couples who cohabitate expect—or at least claim to want—something akin to a fifty-fifty split of domestic chores and financial responsibility, what's often referred to as an "egalitarian marriage" (as opposed to a "traditional marriage," where one spouse or partner is the breadwinner and the other stays at home). Research indicates that, at least at first, modern heterosexual couples do exactly that: support each other's careers and split household duties equitably. But later on, particularly after having children, things change—even among those who said they wanted to keep things equal. According to the New Parents Project, a longitudinal study by researchers at Ohio State University, men perform five *fewer* hours of housework a week after having kids—despite working the same number of hours outside the home as their partners. That sudden shift (and the attendant stress and resentment) was a theme that came up and up again in my own research.

Like with Mia Fischer, another married mother of two boys, ages five and eight. "I take care of most of the logistics and planning for our family—which is fine," she said. "But we still end up fighting about simple things, like 'Can you take the kids to this thing at this time?' I feel like I ask for help as a question, but to my partner, those requests sound like demands. Which, in a way, they kind of are."

"Well, you're asking for help because you need help," I offered.

"Exactly. And I feel like I should *be able* to ask. It's not like I'm overscheduling us—we are not that scheduled. I think this is societal. Men think that they're doing so much because the generations before did so little. But it's not actually anywhere close to being equal. And it just pisses me off."

If there's anyone who understands this conundrum, it's Eve Rodsky, author of *Fair Play*, a system for rebalancing domestic duties she created after having become the default (or what she calls *she-fault*) parent following the birth of her first child, Zach. "Because Seth and I hadn't pre-negotiated how to share in the domestic workload before Zach came along," she writes of her husband, "it defaulted to me. He'd leave for work in the office, and I'd spend the next eight hours boiling bottles, doing dishes, folding laundry, restocking the nursery, running to the grocery store, picking up prescriptions, preparing meals, tidying up, *and* entertaining and attending to my little one. . . . He made efforts to extend a hand but ultimately retreated because 'I can't do anything right.' The bickering between us became part of our new family routine, and when I considered returning to work, the idea of juggling a challenging office job with the ever-expanding demands of domestic life seemed impossible."

Fair Play, which has since spawned a successful podcast and a feature-length documentary, is more than a system, however; it's also an investigation of the societal issues Mia was talking about, the fact that women continue to perform the bulk of childcare and housework, even in two-income families, largely thanks to outdated ideas about gender roles. (Perhaps not surprisingly, research indicates that same-sex couples split up housework much more equitably.) Aside from the patent unfairness, this puts a very real strain on relationships.

"What's for dinner?" Eve asked me by way of example. "When is the kid's soccer game? Where is the soccer bag? When is the babysitter coming? What are we doing this weekend? Why don't we have any snacks?"

I could feel my anxiety building with each new question she tossed out, rapid-fire.

"When all the decision-making falls on one person," she continued, "they are bound to get burnt out. When you are holding all the cards, it's easy to drop the ones that are most important to your mental health: self-care, friendships, date nights, and so on. Your relationship can start to feel robotic. You lose the things that make you *you*."

A huge part of Eve's work—and a fair bit of content in her book—is aimed at helping couples get comfortable even *broaching* the topic of housework without anybody getting defensive. Before attempting to introduce the Fair Play system, for example, she suggests establishing a weekly or even nightly touch-base with your partner. "Communication is a practice that a lot of couples do not exercise enough," she said. "Choose a time when cognition is high and emotion is low—meaning, the kids are in bed and all distractions are put away. Set a timer for ten minutes and use that time to check in with one another. How was your day? How are the kids doing? What does the rest of your week look like? The first few check-ins might feel awkward, so it's always helpful to bring in a short-term reward substitution, like your favorite ice cream or tacos."

Once you're comfortable, she suggests, you can dive into more detail about who does what—and how that might need to change.

But an even better idea? Starting the conversation early on in your relationship—like, way, *way* earlier than you think might be necessary.

"We didn't think we needed to talk about it," Noelle, yet another married mother of two, told me. As required by their church, she and her husband, Miles, had undergone premarital counseling—of both the explicitly religious variety (conducted with their priest) *and* with a secular therapist. "I knew we'd talk about finances and family planning. But it never even crossed my mind to ask about, like, 'Do you leave the toilet seat up when you go to the restroom?'"

"What kinds of things did you discuss?" I asked.

"The questions she asked were really interesting, actually," she said of the secular therapist. "Like, 'What was your dad's role in the household?' Or, 'What did the responsibilities look like for your mom and dad?' It was a reflection of our lives and where we'd come from, but in a way that we would never have talked about—and had never talked about before. Especially since we come from such similar backgrounds. So her questions forced you to articulate—like, for example, my dad always took out the trash. Does that mean I'm just assuming

Miles is going to be the one to take the trash out? That's maybe a stupid example."

"It is *so* not stupid," I practically yelled at her. "I just spoke with a woman who literally said, 'When my husband runs the dishwasher, and I wake up in the morning to a clean kitchen, it makes me want to have sex with him.'"

And yes, I was talking about Willa—the former magazine editor whose mother had been a stay-at-home mom. (And yes, she really did tell me that she was much more affectionate when her partner pitched in.)

"The trash is a stand-in for a much larger issue," I said. "It's about expectations, how things were done in your own home growing up, and your ability to communicate those expectations. When your husband doesn't take out the trash, do you become resentful?"

"It's funny, that's the exact same speech our therapist gave us," Noelle said. "And I will be very open—four or five years later? The struggles we're having? You do revisit it, you do need to have these conversations again. Because these guys"—she gestured to the baby in her lap—"change the game totally. Things are going to come up beyond the trash. Like, okay. Cool. You can conquer the trash in your first year of marriage. But as soon as you have one, and then two kids, life starts to happen."

The Pressure to Be "Man Enough": A Conversation with Justin Baldoni

There's no shortage of potential topics to dive into when talking with actor/writer/director Justin Baldoni—from his work on-screen (he's perhaps best known for portraying reformed bad boy Rafael on *Jane the Virgin*) to the newly renovated—and jaw-droppingly beautiful— Ojai home he shares with his wife, Emily, and their two children (recently featured in *Architectural Digest*, naturally). But I reached out thanks to his work with the Man Enough movement, a community (as well as a bestselling book and podcast) he founded in order to upend traditional gender roles and redefine masculinity—in part by challenging men to be brave enough to be vulnerable, and strong enough to be sensitive.

You've talked a little about your wife's decision—and it was a very intentional decision on her part—to stay home with your children in the early stages of their lives, and some of the ways you both struggled to make that adjustment. Let's unpack that a little bit.

Justin: Yeah, so for years Emily and I found ourselves in this competition: Who was more exhausted at the end of the day? This is something a lot of husbands and wives struggle with, right? You have one person who is out in the world, who has all the pressure to provide for the family—and generally, that's a man. Let's just look at this through a patriarchal lens. More often than not, that's a man. And the woman, if she chooses not to work and to be home with the children—

R&P
QUESTION
#111

If we have children, who will change the diapers, heat the bottles, prepare the meals, draw the baths, get up in the middle of the night, visit the pediatrician, purchase clothing, and so on?

Hardest job in the world, by the way.

Justin: Oh, yeah. We know the invisible work of women goes unnoticed, and yet it's the thing that allows the economy to flourish, right? Like, the secret to capitalism is motherhood. And it is exhausting being a mother with two young kids. So what we found is that I would get home sometimes, and I'd be exhausted. She'd be exhausted. But neither of us was able to have compassion for what the other person was experiencing. In bearing the weight of trying to provide and build my businesses, I missed how hard her job was. And in taking care of the family and managing the household, she missed the pressure and anxiety I was under.

So what changed?

Justin: We've both done so much self-work, which is, I think, the most important ingredient in making *anything* work—both individuals working on themselves separately, and then coming together. And at first it was hard. It took us really talking to each other, and listening to each other, and loving each other to realize we were both suffering, and internalizing that suffering and projecting it onto the other person, as if *they* were wrong. But I remember one day she was finally able to share with me, and I was able to share with her, and we both had this aha moment. We realized we were both being fucked by the same system—like, this is how the patriarchy actually hurts me, in that I was taught that my worth as a man is entirely reliant on productivity. So I'm out in the world, but deep down in my heart, I want to be with my children. I realized I was actually jealous of my wife and she was jealous of me. That realization couldn't have happened unless both of us said, "Okay, let me share how I'm feeling. And let me listen to you." Since we had that conversation years ago, we haven't had one argument about it since.

You mentioned self-work. What would you say to someone who is maybe new to that concept?

Justin: I think learning how to communicate—it's a skill set. And both partners need the same skill set. So it's okay to say, "Hey, I think we're struggling with communication. Can we bring in a third party?" Unfortunately, for most people—especially young people—that's a red flag. Like, *We need to go to therapy and we're only a month in?* But I believe we have to deconstruct this idea that therapy is only for broken people and instead use it as a tool, right? It's like stretching before a workout. If the workout is the relationship, we have to stretch first, so we don't pull a muscle. That's what I would say. Therapy, learning communication skills, reading books together—this is not a sign that you're doing something wrong, or that you're bad at dating. These are tools that are going to help you create—and have—a healthy relationship.

• • •

Jess and Jeremy, a newly married couple in their late twenties, were recapping their relationship history for me—together eight years, met in college, briefly split after graduation only to get back together a month later—and we'd just gotten to the part where they'd decided to live together.

"And was that a very conscious decision on your part?" I asked.

"Oh, yeah. I almost feel like moving in together was a bigger step than getting married," Jess said, turning to her husband. "Because I think I told you, '*I do not take this lightly.*' Like, 'If those aren't your intentions, then you should not move in.'"

As someone born and raised in New York, I've become intimately familiar with the "real estate merger"—aka, choosing to live with a partner, maybe before either of you is really ready, for the simple reason that somebody's lease is up. In a place as notoriously expensive as NYC, where the vast majority of young people must have roommates to survive, living together seems to make sense. But I'm also familiar with an oft-quoted statistic: that cohabitating before marriage is associated with a *higher* risk of eventual divorce. Reams of studies, conducted over decades, have arrived at that same finding again and again.

And for a lot of people, this is super confusing. I mean, wouldn't it stand to reason that living together first, as a sort of trial, would *lower* your risk? How can you know if you're truly compatible, if you'll actually enjoy living with someone without, you know, living with them? Turns out, this is confusing for researchers, too, in no small part because premarital cohabitation is now much more common. As many as 70 percent of modern couples will shack up long before saying "I do." And for every new study that suggests a risk, another demonstrates the exact opposite effect: that living together first does indeed have something akin to a protective effect. After taking a fairly exhaustive dive into all that conflicting research, however, there's one thing I can tell you that's pretty clearly true: *when* you choose to merge households matters far less than *why* you merge them. Couples who are very intentional about their choice to cohabitate—like Jess and Jeremy—fare much better than those who just sort of slide into it, as was the case with another young woman I interviewed, Mariah.

"I remember I asked if I could put him down as my emergency contact," she said. "I was in my late twenties, we had just moved in together, and I had started a new job—that's why I asked. But he hesitated. My dad is a doctor, and he was like, 'Why wouldn't you want your dad to be your emergency contact?' And I said, 'Well, yeah. He's a doctor. But he's four hours away, and you're here?' So that was one of the things that told me, maybe we're not on the same page about what it means to be moving in with each other, what that commitment means."

I was struck by that—after all that time compiling the questions that make up R&P, and talking to couples, and disseminating the questionnaire, it hadn't occurred to me to ask about becoming someone's emergency contact. "It's interesting," I said, "because when you're talking about moving in with someone, you typically discuss things like rent and utilities, or how much money you both make and how you'll split bills and what furniture you'll buy. But I never thought about the choice to live with someone in those terms. And frankly, if you're taking that step, shouldn't you want to be each other's point of contact?"

I asked to what extent they'd discussed the realities of cohabitation, and what that might mean for their partnership long term. "Did you really talk?"

"I thought we did," she said. "And there were differences—in how we were raised, how we felt about money. But we were passionately in love. I just don't know if we understood the depth of what love means in terms of choosing somebody and making the effort to consciously choose each other. And it got to a point where he clearly didn't want to choose me anymore."

Three days before Christmas, Mariah's boyfriend ended it. "It was heartbreaking for me at the time. But looking back, we were not a match. And I was talking with a friend recently who mentioned—rightly—that it's much easier to break a relationship than to break a lease. Now I feel very strongly that I will not move in with anybody until I either have an engagement ring on my finger or I know that's coming."

"Or until you see that you're listed as their emergency contact," I teased.

"Exactly. Like, if you get into a car accident and after you call AAA you don't call me, then I don't know what we're doing."

The Design Compromise:
A Conversation with Nate Berkus

There's an old *Sex and the City* episode in which Charlotte (desperate to find a husband in those days) meets a man who—surprisingly and shockingly—is *also* desperate to get married. Sean owns an investment firm and a classic-six apartment on the Upper West Side, and soon enough the new couple find themselves at a home goods store, where Sean shows Charlotte the china pattern he's been admiring. She *hates* it.

"Charlotte broke it off then and there," Carrie narrates. "It would never work. He was American Classic; she was French Country."

It was funny and pithy—as all *Sex and the City* episodes were—but it also got at a larger truth: merging tastes and styles and design budgets can be tricky when partners decide to share a living space. *I couldn't help but wonder* (sorry, couldn't resist) . . . is there something in particular that tends to trip couples up? Is it possible that two people can have such wildly divergent aesthetics that they really *can't* be blended?

There was only one person to ask: Nate Berkus. Not only because he's a fabulous designer, but because he married a designer, Jeremiah Brent, and the two are known for having divergent aesthetics.

You've said publicly that you and your husband have "blended" your design styles, and—furthermore—that "it's not worth having the fight of your marriage over a table lamp." But you've also made it clear that you and Jeremiah *don't* always see eye to eye. How do you work through differing opinions without letting things devolve into a fight?

Nate: I've always known there's not "one correct way" to assemble a space. But being married to another designer—whose talent I admire and respect—has taught me a lot in this department. So, first, an absolute *no* from either of us means an *absolute no*. Stop your pitch, stop trying to convince the other person. Whatever the *no* is—a piece of furniture, an idea for decorating, anything— it dies on the hill. But a *maybe* or *let me see what you mean*, those are open invitations to stand up and start pushing furniture around, or to run to one of the sample cabinets in our offices for fabrics and wall-covering ideas.

> **R&P QUESTION #81**
>
> What styles of décor do you prefer? What styles do you dislike?

Jeremiah has said that the two of you actually like the struggle. What did it take for you to arrive at that place?

Nate: I've learned that when design isn't ego-based, when you make the space to allow everyone to be seen and feel heard—whether we're talking about home partners or designer and client—you'll actually end up with a design that's much more interesting than your initial instinct.

You've also found a beautiful way to honor your former partner, Fernando Bengoechea, who tragically died in the 2004 Indian Ocean tsunami, in part by displaying photos of him in your home. [Nate and Jeremiah's son, Oskar, was also named in honor of Fernando, whose middle name was Oskar.] It's not a design question, per se, but what advice do you have for partners who would like to honor the past, without feeling threatened by it?

Nate: I wish that my answer to this question could only be about working on healthy communication, or making sure that how you approach your own grief is framed in a way that honors the love you share now. Or even that having had a great love story and lost it can sometimes prepare you for another great love story. But my truth is that it depends on the inner strength of the person who has to live with the knowledge that they were not your first great love.

● ● ●

It's hard not to be moved by that level of humility; certainly, it puts petty fights about design into perspective. So who knows? Maybe Charlotte and Sean could have made it work, had they been willing to embrace a new aesthetic: American-French, perhaps, or Classic-Country.

R&P QUESTION #77 What type of house or apartment do you prefer to live in? Urban or rural? City or suburbs?

Unless you plan to maintain a long-distance relationship indefinitely, a desire to live in the same general geographic region seems like a pretty fundamental requirement for making things work long term.

Then again, it's easy to forget the multitude of factors that may come into play over the years. And at no point was that more clear than during my conversation with Jo Piazza—you remember her, writer and podcaster extraordinaire, who went from researching marriage to researching infidelity? Not long after meeting her now-husband, Nick, Jo relocated from New York to San Francisco. Then, after a number of years on the West Coast, the couple was ready for a change and headed back across the country to Jo's hometown.

"That was another question we really had to grapple with," she said. "What kind of place do you want to live in? Not so much where, but what *kind* of place? We're both urban people. We don't want to drive a car everywhere. We want to walk as much as possible. If we were suburban people, I'd maybe explore the California suburbs—I do love so much of the nature in California, but I find the cities impossible. So Philadelphia is the ideal urban location for us."

Philly certainly sounded ideal. She explained that she lived in the same neighborhood as four friends from college, all of whom also had children, all within walking distance, while her mother was a mere forty minutes away. New York, to which she and Nick both traveled frequently for work, was an easy commute. "You can be home by dinner," she said. "But it's interesting—one of the biggest fights I've seen friends engage in in the last few years is one partner wanting to leave the city and the other not. I've seen so many relationships held hostage over that particular argument, so it becomes this huge negotiation. I literally know someone who wanted a third baby, and her husband said, 'No, no, no, no, no.' But he ultimately agreed if she would allow them to move to the suburbs."

"And how is their relationship now?" I asked.

Jo clucked her tongue. "Not good," she said. "Not good."

Because that's the thing—people lose jobs, switch jobs, decide they want to be closer to family, need more space. It would be impossible to anticipate all the ways your life and your needs might change (*you don't know what you don't know*, as we've discussed), but you can at least determine if your and your partner's long-term visions align. Perhaps you always presumed you'd return to the burbs when it came time to build a family, or—like actress Jill Kargman—you'll need to make it crystal clear on your second date that you are *never leaving New York City*. Maybe your preference is to relocate often, or to live abroad for a few years—as was the case, and eventually the deal-breaker, for Tracey, a woman I spoke with whose boyfriend hoped to one day live in Hong Kong (a dream she did not share). Even if you're not currently partnered, asking yourself the questions can help bring the vision into focus, as it did for Angela, another young woman I talked to, who was single, still in her early twenties, and living in Hoboken.

"I'm not picturing raising a family here," she said. "I mean, I want to stay in New Jersey. I've become such a Jersey girl. And I would love to live close to the shore—not a beach town necessarily, maybe, like, a fifteen-minute drive away. But if I meet someone who's living here, they might want to stay in this area."

"Which is something you'll have to figure out," I said. "You could fall in love with a guy from England!"

Figuring it out is something Noelle was on the verge of doing, too. "We're going to move back to LA," she told me. "And it's the first time in our marriage that it's like: big decision, different feelings on it. If it were up to Miles, he would stay here forever. But there's a real drive to come home and to be near family. I'm sure you had a decision like that as well, being from two different countries."

And of course she was right. Because back then, where the Brit and I might one day live was still very much up in the air.

6

Health & Medical

It is health, which is real wealth, and
not pieces of silver and gold.
—*Mahatma Gandhi*

It was a Sunday afternoon in New York, one of those gorgeous spring days when it suddenly feels like absolutely everyone has decided to get outside, and the Brit and I were strolling back from brunch on the West Side of Manhattan. He'd flown in for the long weekend, three magical days together. We were in that sweet spot of feeling totally comfortable with each other, yet everything was still exciting and new—sharing food at restaurants (no cucumbers for him, *ever*). I'd introduced him to my favorite smoothie joint, Juicy Cube on Lexington and Fifty-Sixth, where he'd ordered a juice blend called the Blondie (apparently his new favorite flavor—in quite a few realms). And as I delightfully discovered while snuggling on the couch in the evenings, he loved a good rom-com. We rounded the corner and continued along a chain-link fence, the confines of a city ballpark. A Little League game was in session; the ping of a metal bat connecting with a ball rang in my ears. The sidewalk was lined with parents and strollers, a crowd of too-young-for-Little-League tots crowded around a sidewalk ice cream vendor.

"How many kids do you want to have someday?" I asked. I hadn't planned to initiate the "kids conversation." I wasn't in any particular rush. It just felt natural, given our surroundings.

"Two, I think," he said, utterly unfazed. "You?"

"Two."

"Well then, that settles it," he said, grabbing my hand. "We will have two kids." We walked in silence for a beat. Out of the corner of my eye, I could see the Brit tipping his chin to the sky and closing his eyes, enjoying the sun.

"It doesn't totally settle it, though. Like, I don't know how you want to have these two kids."

He turned to face me, raised an eyebrow, and flashed me a devilish grin.

I playfully smacked him on the arm. "I know how you want to *make* them. I meant, I don't know your thoughts on having biological children versus adopting, for example. Years ago, a good friend of mine adopted a daughter from Guatemala, and watching her go through that process, I realized I could absolutely love a child as my own, even if I didn't physically give birth. Could you?"

He took a moment to consider my question. "I'd like to try for biological kids, if you're okay to carry them. We'd obviously make the cutest babies." He brushed my shoulder with his and gave me a wink. "But I know it's not always as straightforward as that. I think if you wanted to adopt, I'd be okay with that, too."

Definitely not that straightforward, I thought. By then, I'd watched a number of friends struggle to conceive. "I'm glad you feel that way. Who knows if we'd have trouble getting pregnant. What about IVF? Would you be comfortable with that, too?"

"Of course. We'll do whatever we have to do. I'm open to all of it."

He gave my hand a squeeze, and though the conversation was light-hearted, it was poignant. We both knew what we'd left unsaid: we were older. We wouldn't have the luxury of working and traveling for years before trying to start a family.

Of course, that was hardly the end of the discussion. On the topic of kids, there is tons to discuss—I knew we'd get to the specifics later, as we worked our way through R&P. But that afternoon, as we, too, stopped for ice cream, there was something else on my mind.

I suffered from neurological motor tics as a kid.

It started around age seven with an errant nose wiggle, hidden easily enough behind my part as the White Rabbit in a fourth-grade production of *Alice in Wonderland*, but less so over the next few years, when I might dramatically raise my eyebrows or perform a funny sort of ill-timed eye roll when stressed. Sometimes I didn't know I was doing it at all; other times I could hide the tics by looking away or incorporating them into conversation, masked behind high energy. I was a social kid with a lot of friends, but still, I wasn't immune to the occasional comment or odd look or question.

It took years and a lot of work to learn to control each tic, but I eventually grew up and grew out of it—which is probably why I'd never discussed it with a boyfriend before. Even some of my closest girlfriends didn't know. With the Brit, though, it was different. There was always a chance of passing the tics down to my children, just as they might inherit my mop-top of frizzy curls, which had earned me the nickname Fuzzy at summer camp.

The Brit's response when I eventually told him? That he loved me and every part of me, and that if our future children developed the same issue, he wouldn't love them any less for it. And then very sweetly, in a show of solidarity perhaps, he started talking about his struggles with procrastination and his tendency to do too many things at once. "Maybe I should get checked out for ADHD?"

R&P
QUESTION
#90 What are your thoughts on going to the doctor? The dentist? Getting regular checkups or physicals? Would you want me to make those appointments for you?

"Health" is kind of a vague and intangible idea, in the sense that it means a lot of different things to different people. Some of us seek to "optimize" our health. We hit the gym, cut out gluten, or "go paleo." We take a self-care or a mental health day. Some of us are fastidious about having yearly checkups; some are fearful. But it's not something we generally think about in the context of *dating* or long-term partnership. And yet relationships have a profound effect on our health, and our health has a profound effect on our relationships.

To talk about that, I reached out to Dr. Mark Hyman, one of the most visible MDs in the country, author of fifteen number one *New York Times* bestsellers on health and wellness and a leader in the field of functional medicine. "I think the main message is that having and building happy relationships—not just romantic partnerships, but friendships—is critical to our health and survival," he told me. "They're one of the key foundational pieces at what we call the bottom of the matrix."

Functional medicine is a holistic model of care focused on addressing root causes of illness, rather than simply treating or managing symptoms, and the "matrix" is a mapping tool meant to help practitioners assess an illness or health concern by taking into account someone's whole body as well as their entire medical history. As Dr. Hyman has explained elsewhere, two people might have the same symptoms with very different root causes, or vice versa. At the bottom of the chart is a place to record notes about relevant lifestyle factors: nutrition, exercise, sleep, stress management, and, yes, relationships and social networks. We talked a little about how the effects of lifestyle on matters of health are especially obvious within the "Blue Zones," five geographic regions across the globe—in Japan, Greece, Italy, Costa Rica, and Loma Linda,

California—notable for very low rates of chronic disease and particularly long life expectancy. "You have deep connections, relationships," he said, "that are prioritized in such a way that some live to be very, very old. And a big part of it is the social connections. If you are deeply connected to another human being, it changes your biology in measurable ways; it changes the expression of genes that regulate immune function, inflammation, neurochemistry. Love is probably the most potent healing force on the planet."

"Given that relationships are such a key area of health," I asked, "why don't we, both as individuals and a society, dedicate more time and attention to them?"

"I mean, our entire culture is centered around achievement, career, being productive," he said. "We're not focused so much on the *being*, more on the *doing*. But at the end of the day, it's not how many emails you've answered that determines the quality of your life. What you'll look back on—what determines the quality of your life and your health—is the quality of your relationships."

R&P QUESTION #95 Do you want to know more about your genetics?

R&P QUESTION #96 Do you want to know more about your future health?

"The vow thing is 'in sickness and in health,' right?" Lolo said. "But what happens when you show up with the sickness?"

I first saw Lauren "Lolo" Spencer on the hit HBO show *The Sex Lives of College Girls*. She stars as Jocelyn, a funny, sexy, wildly confident college freshman—who, incidentally, is not so different from Lolo in real life. (She often refers to the character as "the younger version of me.") The multihyphenate model-actress-author, who was diagnosed with ALS (amyotrophic lateral sclerosis, or Lou Gehrig's disease) at fourteen years old, is also a disability advocate, the founder of the disability lifestyle brand Live Solo, and known for speaking frankly about life, love, dating, and sex.

"Here's the thing that comes with dating with a disability," she told me. "There's a lot of nuance when someone is being honest about what they believe it would be like to be with you, if they're the nondisabled partner." She explained that men have told her, flat-out, that dating her would be a "no-brainer"—if she were able-bodied. "Which is a very honest thing to say, right? And that's hard. That's hard for me to hear. Because I want it to be easy."

During our conversation, two things struck me: just how much Lolo's dating dramas, by and large, sound exactly the same as everyone else's (despite her struggles) and how often her particular romantic challenges are rooted in *communication*. (One of the reasons I especially wanted to chat with her was the frankness she'd displayed on an episode of Jameela Jamil's *I Weigh* podcast, when the topic of sex came up—specifically, the notion that disabled people are often viewed as too "fragile" to do it. "Girl, I just want a little choke," she'd said to Jameela, playfully wrapping a hand around her own neck. "There's that piece of it, too. Everyone's so afraid to have the fucking conversation! It's like, 'Let's just talk this out *please*.' And that's the problem: Nobody knows how to fucking communicate. So you can't even have an adult, decent conversation about these things that people are thinking about but for some reason don't want to discuss.")

Sound familiar?

"In interviews, you've talked about sometimes needing to ask for help in the restroom, even on a first date," I said. I'd read that she uses the tactic as a way to vet potential suitors, as well as a check against "internalized ableism," the tendency of disabled people to hide their needs or try to present as able-bodied as much as possible.

"Yeah, that's definitely been one of the ways," she said. "And I do find out later how terrifying and awkward a position that puts them in. But I kind of don't give a fuck? It's the reality of it. The guy I'm seeing now will jokingly say, 'I can't believe you did that to me. You have no idea the anxiety.' I'm like, 'Yeah, well, how else were you gonna find out?'"

I thought of a story I'd once heard about my friend's brother-in-law, who'd married and had a child relatively young. When his twenty-something buddies would come over to meet the new baby, he'd say, "Here!" and practically drop the newborn into their arms to see how they'd handle it. Sometimes the best way to gauge someone's reaction is to throw them into the fire.

"I like to start conversations that are real," she continued. "I'm not the one, 'Oh, what's your favorite color? Where do you like to eat?' Nah. 'What's your relationship like with your mama? Tell me the reason you and your last girlfriend broke up. Are you healed from that relationship? Have you done the work? Who do you aspire to be? How do you talk to God?' *Those* are the questions I ask."

Part of Lolo's work as an advocate is to debunk ideas about what it means to live with a disability, to normalize the experience simply by showing up as her authentic self, living her day-to-day life, and knowing that who she *is* is enough.

"I always like to remind people—this is something I say in all my interviews—everyone is going to experience life with a disability at some point," she said. "There's no escaping it. Whether it's temporary or permanent, or you grow old into it, you're going to experience life with a disability. So I like to advocate now. Let's start talking about how we would handle our lives if we were disabled people. Let's start asking those questions. And I mean from every angle—architecture, travel, employment, relationships. If we could figure out what those solutions are, things wouldn't be so difficult to experience. God willing, life is long. So let's be practical."

• • •

Showing up as your "authentic self" isn't always easy (even if Lolo makes it seem that way), and yet a theme across virtually all the interviews I conducted was how easy it is to share one's truth when you've finally found the right partner. I spoke with one woman whose first husband was convicted of and imprisoned for embezzlement. She was so embarrassed (even though she'd had no part in the crime) that she didn't say a word about it in her next relationship. But when she eventually met the man who would become her second husband, she told him everything—on their second date.

"That's it?" he'd asked, totally unfazed. "I thought you were going to tell me you don't eat meat."

Certified dating coach Damona Hoffman, the "Official Love Expert" on *The Drew Barrymore Show* and author of *F the Fairy Tale*, became a relationship coach thanks in large part to the transformative comfort she felt upon meeting her husband. "I think all the anxiety that past relationships brought up for me, how much I was thriving on drama, things I thought were romantic or butterflies—really, those were signs of disconnection," she said. "This sounds so corny, but I think of love as sort of like a hammock that holds you and makes you feel like you're both relaxed and supported, and able to just *be*."

The same proved true for my dear friend Marni Blake Ellis, who was diagnosed with multiple sclerosis at age twenty-three. "It must have been, like, our fourth date," she said of her now-husband, KC. "We were hanging out in my apartment in LA, having some drinks. And I told him, and it was like it went right over his head."

"Did you know you were going to tell him?" I asked.

"No, there was no preparation for it at all. And I don't think he really understood what it was to have an autoimmune disease. As opposed to that *other* guy, who rejected me."

Here, Marni digressed to remind me about the time a little old couple in her building set her up with a young man they knew, apparently based entirely on the fact that she had MS and the guy had Crohn's disease.

I burst out laughing. "I'm so sorry, but that was a terrible reason for a setup."

"It was actually going well!" Marni said. "I really liked him. And then he fully ghosted me. He'd met a lot of my friends, my parents. I was like, what happened?"

"Did you ever get a resolution?"

"Well, first, the neighbors in my building were like, 'We think he was scared of your MS.'"

Now I was cackling, thinking of the Crohn's guy scared off by—of all things—an autoimmune disorder.

"But then five or six years later, he called me—out of nowhere. He said, 'I'm so sorry. I was scared. Would you go out with me again?' And I said, 'Absolutely not. I'm seeing someone.' By then, I was seeing KC."

"What was different about *him*? What made you feel like you could tell KC right away? Because I know one of your biggest fears when you were diagnosed was the effect it would have on your dating life."

Marni took a moment to consider my question. "I think there's a lot to say about somebody just based on the way they treat other people. Like when you're at a restaurant, how they treat the staff? I saw how genuine and kind KC was. He was just such a nice, nonjudgmental person that I felt comfortable telling him. And he didn't make it a thing. Whereas that other guy absolutely made it a thing—by not communicating with me. That's the thing about my husband and our relationship. If anything, we *over*communicate."

"When did that start?"

"I think you always have to remember that your partner—your boyfriend, girlfriend, fiancé, whatever—is not a mind reader. For example, when we were dating, I got into a minor car accident, and I remember KC asking if I needed him to come over. And I said no, even though I wanted him to. But *he* didn't know that."

"Then you get mad at him for not coming over," I said, laughing.

"Yeah, they're not mind readers. You cannot expect them to know what you need. So now he'll ask me, 'Do you need me to come to the city with you and sit with you while you have the infusion?'" she said, referring to the twice-yearly treatment she gets.

"And do you say yes?"

Marni smiled. "No, because that's my time now. I make a whole day of it. I go to a café. I have my coffee and avocado toast. It's me time."

"I can't remember—when did you bring KC into the MSquared fold and show him that whole world you'd created?" Marni had long ago started an advocacy group, MSquared: Music Against Multiple Sclerosis, and though we've been friends for decades, I'd always assumed the order was: nonprofit first, supportive boyfriend (later husband) second.

"That came about *because* of him," she said, shaking her head. "That whole first year we were dating, I was having such bad back issues that I couldn't do the MS walk I usually do. And KC was in a band and had introduced me to all these other musicians, and one day he just said, 'We should do something with this.'"

"Marni! I just got chills!" I said. "I had no idea!"

"Yeah, that was all KC. MSquared was literally created at a bar while we were watching his best friend's band play. KC's been at all our events and performed at every one of them."

Opening up was easy for Ivy Lynch, an LA-based music executive, too.

"We met at a very stressful time in my life," she said of her fiancé, Russell. "I was in the middle of a job I was very unhappy in and had been actively trying to leave. I had some construction stuff happening in my home, a functional problem I was dealing with, but my home life was stressful. And my personal life was in upheaval because my mother was very ill, and she lived in Texas. So I was *very* clear from the outset. I said, 'I just need you to understand, I am adulting at a very high level right now. I hate my job, so sometimes I come home and feel really shitty. My mother is very sick, and I'm staring that in the face. My house is not a safe haven.' I had, essentially, three pillars of things that were giving me sleepless nights."

"But you didn't shy away from telling him any of that," I said. "Other people in your situation might have been afraid of coming off as too needy or having too much drama."

"Yeah, it wasn't some sort of calculation: *I'll be forthright, and he either stays or runs.* It was that he made me feel comfortable enough to be clear about all of the things that were stressing me out but that had nothing to do with him."

"What did he do to make you feel comfortable?"

"I think he recognized that in my friend group, and in my job, I'm kind of always the person that gets stuck doing things, because I'm 'the competent one,' or at least the one who's most proactive. And when you're that person, the people around you don't often pitch in or offer to take the reins. So I had a lot of shit going on, and a lot of stuff on my plate. And he showed up during a period where it was far more—I don't want to say *sexy*, but it was important that one of the first things he did was basically say, 'You don't have to do that. *I'll* do that.' Even when we first started dating, just recognizing that I didn't always have to be the one to plan things. He would go, 'Hey, do you like X kind of food? I made a reservation at Y place, and thought we could try it.' I think men would be shocked to realize how the tiniest effort goes such a long way.

"And then in January, I went to Texas because my mother was put on life support. Russell ended up meeting my entire family for the first time at her funeral. This all happened inside of a year, by the way. So he walked into a maelstrom, and he'll be the first to admit that he didn't have experience with any of this. He hadn't weathered any of these life events at that point. His parents are married and in good health. He'd never had anybody close to him die. He'd never had to think about wills and estate planning. He'd never had to make decisions about how to care for a parent. But this is what real life brings you. And he willfully dove in and showed up. You know, I'm not a spiritual person, but I feel like the universe gave him to me at a time when it was clear that I needed some help. It hasn't been all sunshine and rainbows. But the way in which we mesh together and fell into lockstep was easy."

That theme of things being simpler when you're with the right person was also true for Mark Hyman. He's been extremely successful in his professional life, has two great kids, but is twice divorced and has been honest and public about his romantic struggles, which I asked him about.

"I think my view is: all of us get software written when we're kids," he told me. "Our *love software*. And depending on our parents and their way of loving—or not—whether there was trauma or not, it all sort of wires your perspective around love and relationships. So if you don't rewrite that operating system, that software, you're going to keep repeating patterns that keep you stuck in ways that don't let you have authentic, healthy, mature love."

I couldn't help but smile. *Where had I heard that before?*

"I had to do a lot of work on myself. My last divorce, I realized that I had to address things I had long neglected. I had to look really deeply at my past and my own challenges, and I was able to arrive at some insights around why I'd been choosing the things I was choosing, why that wasn't serving my best interests. I think it's really important for everybody to dig into their past, whether it's through self-reflection or therapy, doing workshops—whatever resonates. I think it's important to understand that automatic ways of being, which are often to our detriment, can be rewritten and reprogrammed. So during that process of self-discovery, I got to a place where I was sort of free, where I felt like I didn't need a relationship to be happy. And then someone showed up."

In late 2022, Dr. Hyman and his new partner went public with their relationship.

"We still have issues," he said, "work to do on ourselves. But it's more fluid, and not so burdensome. I think I've got it right now."

R&P QUESTION #86 **How do you like to be tended to/taken care of (or not) when you're ill with something like the common cold?**

Talking about health with a partner doesn't need to be gloom and doom. Think about this: when you're battling a Rudolph-nosed killer cold, when you can barely lift your head from the pillow, how would you most like to be looked after? *I* like to be left alone—to sleep it off and slog through quietly. The Brit prefers to be checked in on and given ibuprofen at regular intervals, and he'll *never* turn down Nigella Lawson's Cold Cure Soup, a *New York Times* Cooking recipe I've mastered for this precise reason.

Knowing how best to tend to your partner, because you *understand* their needs, is an easy way to show your love and demonstrate commitment. Don't skip the question—it's a low barrier to entry—and the answers may be more revealing and surprising than you realize.

7

Children

Simplify before you multiply.
—*Mr. Garry, my seventh-grade math teacher*

I had a friend in college whose mother told me that she'd always wanted three kids; her husband, meanwhile, wanted one. After the birth of their first baby, they decided to try for one more, for a grand total of two children. A compromise.

Then she got pregnant—with twins.

There is so much you just can't plan for, but in my interviews—especially with couples who'd been together a long time or known each other for ages—I often sensed a real reluctance to dive into the details. Their default setting was that they already knew everything about each other. Then they'd do R&P and, invariably, something would come up. Frequently, that *something* had to do with having or raising children.

"We were together fourteen years before we got married," Todd told me, confidently crossing his arms. "So we literally know almost everything about each other."

Todd and Avery had met way all the way back in the eighth grade, gotten together in high school, and stayed together through college, through several long-distance phases of their relationship, as well as Todd's graduate school education, all before saying "I do."

"Okay, so take me through your experience of doing the questionnaire," I'd said. "What do you remember? What stands out?"

"Well, there were a few questions where I was, like—not *surprised*," he admitted. "But maybe, like, *okay*?"

"Which ones?"

"We're not big religion people. And I remember the question about *how would we raise our kids?* So hearing her answer versus my answer..."

"What were your answers?"

"I don't remember," Avery said, and it suddenly occurred to me that she might be hedging, waiting to see what her husband would say.

Todd glanced at his wife. "I grew up Catholic," he said. "But I'm really a lapsed Catholic. I never really *followed* Catholicism. So I said that I would give our kids the option. Like, I'd raise them Catholic, but then if they wanted to follow their own path, that would be okay."

Here Avery chimed in, much more assertively. "I was not raised religious at all. I would say Protestant—I was baptized—but I've never really been to church. My parents didn't want to force it on us, because growing up, they felt like they were forced to be a certain religion—well, maybe *forced* isn't the right word. But they grew up feeling like, *It's Sunday, I have to go to church.* And if you're religious, you should want to go, and believe in it, right? So *I* said, I would follow that. Like, we'll get them baptized, maybe even just to make our parents happy, our grandparents happy, and call it a day."

"And, Todd," I said, turning back to him, "what was your response to that?"

"It's just that religion, politics, those kinds of things don't really come up because we're not religious. We're not heavy into politics, so it isn't usually a topic of conversation. I guess that's why the question stuck in my head," he said.

Avery looked at her husband. "I guess that's why she included it in her questionnaire? So, that's pretty smart."

R&P QUESTION #104   **Would you like to have children? If so, how many?**

The starting point to the "kids conversation" is usually pretty straightforward: Do you want to have kids—or not? But even that question, I soon realized, can quickly become complicated. Plenty of people I spoke with didn't make a firm decision on whether or not they wanted to raise children until they met the person who would become their significant other.

Such was the case with Amy Sparks.

"I never wanted kids," she told me. "I wanted to live my life, do my thing. And then I met Blake. And I was like, *Oh, my God, I understand the appeal now. I want to have kids with you.* I didn't want to just have kids. I don't particularly like kids. I wanted to have children with this person who I adored so much."

"Did you just wake up one day and realize this?" I asked.

"Yeah, truly. I mean, I didn't meet him until I was thirty-three. I had had a very full life of fabulous experiences before that. Done it all, seen it all. Then I met him and fell madly in love, immediately. I was like, *This is the man I want to be with. I want to have a family with him.* And I understood what it felt like to desire more than just an independent life of travel or drinking or whatever it was."

"Had you already told him that you didn't want kids, or did you come to that conclusion before you had that talk?"

"I think I had probably mentioned it, in a not-so-serious way. Like, 'Oh, I don't care about kids.' And then I remember, we were at a bar in the East Village, drinking, and my husband is a musician. His dream has always been to play in front of, like, fifty thousand people. And I said, 'Are you interested in having kids?' And he said, 'A baby would be cool.' And I thought, hmmm, maybe a baby *would* be cool? That was really the impetus. Of course, his immediate line after that," she said with a laugh, "was 'But what I really want to do is play in front of fifty thousand people.' But he planted the seed that that was something he was interested in."

The same was true—in reverse—for Thiago Alves.

"Early on in our relationship," he said of his now-wife, Eva, "she would hit me with statements or questions that made me realize, wow, I'm taking her and our relationship much more seriously than any other before. And one time, we were hanging out with a friend who just simply, off the cuff, asked, 'Oh, do you want kids?' And I immediately said, 'Oh, yeah. For sure.' Almost without thinking, like I thought that's what you were supposed to say. And Eva immediately responded, 'Oh, no. I don't want children.' I was looking over at her, and it struck me: *Wait, do I want kids?* Because I just assumed, in the future, that's what you do? And it made me really deeply reflect, and that was awesome. It was one of those moments where I felt like, *I'm really into this woman, because she's making me think in this totally different way.*"

For others, the choice is much more clear—and the choice is not to.

I've always thought there was so much power in being a woman who decided not to have children, because it's not the societal norm. I spoke to several, including Colleen, a creative director at an advertising agency by day, singer and bass player in a punk band by night.

"I kind of always knew," she told me. "I remember even as a small child, I was somewhat of a tomboy—not that that makes a huge difference. But I didn't want anything to do with dolls. I wasn't just *un*interested; if someone gave me a doll, I got really uncomfortable. One time—God, I had to have been four or five—I was playing with a car, and I turned it on its back to kind of cradle it like a baby—"

"You remember this, or you were told this?" I interrupted.

"I remember this. My mom walked in, and she goes, 'Colleen, what are you doing?' And I was embarrassed. I was like, 'Nothing.' And I started playing with my car again. You know, *vroom vroom*. I remember asking her, 'What if I don't want to have kids?' Luckily, I had very supportive parents. My mom was like, 'Well, then you don't have to.' She never said, 'Maybe you will change your mind.'"

"You *are* lucky. A lot of people would be more inclined to say, 'Just you wait.'"

"Yes. And I mean, I was pretty stubborn about this. I'm the oldest of three girls. I have two younger sisters, and I remember they would always want to play house, and me being the oldest, they would say, 'Oh, Colleen's the mom.' And I would be like, *No, no, no, no, no.*"

"I'm the teacher," I offered.

"Yeah. I would make up stories about how, like, the mom and dad had died, and I'm the older sister who has to take care of you. My sisters really loved babysitting—I didn't. But the funny thing is: kids always loved me, because I'm goofy and animated. The little boy across the street would always want to come play, shoot hoops with me. And I would gladly do that, but I—"

"You can still be maternal, and enjoy children, but not want kids."

"Right. I think that's a really good distinction to make: Just because you don't want kids doesn't mean you're not *kind* to kids, or don't want to spend time with them. And there were times when I second-guessed myself, where I was like, *Wait*, is *this what I want? Am I going to regret it?*"

"What would make you go to that place?"

"Well, I've been married for eleven years. I care deeply about my husband. And whenever I'd see him with kids, I'd be like, *Oh, he'd be such a great dad.* We were very young when we started dating. And initially, he did want kids. That didn't last long. He quickly decided that he liked life with just me. I mean, he's had a vasectomy. He's in."

"But it's interesting to know that at one point, he did want children. Can you take me through a conversation you had about that?"

"So, he's kind of a nerd," Colleen said. "He loves collecting toys. Loves playing video games. And there were times when he would say,

'It'd be really fun to show all this to a kid,' or to, you know, raise a little nerd. But I was pretty adamant that I didn't want to. And I realized, too, that so many of the reasons I thought about doing it were honestly selfish. I used to think it'd be fun to see what they would look like, or to name them some cool name. But it wasn't anything practical. It would have been far more selfish than the choice to *not* do it."

"Which is why I truly applaud you, because I think knowing yourself well enough to understand that is a huge deal. It's not a small thing."

"Right. And I feel like, honestly—I always joke that we're our own children. Because I allowed myself the space to grow up at my own pace. You know, I had some pretty serious health issues. I have ulcerative colitis; I nearly died when I was twenty-one. That was heavy. I had to grow up really fast when I was a teenager, and in college. And after that, I was a little lost. I didn't know what I wanted my career to be. I didn't really know what my passions were. I don't think I would have been mature enough or known myself well enough to have a child until, like, right now—and I *still* don't want one."

Speaking of passions, Colleen and I were talking a little about her punk band when she mentioned that her husband was a member, too.

"Oh, he's in your band," I said casually. "Amazing, you can travel together."

"I'm in *his* band, really," she said. "He was a musician, and he taught me how to play the bass so that I could be in his band."

It was one of the sweetest and sexiest things I had ever heard—and I told her so. "You wanted to learn, so you could be with him?"

"Yeah, and because it was a challenge. You know, I watched him play music for years and years and years. And this is part of what I was talking about, in terms of growing up at my own pace. I didn't learn how to play bass until I was thirty-four. Now I'm in a band that's on a label, that's going to be touring, at forty. I was always a big fan of live shows. I'm guilty of dating other musicians before I met my husband—that was kind of my thing. But I realized I didn't want to be the musician's *girlfriend*. I wanted to be onstage. I think it's really important to know yourself, and I feel like I understand myself so much more because I didn't put a timeline on my life. Having kids would have done that. I go back and think about decisions I've made that I probably would have made differently. I started my career in a really secure corporate environment. If I had had kids, I probably wouldn't have left. I don't think I would have started playing in a punk band at thirty-four. I don't think I would have—I'm in a stand-up comedy class now. It's funny, people assume that those without kids have all this free time. But I am *so* busy. I volunteer with an organization called Girls Rock, which encourages young people to get involved in rock music. And it's so cool to work with those kids and then see them at my shows, wearing my T-shirts. Every choice you make has a sacrifice. Anything that you choose to do, you're choosing *not* to do something else. I really had to ask myself, Am I willing to sacrifice what I love to do? My passions? My freedom?"

R&P QUESTION #116

Do you anticipate raising our children the same way you were raised, completely differently from the way you were raised, or a mixture of both?

The choice of whether or not to have kids is one thing, but if you do decide to build a family, that's when the fun starts—because then you have to raise them. There is no end to the potential questions that will arise. "I don't know if *values* is the right word," a woman I spoke with said, "but—the image of what it means to be a family? Do we eat dinner together every night? Do we eat dinner together three times a week? Do our kids participate in a lot of activities, or do they do just one thing? Is it important that they do art and music? Do we make them do it even if they hate it?"

I'd smiled. It's not always about knowing the answers. Things will arise you couldn't possibly have predicted. Speaking of which, I spoke with Meredith Rossi, an American living in London, about a recent "miscommunication" she'd had with her Italian husband, Leonardo.

"It's still very foreign to us," she said of the London independent school system. "Though we grew up in different countries, Leo and I were raised similarly, in the sense that we both went to the local, coed public school. How our families were involved in our upbringings, however, was very different. Leo's mom was a math teacher, and his dad was a statistician for the local government. Math is in their blood, their DNA. And, fast-forward, Leo was an investment banker, now he works in real estate finance. His sister is an architect."

"Everything is math-based," I offered.

"Right. Math, math, math. And if something didn't come easily, it was drilled into them. Leo would be made to sit in his bedroom, which was like a little prison cell, and do umpteen pages of whatever algebraic equation until he got it. Repetition, repetition, repetition. So then our daughter, sweet little Olivia, who was maybe seven years old—actually, it was the teacher who let us know that she was behind her peers. In simple addition."

"Which to your husband must have felt like *the house is falling down.*"

"Right! So we said, 'Okay. We need to get her some support.' But Leo was like, 'This is math. This is *addition*. This is something we should easily be able to help her with.' Since his schedule is less predictable than mine, I offered to get her started, help her settle into a routine, but he was like, 'No. I want to do this.'

"So he would sit down with her, usually on the weekend, and do a few little worksheets with her. And it would be very boring—just a piece of paper with math written on it. And you've got to make learning fun, you know? I would be downstairs in the kitchen with our son, who was very young at the time, and they would be upstairs with the door closed in our little office pod. After ten minutes, I would hear yelling and crying and just this horrendous situation. And I would sit down there in the kitchen, biting my nails. Like, *everything about this is wrong.* I would wait for another ten minutes to see if things would calm down. Then I would go up there and say, 'This is unhealthy, I'm intervening.' And it would blow up. Leo would be like, 'No, we will stay in here until she gets it.' And Olivia would be looking at me like, *Save me*. We did that for probably a couple of months."

"Was it a pride thing for him?" I asked. "It sounds like, *I am the math person. This is how my family did it and look where it got me. This is on me*. Which, in a way, is very noble."

"Oh, for sure. He meant well. His intentions were good. But I thought of it as a short-term problem. You know, she's six and a half. She goes to a very good school. She'll get there. Maybe she doesn't go to *Oxford* . . ."

"Or maybe she just learns differently?" I added.

"There you go. All of the above. For me, it was a short-term conundrum. Leo was looking at the long-term picture. He went to one of the best schools in Milan, got a job at a top investment bank. So he felt like, *If she doesn't have the proper foundation, she's going to fall behind*. And I kept saying, '*I* didn't go to a *top* school. *I* didn't become an investment banker, and *I'm* happy. I love my work. Not everyone has to work at Goldman Sachs.'"

"You're also super successful." I laughed. "Like, *hello*?"

"Well, thank you."

"How did you resolve the issue? You go in there, you split the two of them up. You say, 'We're done for the day,' right? You save Olivia?"

"Actually, it reached a point where I wrote him a letter."

"*This* is what I wanna hear about," I said, settling in.

"Yeah, so there was one day where I was just like, *Enough is enough*. And I literally sat in the next room and wrote down verbatim what I was hearing each of them say, and gave him the letter that night. I was like, 'This cannot continue. And if it continues, we're going to counseling.'"

"What was his response?"

"I don't think he said much that night. We talked about it more in the following days. And I don't remember the exact sequential order, or quite how much time passed, until we found what ultimately became a very healthy solution, which is a math club called Kumon."

"I've heard of that," I said.

"Yeah, and you know what? Credit to Leo, because we found out that Olivia's best friend had been doing Kumon, so he researched it, and called up the teacher, they have a little trial thing, and two and a half years later, Olivia's still using it. She's in the top math set in her year group. Our son is doing Kumon, too. Now it's just part of the routine, and Olivia's confidence in herself is night and day from what it was three years ago. So, everything in life is about communication, finding the right compromise, right? How did we find the right compromise for Olivia? First it was my way or your way. It's either A or B. But then sometimes you have to explore a C, D, or E option."

"In this case, option C worked for you."

"C worked. But it takes calm and courage and compromise. And I think when partners let things fester, the longer things fester, the more stubbornness sets in."

On Mismatched Parenting Styles: A Conversation with Dr. Vanessa Lapointe

Parenting: the easiest (and highest paying) job in the world. Just kidding—it's only the exact opposite. And while raising a tiny human is hard enough on a good day, it only gets tougher if you're at odds with the person you're raising them *with*. Which is exactly why I reached out to psychologist and author Dr. Vanessa Lapointe—she's not only a renowned parenting expert, but also someone who once struggled to get on the same page as her partner.

You've said publicly that when you were still married to the father of your children, the major source of disagreement between you was parenting. What happened?

Vanessa: You know, I was bright-eyed and bushy-tailed, and I thought you could learn all that "relationship stuff" from a textbook—which you cannot. I had not gotten down to the nitty-gritty of examining my own inner workings. Like, who am *I*? So I married somebody who—we came from such different perspectives in terms of who people are, never mind who children are. We also had incredibly different upbringings. I think our wounds came together in this synergistic kind of way. And then, right about the time that we had children, I discovered the work of [developmental psychologist] Gordon Neufeld.

R&P
QUESTION
#126

How will we handle
parental decisions?

I was devouring his material, and it was lining up with a lot of things that I had studied and experienced. And I remember, I convinced my German engineer husband to come out to a Neufeld event, whereupon this woman sat down with her infant—and she was part of the diaper-free movement.

Oh, gosh.

Vanessa: So this baby was uncovered from the waist down, and my husband looked at me like, *Where did you bring me?* He was having none of it. And then it was on. Meanwhile, I completely missed the boat in terms of what was actually happening for him, and how probably traumatic it was for him to even have children, because the act of parenting became a trigger that launched him into all this reactivity. So we had increasing challenges in the marriage, and it ended very loudly.

How does someone head that off, or avoid that fate? Looking back on it now, are there things you would have done differently?

Vanessa: I think about this a lot. With my own children, I think about how one day in the not-too-distant future, they're going to start dating the person who will become their partner, and I desperately want them to not have the experience their dad and

I did. So, I think really understanding who your partner is, and where they've come from—not as a deal-breaker, but being able to hold space for how they show up—is important. Not reacting with judgment, responding with compassion . . . I think you only share the vulnerable parts of yourself, you only allow yourself to be *truly* known by another person, when they create an environment that allows you to be vulnerable. But when we had kids and it all went sideways, I was on him. Like, this fierce, angry, *I can't believe how awful you are*, right? So there was no space for him to admit that he needed help, because I shamed him.

It can be so difficult to approach our partners without judgment.

Vanessa: Yeah, I think I've really landed on the idea that everybody, all the time, is doing the best that they can, given the circumstances they've come from. And your early childhood, particularly your first six, eight years, really shapes you. I guarantee—even if you're like, "Nope, I'm going to do it differently. I'm going to do it better than my parents"—when you have children, you *will* hear your mother or father coming out of your mouth.

Which is *terrifying*.

Vanessa: Right? It's like, why and how and where did that come from? So for each of you, it's really about asking yourselves: Where did I come from? What were the messages imparted to me by my own parents? And it's not about blaming anybody; it's about being accountable to your own program and your own story. It's about understanding: I'm not here to fix my partner or fix the way my partner is going to show up and parent. I *am* here to bear witness to that person becoming who it is that they're meant to be.

Learning to Trust the Struggle:
A Conversation with Zain Asher

CNN International news anchor Zain Asher has described herself as "Nigerian by blood, British by birth, and American by residence," but the award-winning journalist's path to success was anything but certain. When she was just five years old, her father was tragically killed in a car accident; her mother—a Nigerian immigrant living in South London—was suddenly tasked with supporting and raising four children on her own. Through sheer grit and determination, amid the pressures of poverty and prejudice, those four children would grow to exceed all expectations, becoming a journalist, a medical doctor, an entrepreneur, and an Oscar-nominated actor. Her mother's remarkable strength and sacrifice are laid bare in Zain's stunning memoir, *Where the Children Take Us*, but I hoped to chat about the ways Zain's background shaped her own thoughts about parenting.

R&P QUESTION #102

What values do you want to instill in your children?

I've read your beautiful memoir, of course, and your mother is such a force. I'm thinking of the moment she takes you to visit Oxford University when you were just thirteen, points to other students, and says, "That could be you someday." And it *was* you—you did go to Oxford. Can you talk a little about how her tough-love approach not only influenced you, but influenced your own thoughts about raising children someday?

Zain: You know, when you're an immigrant in a foreign country, and you lose your husband, when you're battling discrimination and poverty, your biggest concern is making sure that your children experience something better. So when it came to raising us, my mother was often thinking much more about the long game. Everything she did was about asking herself, *If I teach my children this now, how will it impact them five or ten or even fifteen years from now?* She was always thinking about the future. Even down to deliberately plastering our bedroom walls with newspaper clippings of Black people who had achieved extraordinary success to show us what we could achieve someday if we applied ourselves. I remember her going through my school curriculum when I was seven, so she could teach me what I needed to learn beforehand. As a result, I was top of the class. Those were some of the inflection points that completely changed the trajectory of my life and influenced the way I would raise my children.

I imagine one of those inflection points was returning to Nigeria? [Between the ages of nine and eleven, Zain was sent to live with her grandparents.]

Zain: Absolutely. And that's common, by the way. A lot of Nigerian families send their children back home for a few years to teach them discipline and resilience. The thinking goes: "If my child can survive fetching drinking water from a river, washing their clothes by hand, or having to clean toilets in a school with no running water, they can handle anything life throws at them in the US or the UK."

And I take it you share that belief?

Zain: Yes. Even as an adult, every time I go back to Nigeria, it renews a certain resolve, a certain fire in my belly. Let's say I get sent there for work. I'll usually experience several days of intermittent electricity, of the power going out. I could be doing a phone interview with someone, and the call will drop five or six times in fifteen minutes. Some people literally have three cell phones, one for every network. I've always thought, *My God, to do business in Nigeria, you have to contend with so much!* And despite all of this you still have to meet your deadlines or file your report, or show up to work after sitting in something like seven hours of traffic, which is common in Lagos. Having experienced that, it is impossible to take the advantages in America for granted. I often think to myself, *I cannot waste what I've been given here.* It's also easy to see that some of the world's most successful people have experienced a fair degree of hardship, and that instills in them a certain level of resilience. So, the way I approach parenting is through the lens of giving my child as much love and as much of a nurturing environment as I possibly can, with the understanding that there is so much value in struggle. The hardest thing—given my background—is that my kids are a lot more privileged than I was. They have a mom who works for CNN. My husband is a journalist, too. We live a comfortable life. So, it's a very tricky line, because you don't want your children to experience so much hardship that it interferes with their self-esteem, their belief in themselves, but you want to give them just enough that they understand the value of hard work, the value of persevering, overcoming. I don't want to raise kids who have everything so easy. That's just my own personal thing.

You mentioned your husband, Steve Peoples—chief political writer at the Associated Press—but I know the two of you come from very different backgrounds.

Zain: It's funny—he's American, from New Hampshire. His childhood was less about resilience and survival, and more about emotional support and nurture. So our initial perspectives and approach to child-rearing were very different.

So how did you broach this conversation with him, about your desire to instill in your kids some level of resilience?

Zain: I don't think it was a sit-down. Like, *Let's discuss parenting.* But as he got to know me, and my past and my background, how improbable the life that I live now is . . . I think he was inspired by that. He's also white. He understands that there's no way his children will ever have the exact same childhood that he did. America is a very different place for young white boys compared to young Black boys. He understands that if you're raising a young Black man, there needs to be a bit more intentionality. So, he did a lot of work. And seeing news reports of police brutality affected him in ways it hadn't before. If you have a Black child, it hits way closer to home. So he had to reeducate himself.

I wonder, did you *ask* him to do that?

Zain: No. But the thing is, I'm not American. I *also* had to educate myself, because race is very different in the UK. There are elements that overlap, but we were both educating ourselves. I think I also got really lucky, in that he was very humble in this particular area, and very willing to learn. You know, he's been with me to Nigeria. For our wedding, he spoke in my native language, Igbo.

I mean, if that's not commitment to a partner . . .

Zain: [nodding and smiling] I was single for a long time. And I always tell my single friends that getting married and finding a partner is actually a spiritual endeavor. I mean, people think you go to a bar, you meet someone, or you go to a party . . . No. This is a spiritual endeavor. Sure, you can meet somebody and find them charming and attractive— but that is not enough. Like, really, who *is* this person? You need to have a full 3D picture of their psychological résumé.

So, is there a Nigeria in the future for *your* kids? Do you ever think about sending them?

Zain: I've thought about it so many times. The catch for us is that my grandparents are no longer alive—and you don't send your kids to Nigeria to live with a *stranger*. But if my mom were to move back? Now we're talking.

R&P QUESTION #105   **Do you want or need to be married before having children?**

It's no secret that times have changed—people are waiting longer than ever to get married and are more likely to cohabitate before marriage, and more and more are opting not to get married at all. Or, in some cases, not to wait around for a partner before embarking on parenthood. I chatted with Lori Gottlieb about this notion of doing things "out of order" and, frankly, expected her blanket endorsement—but what she said surprised me.

"I think the message that people are getting really young—like, in their twenties—is that you can do anything. You can have kids first and then get married; you can have kids and never get married. And I think it's great that people have options, that nobody is pigeonholed into that old model: you know, by your late twenties—or midtwenties, even—you're married, and then you have kids by thirty, and so on. Nobody has to live that model, at all. I want to be clear about that."

I sensed a *but* coming.

"But I think this is confusing to a lot of people. I think what happens is, people don't really think about how to create the situation they actually *want*. I hear so many people in their twenties say, 'I really want to find my person. But people keep saying I'm so young or I should date more.' Or, they met someone in college, but for some reason feel like that's not good. They think they're supposed to have all these options. Or they just don't take their twenties seriously. There's a great book by Meg Jay called *The Defining Decade*, which I recommend to so many people in their twenties, because if you don't do the work now, it's not like you're going to wake up at thirty and say, 'Okay, now I'm ready. Here we go.' It doesn't work like that.

"It's important to be really intentional about asking, What do you want for the rest of your life? Who are you dating? And why? It's not, 'Oh, let me just date these losers.' Or, 'Let me just date these people who don't want the same things that I want, because I'm just supposed to be having fun.' Why do you have to have 'fun' with someone who is nothing like the person you want to be with? I think what happens is, a lot of people end up unhappy because they don't have what they want, because they didn't make choices that would lead them in that direction. There's a lot we can't control. But there's a lot we *can* control. I also think there are things we can control *earlier on*, that we really need to pay attention to. Just like in your book, you're saying, *Pay attention to these things before you marry someone.* So I just want to flag that."

Despite Lori's warning, sometimes being intentional *is* about letting go of the dream of finding a partner. To talk about that, I called a friend of mine, Justine Dermont.

"Dan and I met when I was twenty-one, and right away I fell in love," she told me. "It was my first love. It was a *big* love. And he was, you know, a twenty-four-year-old guy working in finance."

"Enough said." I laughed.

"Yeah. I thought of him constantly, I saw a future for us—*and he was a twenty-four-year-old working in finance.* We dated on and off, but mostly off, for about two and a half years. But he was not a good boyfriend, and I was a desperate girlfriend. I don't know if you remember the old *Sex and the City* episode—"

Seriously, always topical.

"—where Samantha was dating 'We' William. He was like, '*We're* going to go to the Hamptons this summer. *We're* going to do this, *we're* going to do that.' And then nothing ever happened? Dan was very much a 'We' William—and I believed him. I would hinge my whole everything on something he'd said . . . 'Oh, we'll do this next month.' And he wasn't a bad guy. He was just a young guy. And I was young, and very ready to believe somebody that I cared about deeply. But also—I've never played it cool in my entire life. I never made it a secret of how deep my feelings were. And I think that was intimidating for somebody who was twenty-four and new to the city. He was new to his paycheck. So we broke up for the final time, and I really did not think it would be the final time because it never had been before.

"So I was miserable. And we had tried to be friends. He thought, *Oh, we should still be able to talk every day.* And we *were* such good friends, which was always something that confounded me. Because I felt like, *If we have this romantic chemistry, and we're best friends, why do you want anybody else? Why do you not think this is the best?*

"So we broke up the final, final time, and within six months, I said, 'We're not friends. We can't be. *I* can't.' So we would speak once every few months. And then as it went along, every couple of years. And then we hadn't talked in probably ten years."

"I mean, it's crazy," I said, "because *I* knew about him, right? I remember hearing about him."

"Oh, he was always the one who got away. So, fast-forward, I was forty-one, almost forty-two years old. And I decided to get pregnant. I'm in the process of picking a donor, going to a fertility specialist, and it was during the Kavanaugh hearings, and I had written a tweet about Christine Blasey Ford. And Dan liked it. Now, I did not know he followed me on Twitter. I did not follow him on Twitter. I had not even thought of looking him up on Twitter. We're talking about someone I had dated eighteen years earlier. We were Facebook friends, but in the way that everyone you've ever met in your life is your Facebook friend."

"Or everyone you *haven't* even met," I said.

"Or haven't met. Right. So he liked this tweet. And I remember calling a friend of mine and saying, 'It's the weirdest thing. The guy I was so in love with, you know, fifteen, eighteen years ago, just liked this tweet of mine. I didn't even know that he was a liberal?' And she said, 'Don't even make this a thing. You're on a whole other path right now. Don't even make it something you're thinking about.' I thought,

You're right. I'm having this baby. I'm doing my own thing. And maybe a few months passed. I picked a donor, and I was going to all these fertility appointments—and even though I was almost forty-two, I got pregnant on my first try with IVF, which was *amazing*—and the day that I was walking from my apartment to the clinic to have the embryo implanted, my phone rang. And it was Dan."

My body exploded in goose bumps. "Justine! Are you kidding me?"

"I *know*. The last time he'd called, which had been around ten years earlier, he called because someone we both knew had died. So I answered the phone not really knowing what this was going to be about. And he said, 'Hey, too much time has passed, just wanted to say hi. What are you up to?'"

"What did you say?"

"I was like, 'Oh, nothing. I'm headed into an appointment.' I made it sound like a work thing. 'Let's chat later.' Went, got pregnant. And either he called me back, or I called him back. I can't remember. But we started talking every day. And the difference this time was that I could tell he was getting more and more invested. And I—it's not that I didn't care. I did. But there was this part of me that also didn't care. Because I was about to become someone's mom. And like, *Dan Henbury isn't going to be involved in that.* So this can only be fun. I was enjoying myself immensely talking to him, but felt like, *None of this matters to my future.* What mattered was the baby. Plus, he was living in Florida at the time. It just didn't seem like anything."

"What changed?"

"He was in Florida. And I was in New York, and he kept inviting me down. And I didn't want to see him. I mean, I looked pregnant immediately. I was also forty-two years old. I didn't want to jinx anything. And then it got to a point where he was pressing hard about seeing each other. I had wanted to wait until twelve weeks, just because everybody does. But I think I told him at eight or nine weeks."

"What was his reaction?"

"I said to him, 'I want to tell you something that I'm really, *really* happy about. I know it's going to come as a big surprise, because it's been happening the entire time I've been talking to you, but I've been really protective of it.' And then I told him. And he responded in a lovely way. Like, 'I'm really happy for you. That's wonderful. You're going to be an amazing mom.' But it was a short call. And we got off the phone."

"Did you feel sad after or . . . ?"

"No, because I wasn't invested in it being anything. But then he called back the next day and said, 'I still think we need to figure out when we're going to see each other.' And that was that. From the moment he said that, we were a couple. From the moment my son was born, Dan was Daddy."

"Is there any advice you would give to people who are in your situation? Who have a chance to give it a go with someone whom they really cared about in the past?"

"Actually, my bigger piece of advice," she said, "is that if you want to be a parent, pursue it, and the chips will fall into place. Maybe not in the order you expected. But your family will fall into place. I have another friend who—I think in part inspired by my son—ended up getting pregnant on her own, and it's not like she's reconnected with a past love, or even met anyone. But now she has a six-month-old, and she feels like her family is falling into place. That's the biggest thing I would tell somebody: don't worry about the order of the pieces. Just pursue what's in front of you. Have a baby if you want to have a baby; it doesn't mean you won't have a partner. It just might not happen in the order you expected."

"When you decided to pursue a pregnancy and become a mom, where was your head at in terms of finding a partner?" I asked. "Did you have to get to a particular place before you decided to go forward and have a child?"

"Yeah, I got to a point where I knew this was going to be out of order. And maybe I would never get the man. But if I never got the man, that wouldn't be the saddest thing in my life. If I never had a *baby*, that would be the sad thing. Once I realized that—that what I really wanted was a child—I felt like, *If there's a man later, then wow, what a great bonus.*"

"I love that," I said. "I *love* that."

8

Careers

Adults are always asking little kids what
they want to be when they grow up,
'cause they're looking for ideas.
—*Paula Poundstone*

Three years before the Brit and I met, I started writing a novel. As a television producer, I'd always been a storyteller, but I was focused on telling other people's stories. I wanted to craft something of my own. The process, from gleefully typing the first words to learning about the industry, to searching for and securing a literary agent, landing a book deal, tackling approximately eighteen thousand rounds of edits, to (finally) publishing, took four years of work—most of it during late nights and weekends.

Shortly before the book's release, I was walking along West Tenth Street in the Village, one of my favorite blocks in the city (renowned for its charming town houses, including Mark Twain's former residence) when the realization that I would soon be an *author* stopped me cold. I actually closed my eyes and drank in the moment.

Of course, by then the Brit had read the manuscript—and he still swears that I modeled the protagonist's love interest after *him*. "Bret" is a numbers guy who works in finance, has an exposed brick wall in his New York City apartment, and shows up at the main character's door with flowers and vitamin C when he learns she's battling a cold. The Brit, meanwhile, is a numbers guy who works in finance, had an exposed brick wall in his London flat, and once brought me roses and a bottle of grapefruit juice when I was under the weather. And yet I'd written all those details long before we'd met—so maybe I manifested him?

As a finance guy, he didn't know anything about television or publishing, but wanted to learn all that he could to better understand my world. He never once belittled or questioned my choice to write an entire novel with no guarantee it would see the light of day; he often watched rough cuts of TV shows I was working on to see what they were like before they were fully edited. And when I decided to throw a launch party for the book—taking it upon myself to find a venue, wrangle bloggers and members of the press, and scour New York for the perfect food and refreshments—he was right by my side, stuffing gift bags, making sure no last-minute detail went overlooked.

We weren't physically together for much of the party, but I felt him with me the entire time. I would look at him from across the room, and our eyes would meet; he'd give me a wink or a nod of encouragement, perfectly content to support me from a distance, to stand back and let the fanfare happen around him.

"I think you want someone who accepts your ambition from the very start," my friend, the journalist Jo Piazza, said. "Nick was so proud of everything I was doing, whereas I'd had boyfriends in the past who did not build me up. When Nick introduced me, it was like my publicist introducing me—*and she did this and this and this*—he was just so proud of it. I think listening to the way people talk *about* you is just as important as listening to how they talk *to* you. What they're saying about you and how they're saying it shows how much they respect the things you're doing."

That was something I'd noticed about the Brit, too. Whenever we met new people and someone asked what he did for a living, he would immediately deflect: "Oh, you don't want to hear what I do, you want to talk to my girlfriend—because she's amazing."

R&P QUESTION #142   **If we have children, how would that impact our careers?**

"So, what do you do?"

It's one of the first things people ask in social settings, one of the most basic and foundational pieces of demographic data (alongside age, gender, level of education, and marital status), and though we tend to overly define people by their jobs—see above: he's "a finance guy"—it's nonetheless true: you can typically learn a lot about someone based on how they spend their nine-to-five.

But how important is someone's career *really*? Once you get the basics out of the way—are they a doctor? teacher? dog-walker?—once you confirm that your prospective partner can support themselves, how much more is there to actually talk about?

Putting it plainly? *A helluva lot.*

Your career might actually dictate your dating pool, or play a role in your choice of future life partner in ways you hadn't even thought about. Nearly 20 percent of medical doctors, for example, choose to marry other medical doctors. In fact, and according to a *Washington Post* analysis of the Census Bureau's American Community Survey, MDs are more likely than any other type of worker to marry within their own profession—but that may have less to do with a shared passion for medicine and more with the sheer amount of time it takes to *become* a doctor. "Given that prime marrying age in America is twenty-eight for women and thirty for men," the article states, "doctors are likely to be looking for love when they have the least time to find a spouse outside the workplace."

Similarly, college professors are more likely to marry college professors; lawyers tend to marry lawyers (as I well know, having grown up with two attorney parents). And, fun fact: restaurant and hotel managers are also very likely to marry their own kind (roughly 14 percent of them do)—which can probably be chalked up to sharing a social circle and working nontraditional, often late-night schedules.

What you do for a living doesn't just influence whom you'll meet—it can play a role in determining *when* you want to settle down, a fact that came up during my chat with Barbara Corcoran. "Mr. Mark Cuban told me that he was involved in two long-term relationships where the women were really serious and implying that they wanted to get married," she said of her *Shark Tank* costar. "And he told them, 'Listen, my priority is my business. That's number one in my life. If you can settle for that, we can keep going. But if you can't, we're not meant for one another. My priority is my business.' Later, when his business was in order," Barbara continued, "his priority then became his now-wife and kids. So it has a lot to do with timing. If anyone had asked *me*, 'What would you say is most important in the pecking order of your life?'—from the time I was twenty-three until I was forty (when I was first married), I would have said my business. Not kids, not a husband. If someone is willing to sign up for that and take a back seat, like my husband, Bill, happily did, that can work. But without that agreement in advance, I think you're in for a surprise."

Beyond life stages and ages, it's important to confirm that your goals and ambitions are aligned—which seems like a fairly straightforward prospect, but can present an easy enough trap to fall into. Over and over again in interviews and in my research more generally, I was confronted with the phenomenon of "dating someone's potential"— loving someone not for who they are, but for who you hope they'll be—the dangers of which were made abundantly clear by relationship coach Stephan Labossiere (better known by his online handle "Stephan Speaks") during an appearance on a popular podcast: "Unfortunately, the potential you see, they may not see in themselves. Let's say a guy is a plumber, and he's making sixty grand—but the woman he's dating wants a six-figure man. She says, 'He has *potential.* He can own his own plumbing business!' But . . . everybody's not built for that. They're not wired for that. He is happy and content making sixty grand. . . . [So] if you now try to make him be more than that, he will start to resent you. And you will resent him if he's not moving his feet fast enough."

Perhaps the most important question to ask when it comes to careers, however—in particular and especially if you are a woman who intends to have children—is how much your partner intends to help with housework and childcare.

America is the only developed country in the world without universal and guaranteed paid family leave. The burden of care, meanwhile, falls disproportionately on women, which translates to lower salaries, fewer promotions, and slowed professional growth, a phenomenon known as the "motherhood penalty." During the pandemic, literally millions of women—many, many times more women than men—left the workforce entirely, because *someone* had to stay home with the kids and supervise their remote learning. This harsh landscape is why Sheryl Sandberg, former COO of Facebook (now Meta), famously said that the single most important career decision a woman makes is deciding whom to marry. It's why the journalist and novelist Caitlin Moran, in her bestselling book *More Than a Woman*, argued that all too often women marry their glass ceilings.

"It feels . . . unfeminist," she wrote, "to tell bright, hardworking, joyous women that it doesn't matter *how* incredible they are, how many degrees they get, how many businesses they start up from scratch—if they then shack up with a self-pitying woman or man called Alex who's not very good at replying to texts; 'freaks out' when they have kids; doesn't use the washing machine because 'I'm just not good at stuff like that'; always has to see the guys on the weekend to 'wind down'; and flies into terrifying rages (e.g., he or she can't find their favorite suede jacket)—they are doomed. . . . [But] of all the married women I know who have children, all the ones who are successful in their careers (and are happy) are—*without exception*—the ones who married, for the want of a better term, 'good men' or 'good women.' Gentle, clever, kind, funny people, usually in cardigans, who just *show up* for everything. Ones who at a *bare minimum* cut it fifty-fifty with the housework, childcare, and emotional upkeep."

Without a plan, without conversations with and buy-in from your partner, "you can virtually guarantee that *you* will be the one taking PTO when your child is sick," a high-powered publicist I spoke with told me begrudgingly, "even if you've already used up your PTO. *You* will be the one missing the chance to give a keynote address at a very important conference in order to care for your son, while *your husband* travels out of state for his own conference—one he's merely attending, not speaking in. That may or may not be a hypothetical scenario."

Even if you do have a plan, circumstances may arise that you hadn't accounted for. Such was the case with Darya Barzani, a Kurdish immigrant raised and living in Brooklyn.

"My husband is very traditional," she told me. "He's Sicilian. You know, the wife is supposed to stay home, raise the kids, the whole nine yards. Well, I always laughed at that. I didn't realize he *meant* it. That it actually meant *a lot* to him. So he wanted me to stay home with our son, which I did for the first three years. And I was completely financially dependent on him."

"Why did you agree to that?" I asked. "Was that something you wanted, too?"

"The first year, yes. But then it kind of extended."

"Why, what happened?"

"My son had severe breathing problems. We wound up in the hospital so many times; he was hospitalized for weeks on end. I was terrified of sending him to daycare, because a simple cold could land him in the ICU. So that was the deciding factor. But it was extremely difficult to stay home for those additional two years. I was going insane."

"Hardest job in the world, being a stay-at-home parent," I said.

"Exactly. Anybody that does it and loves it, God bless them. I just couldn't do it."

"So what changed? Because obviously," I said, gesturing to her surroundings, "you went back to work."

"We finally found the right doctor and were able to get to the root of my son's health problems—and treat them. He was able to go to school, and I was comfortable sending him. And that's when I started looking for jobs to get back in the market."

"Was your husband resistant, considering his more traditional view of a woman's place?"

I braced myself for Darya's answer—given her husband's background and preferences, I was sure her transition back to the office must've been rife with drama.

Instead, she smiled. "He was actually really supportive. He thanks me every day for staying home as long as I did, and understands how much I sacrificed."

Building a Strong Foundation: A Conversation with Danielle Weisberg

At just twenty-six years old, Danielle Weisberg quit her job at NBC News (alongside friend, colleague, and then-roommate Carly Zakin) to launch theSkimm, a subscription-based daily brief breaking down the most important news stories into a conversational, digestible format. More than a decade later, theSkimm has blossomed into a full-scale digital media company (there's an app and a podcast in addition to the flagship newsletter), while Weisberg and Zakin are still working together as cofounders and co-CEOs. Given their more than twelve-year partnership, I was curious how the lessons they've learned might translate to a more *intimate* sort of union.

You're married now, but you were single when you launched theSkimm. I'm wondering if any of the experiences or conversations

you had when starting your business affected how you approached building a relationship with your romantic partner?

Danielle: In a lot of ways, Carly's and my first marriage was to *each other*. At the time, leaving my job and starting theSkimm was the biggest and most important decision I had ever made. It's still the longest partnership either of us has had. And we often joke that beforehand, we essentially created our own version of a prenup. We had to align on our values and our desired outcome. We discussed what we would do if we disagreed, if someone needed time off, what success looked like to each of us, what our priorities were. We've also continued to check in regularly to make sure we stay aligned. So, yes, having gone through all of that, having been forced to have those hard conversations, did actually prepare me for my relationship—I'd already thought about what I needed and wanted, and had experience communicating that to a partner.

R&P QUESTION #135

How does your career lend itself to being in a relationship?

Speaking of communication, you built a company that's meant to *inform*. What have you learned about communication more generally?

Danielle: It's been the key to our success. With Carly, I learned how to lay down the foundation for a strong relationship. And with our audience, we were very specific about the tone and voice of our newsletter. We had to train ourselves to communicate in a way that resonated with readers while staying authentic to the message we wanted to get across. I really do look at it like strength training—the more you exercise your communication skills, the stronger they become. Pushing myself to be a better communicator in business, learning how to be clear and concise, gave me the skill set to ensure I was speaking up about my needs with my partner.

I really admire the work you've done via theSkimm to foster transparency and openness regarding paid parental leave. How might you recommend broaching that same topic at home? When should couples start talking about what will happen when a baby is on the way?

Danielle: One of the reasons we launched #ShowUsYourLeave and #ShowUsYourChildcare is because a lack of support continues to push women out of the workforce; the expectation is that women will take on that burden. So start talking *way* earlier than you think you need to. Build that foundation. That doesn't mean you have to come up with all the answers right then and there; it's about starting the dialogue. The exact details around timing, logistics, and circumstances if and when you start a family will come into focus, but the first step is making sure you have that open line of communication. That's true in professional partnerships, too. I went on paid leave—twice—during the pandemic era, and Carly and I created a plan that worked for both of us. I wanted her to feel confident running the business on her own and making decisions on our behalf, while she wanted me to feel at ease taking time away, and made sure I didn't feel like I had to check in or sacrifice that time with my family. The level of understanding and appreciation we have for one another is a direct result of the groundwork we laid from the very beginning. Running a business is hard enough—not having a strong foundation and trust is not something we have time for. It's why we've always prioritized our dynamic.

R&P QUESTION #130 How important is your career in terms of your identity?

"It's funny, we'd both always heard the advice that in a marriage, you're going to have to take turns with your ambition," Lauren said. "And both of us were like, *Nope, sorry.* We're going to go full speed ahead and see where it lands us. And, yeah, we're married. We have two beautiful children. We have careers. But I realize now—that was a little foolhardy."

Lauren Smith Brody is the author of *The Fifth Trimester* (as well as a consulting firm by the same name), which aims to ease the transition back to paid labor following the birth of a child, provide support for all working caregivers, and foster gender equity in the workplace. She knows firsthand the challenges of navigating flextime and mom guilt and scheduling childcare. But this is her second career, which she embarked on after an unexpected development in her professional life—one that it hadn't occurred to her to plan for.

"My husband and I met in college," she told me. "In writing workshops at Penn. Beautiful campus, but the writers met in this little run-down house that had not been renovated. All the furniture was stuff that had been dragged in off the corner; you know, grandma's fifty-year-old, falling-apart chair. After graduation I applied to a program that took me to Radcliffe for six weeks and he got hired at *Philadelphia Magazine.* I go to Boston, he stays in Philly. But I know that *after* Boston, my goal is to land a job in New York, working in publishing. I have that job by Labor Day . . . and, within three months, get laid off."

"Best laid plans," I said, laughing.

"Right. And in retrospect, that was a harbinger. Meanwhile, my husband is getting lots of opportunities in Philly working on stories about medicine and science and ethics. But he starts realizing, looking ahead, that his career path would be too unpredictable when he eventually had a family. At least in medicine, he'd know the path forward: do a post-bac, take the MCAT, go to medical school, do a residency. Granted, that's more than a decade of work. I, on the other hand, wanted to be in magazines. I was going to work like crazy, get promoted, and move up the masthead. And it worked! I rose up *very* quickly. Soon enough he was applying to medical school, and then I dragged him to New York kicking and screaming. Every fight we had for the first two years was about me and New York."

"I sort of love that you took a stand about that, though."

"It was really a dream of mine," Lauren said. "And I knew that *his* dream was movable. Mine wasn't. The entire industry was in New York. But then fast-forward a decade. He's now through residency, but I was the breadwinner. I'd been making many times his salary. And then the publishing industry just collapsed around me."

It's funny to reflect on how fast things change. I shared with Lauren that I remembered a time not so long ago when I couldn't have imagined going anywhere without a magazine in my bag.

"This makes me sound so old," she said, nodding, "but I remember at my second job out of college, my coworker turned to me one day and said, 'Have you tried this new thing called Google?' *That's* when I started. And I just did not see the writing on the wall, because I was so in love with paper magazines. So we sort of did it my way, but my husband and I have had this funny flip-flop. Now he's the primary breadwinner."

"So to your point, you couldn't see the writing on the wall—I'm wondering what conversations might have been helpful to have with your husband, given that you didn't see this coming, and couldn't have planned for it."

"For one thing," Lauren said, "I think the conversations you have around careers should be about more than just *ambition*. Like, how are we going to evolve? How are we going to build in room for evolution? Because circumstances can change based on outside forces that we don't have a lot of control over."

"What sorts of forces?"

"So, the economy, right? Whether you're growing a career and investing in an industry that has some inherent risk to it. The amount of structural support available when and if you decide to become a parent. Laws that are there to support you—or not. Honestly, if you live in a place like California, you might approach these conversations differently than if you live in, say, Texas. In California, both parents essentially have access to months of paid leave if they need it. In Texas? *Zero.* Depending on where you live, you may or may not qualify for FMLA [the Family and Medical Leave Act, which entitles some workers to twelve weeks of *unpaid* leave]. You might ask, 'When one of us has a job opportunity, what kinds of things are we considering *beyond* just salary?' What if that opportunity means moving to a different state? You might ask, 'How much of my value in our relationship is determined by the amount of literal cash money I bring in? How much is determined by *unpaid* work?'

"Some of the most interesting and valuable jobs," she continued, "teaching, let's say, are not highly paid, but perhaps offer more flexibility for unpaid labor performed in the home. A lot of us are attracted to those jobs, but how are you going to avoid associating your value with your compensation? You know, it's very hard to say that doing the laundry every day has the same value as—I don't know—being an entertainment lawyer, but if it all contributes to the same whole, and to the same ultimate goal, then it all counts. That can be difficult to see when you're building a career early on, before you've built a family."

"Basically," I ventured, "it's about understanding that what *you* think is most important—a certain job title, a certain salary—might change dramatically when you factor in the realities of running a household."

"Right," Lauren said. "A lot of the work I do now is helping people redefine how they measure success. For example, I work with a lot of attorneys, and they are completely conditioned to measure success in six-minute increments. But as new parents, it's about asking: How else can I measure success right now?"

On Finding a "Teammate in Life": A Conversation with Kandi Burruss

On the fourth season of Bravo's *The Real Housewives of Atlanta*, Kandi Burruss—the Grammy Award–winning writer, singer, actress, and entrepreneur—revealed her relationship with Todd Tucker, then a behind-the-scenes producer on the show. In the years since, the couple (who were married in 2014) have partnered on a range of business ventures, from a soul food restaurant to a touring musical to a fleet of spin-off shows. We discussed navigating two big careers while growing a family—I wanted to know how they seem to do it all!

You've referred to your husband as your "teammate in life." I love that. Can you tell me more? What does that mean to you?

Kandi: For me, a teammate is someone who supports you in everything you do, motivates you to go harder for the things you want, and backs you up when you need support—especially in moments of negativity; they can talk you out of allowing that negativity to take over. There have been times when I felt defeated, but Todd shows me that you're never defeated, that there's always a solution, and helps me find those solutions. I feel like women often become the support for our partner's big aspirations and goals, while putting our own dreams on the back burner. But Todd supports my dreams and helps me figure out ways to achieve them, and vice versa. That's what I mean by being a teammate: getting behind each other's individual goals, as well as our goals together. We definitely lean on each other around the house, too. Todd is great at helping the kids with homework, and I love getting them ready for bed—but we always work as a team.

R&P QUESTION #141

How can we best support each other in our respective jobs or businesses?

You've also said the secret to your marriage is "great communication." Was that something you had to work on, or did it come naturally?

Kandi: I'm not normally a person who talks when I'm upset; I normally shut down and get quiet. In past relationships I would get in my feelings, shut down, and eventually cut people off. Todd understands that he may need to give me some time to calm down, but he always confronts the fact that there is a conversation that needs to be had. We're able to talk through things because he is a great communicator who encourages me to express the things I would usually shut down on.

What advice do you have when it comes to finding a partner who will be supportive of, rather than intimidated by, your success?

Kandi: I think you should talk about your dreams and goals early on. You want to see if they're supportive—do they take you seriously when you talk about things you're passionate about? Some people will try to minimize your dreams, instead of encouraging you with opinions and suggestions. You have to show interest in that person's dreams and goals as well. And remember that relationships shouldn't just be based on the fuzzy feeling you get when you first meet. Figure out if you have common goals that will bring you closer and think about the things that will keep you both motivated.

• • •

I circled back with dating coach Damona Hoffman—she's based out of LA and has worked with a slew of highly successful women—when she brought up a hard-to-believe (for *me*, anyway) statistic: one in five engagements *don't* end in marriage.

"I find it interesting when people tell me they've been engaged before, or they've been engaged three times but never married," she said. "I'm just like, *how*? Because by the time my husband proposed, there was absolutely no question in my mind. It puzzles me that people could get to the point of this grand gesture and this huge decision . . . People will put more time and money and investment into what they're going to *wear* than the person they're going to spend their life with—which impacts *everything*. Your family, your finances, your mental health—"

"Your career," I chimed in, "especially as a woman."

"Yes, everything is impacted by this one decision. To me, it's the most important decision you will ever make. And honestly, I would not be here today—doing this interview with you, and on this particular topic—if it wasn't for my husband. He supports me 100 percent. When dating, we're often addicted to a certain chemistry, a negging and an antagonistic vibe, the highs and lows. So when you're in the right relationship, it can almost feel like nothing's happening because it's so steady and reliable. But—look, I do a lot of yoga. They talk about the balance between freedom and stability; you have the foundation of your poses, and that allows you to do some of the more playful and experimental stuff. I look at marriage and relationships in the same way. If you have a solid foundation, good communication, clarity on values and goals for the future, and mutual respect, then you can kind of go anywhere because you feel seen, you feel safe, and you feel supported."

9

Money & Finances

> Opposites may attract, but I wouldn't put my
> money on a relationship of financial opposites.
> —*Suze Orman*

As my relationship with the Brit progressed, I started to spend more and more time in London—by then, I had the more flexible schedule. And sometime in the fall, we hit what felt like an important milestone: hosting another couple for dinner, at the Brit's flat.

I'd recently met Liz through some New York girlfriends, who thought the two Americans in London might hit it off—and they were right. Over dumplings and sesame chicken at a Chinatown restaurant, Liz and I had breathlessly swapped stories about our pasts, our families, our partners. It was clear, even then, that a lifelong friendship was forming. Subsequently, the Brit had met Liz, but neither of us had met her husband, Macaulay, who went by Mac.

The barrel-chested Scot with the lilting brogue was not quite what I'd expected. He had a booming voice, a hearty laugh, and the physicality of a rugby player. He thrust a bottle of wine in my face when I opened the door and gave me a warm hug, and peppered his speech with wonderful little Scottishisms, like "aye" and "wee" and "nae." The conversation flowed easily, and we seemingly had an abundance of things to talk about, until—in the middle of dinner—the evening went right off the rails.

"Liz invited me to join her next girls' trip in Grenada," I announced to the table.

"They will love you," Liz chimed in, sweetly. "It's such a great group of women. All working moms, and just really nice people. Everyone's super helpful. Like, literally a girl squad."

The Brit smiled as he piled a mound of green beans on his plate. "What I wouldn't give to be a fly on the wall of that Airbnb."

"Oh, I can sum it up for you," Liz said, holding up her hand and counting off the regular topics of conversation on her fingers. "Sex, lack of sex, period pants, why middle-aged women love Harry Styles— which, personally, I still cannot tell you—and superyachts."

"Never mind. I'm good." The Brit laughed, at the exact same time that Mac said, almost under his breath, "I hate the superyacht game."

I passed the beans to my right and reached for the rolls. "Dare I ask what this game is? Is it like the *what-would-you-do-if-you-won-the-lottery* game?"

"Sort of, yeah. I mean, where would you go?" Liz said, eyes wide and sparkling. "How big would your yacht be? What amenities would it have?"

She paused to take a sip of wine and turned to the Brit. "Just to be clear, I come from a working-class family in New Mexico, and I've had a job since I was fourteen. This is not at all coming from personal experience."

We both laughed, and I briefly thought of azure waters off the coast of southern France, of diving off the bow into the sea—although, can you really dive off the bow of a superyacht?

"It's just such a waste of your time together," Mac said, snapping me out of my daydream. "Like, how is that even fun? You do realize how bad superyachts are for the environment."

I perhaps should not have been surprised, as Mac was an entrepreneur in the green energy space. I'd heard plenty from Liz about his start-up business, the passion and the hours he'd invested to realize his vision and to make it profitable—as well as the sacrifices *she* had made in support of that vision. In the earliest stages, they'd kept their family afloat thanks to her salary. But then he just kept going, picking at her.

"What a ridiculous conversation," he continued. "*Superyachts.* Do you know how obnoxious that is?"

"It's a game," Liz said with an eye roll. "Lighten up."

"If you think that's a game, if you think that's a good use of money," he shot back, shaking his head. "It's just really unattractive, Liz."

The Brit and I locked eyes, and I realized I was suddenly holding my breath.

"Well, I'm sorry you find me so unattractive, Mac," Liz said. "But you didn't think it was unattractive when I was paying the mortgage so you could start your business. You didn't think it was unattractive when I let you sleep until noon on the weekends while I watched the kids, even though I'd worked a full week, too. It's only unattractive when *I* want to do something. I can't even get you to agree to a fucking vacation!"

She stood suddenly, the scrape of her chair across the floorboards the only sound in the room, and started gathering plates, stacking silverware haphazardly atop them, and heading toward the kitchen. "I'm going to bring out dessert," she said.

We had somehow ventured way beyond superyacht territory; the Brit and I were watching a couple that had been married for more than a decade lay out their financial differences—and a whole lot more—right in front of us. It was very uncomfortable, and I ached for my friend. But just as I was about to push back from the table, the Brit gave me a wink and quietly excused himself. While I chatted with Mac about sustainability and renewables, guiding us back to more neutral territory, I could just see into the corner of the kitchen, where Liz was taking a few deep breaths, calming herself down, and the Brit was gently putting his arm around her.

I fell in love with him just a little bit more in that moment, with his kindness and compassion. I didn't ask him to comfort my new friend; he'd done that all on his own. *That's the kind of man I want to marry*, I thought. *This* is *the man I want to marry.*

Later that night, with a full belly and a full heart, I snuggled close to the Brit, laid my head on his chest, and quietly asked, "What would you do with your superyacht?"

Ah, money.

Root of all evil. What makes the world go round. Often cited as the primary (if not the number one) reason for divorce. And though it's long been considered impolite to discuss, money came up in virtually every conversation I had with every expert I spoke with, regardless of their field or specialty, even when I hadn't intended to talk about it at all.

"When I was younger, there was somebody who wanted to marry me who just did not have his financial life together," Lori Gottlieb told me, "and I remember my parents saying, 'You cannot imagine what it will be like to try to raise a kid, to try to have a house, to live your life.' Just the basic things. And I was like, 'They just don't understand!'"

"I love him!" I added.

"Right. 'He's so fun! He's so quirky! He's so *different*. I don't want to marry an investment banker!' But it's not one or the other. It's not that you have to marry a 'boring' accountant or you get the 'quirky' writer. It's almost like that binary that people have in high school," she said. "My son's in high school, so I'm thinking a lot about that right now. We were watching *Freaks and Geeks* the other day, and it was like, *Can someone be attractive and* also *interesting and smart?* Yes! We put people in categories, like the person who's really fun, but they're not going to be financially successful. Or the person who's financially successful, but they're a bore. It's not like that! And when I was young, I didn't understand that."

"I think that's a hard lesson to learn, especially when money is something most people are so reluctant to discuss," I said.

She emphatically nodded her head. "People think that talking about money makes you shallow. It does not. It is so real. It plays out every second of every day of your life."

Then she left me with a plea for my readers: *"Please* do the questions about finances."

Aside from an aversion to talking about it, I think couples are frequently tripped up, too, by the fact that "money" is really a proxy for your *values*—what you deem important (or not). In other words, understanding how someone feels about money is a much bigger and more nuanced conversation than asking "How much do you have?" or "How much do you make?" Things are further complicated by the fact that we also often lack a cold, hard understanding of what things truly cost.

In the spring of 2023, for example, *New York* magazine ran a cover story entitled "How Much Is That Lifestyle in the Window?" in which nine young people—all single, all childless, all thirty or under—were asked about the lives they were picturing for themselves ten to fifteen years in the future. The magazine's reporters then got to work researching and totaling up exactly what those lives would cost. It's no secret that New York is a notoriously expensive city in which to live; in explaining the project, the authors included a bit of an ominous warning: "The purpose of presenting these receipts isn't to shock or horrify."

And yet for many, the results were pretty shocking and horrifying.

Aliya, for example, the thirty-year-old corporate lawyer featured in the article, would have to pull down a little more than $700,000 a year to afford the life she'd imagined (after a one-time payment of $1.25 million toward her ideal abode: a Brooklyn brownstone).

"I think a lot of people don't realize how many of their life plans are financial in nature," Chelsea Fagan, founder and CEO of the Financial Diet, a financial media company, told me. "People have a tendency to treat money as an afterthought, but it's very important to frame these things as, first and foremost, financial decisions. An example is whether or not to have children. Not enough people look at the decision to have a child as a *financial* decision. Whether you want to own a home, where you want to travel, if you want to go back to school, the kind of career or the hobbies you want to pursue—we have a tendency to avoid thinking about things in terms of money. It feels unromantic. It feels overly practical. But ultimately, it's in not preparing for things financially, or not understanding financial demands, that we find ourselves in really tough positions, which then becomes one of the leading reasons people divorce."

R&P QUESTION #157 — **How should we handle our long-term financial planning?**

I hate to break it to you, but Liz and Mac divorced.

In fact, that night in the Brit's flat was the beginning of the end. As Liz later told me, she and her husband had always been misaligned about money; what he considered "hoity-toity" or over the top or just plain too expensive, Liz had thought of as perfectly affordable. The misalignment didn't mean much when they were young and just starting out and didn't have much; it was thrown into sharp relief when Mac's business took off, and they suddenly had more disposable income than they'd ever dreamed.

Finances were also the breaking point for Franchesca Ramsey.

Perhaps better known by her online alias, Chescaleigh, Franchesca is a writer, actor, sought-after speaker, and creator and host of the award-winning web series *MTV Decoded*—and the list goes on. We met years ago on the New York entertainment circuit. I reached out to chat in part due to the frankness with which she'd addressed her divorce publicly, and in part because she and her ex-husband had worked together on a podcast *specifically about their lives and relationship,* and yet still didn't speak about a number of important topics when they were together. Money was one of them.

"I didn't go into my marriage thinking, *I'm going to make more,* or *I'm going to have this career,*" she told me. "I was twenty-three years old when I started dating my ex. We divorced when I was thirty-five. So much has happened, you know? So many things transpired. But I think finances are a taboo topic. It was only through our divorce that I learned a lot about how my ex felt about needing to be the breadwinner. He might not have wanted to fully cop to it, but he insinuated it. But I think the biggest thing I realized is that there were a number of times where we were both unhappy, and we didn't tell each other."

"Why?"

"Largely out of fear," she said. "I think as a woman, there's the fear of coming off like a nag or being too needy. And I think for men, there's this idea that airing grievances makes you sound weak, that men are supposed to be stoic. Even now, I still feel like, *Wow, maybe our relationship would have taken a different path if these things had come to light earlier?* Does that mean we would have stayed together? I don't know."

"Maybe you would be talking now," I said, knowing that she and her ex were not in contact.

"Maybe we would be talking. Maybe we wouldn't have gotten married? Maybe we would have ended the relationship earlier because we realized we both wanted different things. There are so many things that we don't talk about until it's too late, until there's some blowup. That happens in platonic relationships, too, when people don't feel confident enough to advocate for themselves, so they let the thing fester, and fester, and fester. And by the time you say something, it's too late to resolve it. We had that in therapy, where it was like, *Five years ago, you said X, Y, and Z.* And I'd say, 'I don't remember that.' Or, 'I remember it differently.' And I was guilty of that, too, saying I was okay with things when I wasn't okay with them. So instead of course correcting, we just continued on that way until it got to a point where it was like, *We can't do this anymore.*"

"What do you wish you would have known, or discussed?" I asked.

"I would say, things that you should talk about are like: What is your metric for a 'lot' of money? And what do you consider quote-unquote cheap? Because someone might say, 'Oh my God, I found this great pair of shoes. They're so cheap. They're five hundred dollars.' You're like, 'What? Five hundred dollars is not cheap to me—that's a ton of money.' There's also the person who will cut corners to save two dollars. You know, 'This milk only expired last week!' It's not a criticism; it's just that what seems like a little or a lot of money is going to be different from person to person. So being really honest—would you feel comfortable spending this much money on vacation? Are you a Best Western or a White Lotus?"

"Or, do you want to spend money on vacation at all?" I added.

"Right. Do you want to *go* on vacation? Maybe you would rather save that money and go out to dinner once a month? Are you a go-out-to-dinner person? Or are you a stay-at-home-and-cook person? Are you an Uber or bus person? All of those things will help determine if you're able to live together, and, like, the longevity of your relationship."

"And you might do things differently ten years on," I said. "Life happens. Good things happen. Tragedy happens. But it's not like we're having this conversation for the first time. We're *revisiting* the conversation. There's a comfort in that. 'We talked about finances. Let's talk about it again.' It's not like, *Ugh, can we talk about money?*"

"Yes!" Franchesca said. "I think maybe setting up a system for regular check-ins, the same way we have a yearly review at work. We don't necessarily do that in our relationships. Or like we do our taxes every year. Why don't we have a yearly check-in about, like, what's on the agenda? Are we going to visit relatives? Last year, we went and saw your family. Or we went wherever, spent a lot of money, and I wasn't super happy with the trip. Let's not do that again this year, right? Instead of waiting until the last minute, and then it's a big freakin' thing."

R&P QUESTION #166   Would you help your parents/siblings/friends financially if they needed it? Would you expect them to pay you back?

If you want to talk about money, you go to the queen of personal finance: Suze Orman, as famous for her tough-talking, no-nonsense emphasis on personal responsibility as for the witty aphorisms she dispensed on her long-running, eponymous CNBC show. "I always say, Lindsay, that you cannot fix a financial problem with money," she told me. "That's why most people who claim bankruptcy once claim it twice. That's why most people who get out of credit card debt go right back in. The problem is never with money. I always say, you have to go within to see why you're doing without."

She has a wealth of knowledge and offers tons of practical tips for managing your money as one half of a couple.

For example, want to know how to split the bills?

"Everybody says, 'Oh, fifty-fifty,'" Suze said. "That is *not* how you do it. You never split things fifty-fifty, you split them according to what you make in relation to your bills." In other words, if someone earns twice as much money, they should be paying twice as much rent. "It's not equal amounts of money, it's equal percentages."

Wondering if you should share bank accounts?

"I still get thousands of emails from women who feel like they don't have the money to leave a bad relationship. So they stay, out of fear. And in the end, that fear deprives them of a free life. So I am not one who believes in joint accounts. You can have a joint account for joint bills, but you only put in the amount needed. At the very beginning of my relationship with KT," she said of her wife, "we made the decision that we were never going to have a joint account, ever."

What about stay-at-home parents? Where should their money come from?

"Whatever the breadwinner is making gets split. First, you pay the bills. If there's anything left over, fifty percent goes to the partner staying at home, the other fifty percent goes to the breadwinner."

I'd grown up listening to Suze preach about the importance of financial literacy, about how important it is for women in particular—especially those leaving the workforce to raise children—to maintain financial independence. (Incidentally, I spoke with *three* women who revealed that their first husbands had ruined them financially; two of those husbands went to prison for fraud.) And yet I wondered what effect separate accounts had on a couple's communication; if keeping your money separate from your spouse created an opportunity for subterfuge and secrecy. "If you maintain separate bank accounts," I asked, "to what extent should you discuss those accounts with your partner?"

"Every single month, KT and I go through our separate accounts together—savings accounts, investment accounts. We look at what we have this month in comparison to last month. Did it go down? Did it go up? But *KT* has to call the financial adviser. I don't want to make her financial decisions *for* her. She wants to buy stock, she wants to sell stock—that's her decision, her money. But we go through it together."

"In other words: separate accounts, joint conversation," I said.

"That is correct. We know exactly what we have as a unit, as well as separate entities."

"Do you think it's important for potential partners to understand how the other's family viewed and talked about and spent money?"

"*Are you kidding?*" she said, emphasizing each distinct syllable, just as she did for years during her famous "Can I Afford It?" segment, whenever she'd reject someone's wish to frivolously spend their money by shouting, "De-*nied!*"

"Look, I have relatives that—I have a hard time with some of their money habits, I do," she said. "And sometimes that might be a discussion between me and KT. We discuss it, and we talk about it, right? It will absolutely come into play. Is it possible that you're going to have to save them? Are you the one who's going to have to make sure they're not kicked out of their house or their car? So you better understand the relationships, because you're marrying into that; all of sudden, they are your in-laws. I mean, how many emails do I get about *my husband wants to take money out of the 401(k) or refinance the house—which we own outright—so we can support his parents.*"

And sure enough, I came across that scenario when speaking with a young, newly married couple, Cynthia and Brandon.

"The one area where we differ is that Brandon's more generous than I am," Cynthia said. "Brandon feels like—we're so fortunate. We should be helping our families or helping our siblings. Whereas I'm like, we're just starting out. We don't have a family of our own yet. And we don't know—to your point earlier—if we do have trouble having kids, that's really expensive. I would rather save it for ourselves."

"You knew that was a point of differentiation before the questionnaire?" I asked.

"Yeah. And I'll acknowledge that I get a little mean and judgmental. I might say, 'Why are you doing that?' Or, 'It's not your job to do that,' instead of being a little more empathetic. I know it defaults to a fight when I come in with that tone."

Cynthia and Brandon kind of looked at each other, and I sensed that something was brewing just below the surface. Finally Brandon took a deep breath and said:

"Yeah, so basically my brother racked up a lot of credit card debt. He compounded that with some sports-betting issues, lost a lot of money, opened up new zero-percent-interest cards, kept it rolling. And he was actually doing okay. He was staying on top of it, not paying any interest on the debt. But then he injured his leg and had a botched surgery. Now he's got medical expenses racked up, now all the debt's on him at the same time. His credit tanked. He can't open up any new cards. He's got twenty thousand in credit card debt racked up at 25 percent interest, and I'm sitting here working a cushy software engineering job . . ."

When Brandon broke down into sobs, it took everything I had not to cry with him.

"Which I empathize with," Cynthia said, her tone considerably softer. "I love his brother. I don't want to see him suffer. But also, he made decisions that led him to this point, and it's not our job to bail him out. The medical part definitely compounded it. But I also want to see him take some responsibility. He's talked about getting a new job to better his financial prospects, but he hasn't really done anything. I was coming at it more from the sense that, there's a lesson here. He has autonomy. He is in control of these decisions. So we aligned, we decided to help him out, give him the money, but this is it. You're not going to be there again to bail him out."

Brandon wiped his eyes and nodded his head. "Yeah. It's like, 'You continue sports betting? I'm not covering that.'"

R&P QUESTION #155

How was money modeled for you growing up? How did you learn about spending and saving? Was money discussed in your childhood home, or was that considered a private or off-limits topic?

Just as Suze had reacted kind of dramatically when I asked if couples should talk about their families' attitudes about money—*Are you kidding?*—so had Chelsea Fagan.

"Oh my God, that is one of the most toxic aspects about money and relationships that never gets addressed," she said. "This bothers me so much. I was actually just talking about this with a friend who came from a similar situation as me. I grew up low income. My husband was upper middle class, and the people around him, *very* upper middle class. Everyone in his family went to a good school. They're doctors, they have multiple homes, he learned to ski . . . And for me, that was a big source of angst early in the relationship. It's hard not to have that feeling of, *You live like this? Like,* this *is normal for you?*

"People who come from wealth will often have a kind of laissez-faire attitude about money, because they know there will always be more. They can always rely on someone, there's an inheritance coming in a lot of cases. Whereas a lot of other people will have to support family members, they have to send money back home. I do think it's possible for people from two different backgrounds to come together and overcome that kind of baggage, but I also think not enough people talk about that, or think about it."

"How did you and your husband handle it?" I asked.

"One of the big changes was that my husband used to downplay his family's wealth. Like, 'Oh, you know. We were fine. We were comfortable.' At some point I said, 'I feel like I'm being gaslit here. You guys had *money*. I understand that that wasn't clear, because it was normalized for you. But you have to recognize it now.' Even recently, we were at an event with extended family, and everyone was talking about their country home. I was like, *Do you get what I'm saying? This is not how 99 percent of people live.* Now there's a lot more lucidity on his end, an awareness that if you're coming from a higher socioeconomic position, it is very much on you to make strides to bridge that gap by acknowledging it. Like I said, I grew up low income. Now I'm high income, and that has made me so angry at a lot of wealthy people who pretend like it's normal. Life is so different when you have money; it impacts every aspect of your life. And if that's how you grew up, the least you can do for the people around you is be honest about it."

"And yet, *so* many people struggle with that," I said.

"Yes. And I think part of the reason," Chelsea said, nodding her head, "is that if you came from less, or you aren't as comfortable with money, or you don't have a good relationship with it, it becomes a topic you're embarrassed to speak about. I remember I was dating a guy who had a lot more money than I did. We would go out to restaurants, and one time we were ordering and I was worried about what he was having, because if we were expected to split the check, I knew I couldn't cover it. So I was like, 'Oh, that's okay. I don't need this blah, blah, whatever. I'm trying to, you know, be on a budget.' And he looked at me and said, 'Why is it always about money with you?' At the time, I was very chastened. I was like, 'You're right. Absolutely. It shouldn't be about money.' Now I know I should have thrown a glass of wine in his face and walked out of the restaurant. But it took me *years* to be able to talk with my husband openly, because it was so embarrassing.

"That's why it's really incumbent upon the person who has more financial privilege to accommodate the other. Unfortunately, in a heterosexual couple it's usually the man who has the privilege, or who has more financial access than his female partner. I think part of the reason these relationships *do* often fail is because there isn't that accommodation made. The person who has more will often be deferred to; what they consider normal will be taken as the normal. And it's not hard to understand why—that's how we treat people in general in our society. The more money they have, the more respect we give them. That's partly why I really believe that a huge component of healthy finances is having at least some degree of separation. If everything is *too* combined, it's easy for the person with more to have way too much leverage."

"I want to pause for a minute," I said, "and define the word *accommodate*. Because at first I thought of dating: *Oh, the person with more money is paying for the dinners and paying for the movie and paying for the subway or the Uber or whatever.* But I think what you mean is, have a discussion—i.e., *Listen, we come from different places, but I don't value you differently.*"

"That's right. But the truth is that very few people with more privilege really do the work to make it an egalitarian relationship. It can happen, it's just not that common."

You *can* overcome different financial backgrounds—as Chelsea and her husband did—but sometimes coming from similar circumstances can bring you together in ways you couldn't have expected. Such was the case for Claire and Finn, who were just a month or so out from their wedding when we spoke.

"Before we moved in together, I made us whiteboard our finances," Claire said. "I was like, 'We are having this meeting.' I actually googled how to start talking about finances with your partner, because I wanted to do it right. Also, I was thinking, *We're going to get engaged soon.* Joke's on me—it was two years later."

She looked over at Finn, who flashed her a sheepish grin.

"But I knew I wanted to start saving for a wedding," she continued. "So I had us write down the three things that were most important in terms of spending—or saving—money. You write yours. I'll write mine. And they were different."

"Mine were house, kids, wedding," Finn said.

"And mine were wedding, house, travel."

"Were you surprised?" I asked.

"I was," Claire said. "Because I just felt like a house is so expensive. I was looking at it through an entirely different time lens. And I wanted a big wedding."

"And *I* was totally on the wavelength that we could go to the courthouse, get married, and at our five-year anniversary just ball out, because with the money we would've used for a wedding, we'd have a house. So that's what I wanted. It was only when she said—"

Claire laughed and interrupted: "I was like, 'Hell no, I'm not getting married in a courthouse!'"

"Before going into this meeting, did you know how much money each of you made?" I asked.

"Well, I had an idea—"

Claire laughed and cut him off. "No. I think we had an idea of each other's ranges. And it's hard. It's like, if you're the person who makes more money, you want to be sensitive to someone making less. If you're the person making less money, you don't want to feel inferior, but a lot of times you do. It's this cycle that we create. And it's because money is such a closed-off topic."

"But that's what was helpful about the whiteboard," Finn said. "It opened the door to other conversations, because there's such a cloud over the idea of talking about it."

Just as I was wondering what other conversations they might have had, Finn looked at Claire, sighed, and said, "I came from a lot of wealth growing up, and then my parents lost it all. I think it was our third date when Claire was like, 'Oh my God—'"

"Same thing happened to me," Claire chimed in.

"Yeah. 'That happened to me, too,'" Finn continued. "We joke that COVID was a fast pass for our relationship. But to me, when I heard that . . . I was like, *No way.* Because you can't really understand what that's like unless you've been through it. My way of dealing with it is that it means nothing to me now. I don't care what fucking shoes you wear. The concept of having a watch that costs more than someone's rent . . ."

He paused, shaking his head.

"How did this come up?" I asked. "What happened on your third date?"

"Well, Claire wanted to take me—it was a nice rooftop bar. But they couldn't seat us right away, so we were standing on the balcony, listening to music, and we like to people-watch, right? And I don't know who opened the door, some guy." Finn paused to look at his fiancé. "I think we may have been a couple of drinks in—"

"I think we were just drunk." Claire laughed. "I remember this date. It is crystal clear in my mind. We saw these people wearing Gucci shoes, and they were kind of fake flexing. That's what opened the window. You said to me, 'Look, I've had all that.'"

Finn paused to give me the rundown of the story: His father, then a young graphic designer trying to get his fledgling company off the ground, would show up at a particular film executive's office, trying to get a meeting. The executive's secretary was the woman who would become Finn's mom. "Eventually, he asked her out on a date," Finn said. Once his father became successful, he encouraged his young bride not to bother finishing school, not to bother working anymore—he was bringing in plenty for the both of them. And eventually he became *very* wealthy. "We were going on fancy vacations, having gift boxes sent to the house. We would have elaborate Super Bowl parties, parties all the time," Finn said. "But eventually I realized that the foundation of my whole family was money. Once it was gone, my family—well, I didn't really have one anymore. I had a birthday in August. No message from my sister. No message from my dad."

"What exactly happened, if you're comfortable sharing?" I asked.

"To try to get his next company started—retirement money, gone. Money on the house, gone. College fund, gone. In hindsight, was it something that should have been a conversation? Absolutely, but there wasn't one. My mom later told me: 'He never talked to me. I would have gone back to work. I *could* have gone back to work.' But it wasn't even put into the ether that there was a problem. There wasn't any communication whatsoever. Until my dad was like, 'We need to make a mortgage payment or we're out of here.' I was like, 'Well, fuck, sell the cars.' Got that mortgage payment. We were out the next month anyway, because we were behind. I remember packing up the house in a U-Haul in the pitch dark of night, because my parents didn't want the neighbors to see that we were getting the fuck out of Dodge. And Claire was like, 'I remember the same thing.'"

"And we used that as kind of a jumping-off point," Claire said. "When we did the whiteboard thing, Finn was like, 'My parents never did this.' *I* never want to be in that situation again, and knowing that Finn doesn't want to either, it kind of aligned us. We both never want to be in that scenario. We never want to overstep so much."

10

Weddings & Marriage

When I'm married, I want to be
very much married.
—*Audrey Hepburn*

Six months or so into our relationship, the Brit and I took our first trip together: skiing in Vermont over Valentine's Day. We picked a small town called Stowe, close enough to drive to for a long weekend, far enough away to feel like a proper getaway. I borrowed a pair of hot pink ski pants and a white jacket from two different friends, and we loaded up the car with our luggage, snacks, the Brit's road-trip-ready playlist, and the gift I (secretly) had for him.

How do you buy a Valentine's Day present for a man who doesn't really want for anything? The Brit isn't really a "stuff" guy—he's not into accessories or cologne, and if all went well, I figured I had years ahead to buy the books he wanted or a sweater he needed. I was aiming for something more thoughtful and landed on "sleep notes." We had a long stretch of not being able to see each other coming up: sixty-five days. So I'd gone to a stationery store, purchased tiny envelopes and cards, stickers, and colored pens, and written him a note to open each and every night until we'd next be together.

I was hoping he wouldn't think it was *too much.*

The six-hour drive took us eight, as we got caught in a snowstorm. (There was also an impromptu stop at Taco Bell, which the Brit loved and couldn't, at the time, get in London. The man must have ordered the entire dollar menu, and the car hilariously smelled of chalupa for the duration of the weekend.) Still, the playlist he'd made went unplayed. We never once even flipped on the radio—which surprised us both. Instead, we talked the entire way. Eight straight hours of near nonstop chatter. We were just happy, even when the snow hit and we were navigating unfamiliar, icy roads in the dark.

I'd spent a long time searching for the perfect accommodation, and found it in Edson Hill Manor, a gorgeous bed-and-breakfast nestled into a hillside just outside town. We finally rolled up the winding drive, past horse stables and a frozen pond, lights twinkling in the trees. It was like something out of a Nancy Meyers movie. The smell of woodsmoke was in the air, and though there was record cold that weekend, I don't remember feeling so much as a chill.

The next evening, after a day on the slopes, we were lounging in our cabin with our feet propped up in front of the fire when I decided to retrieve the little blue box tucked away in my suitcase. The Brit raised his eyebrows as he took the box from me, opened it, and slowly started to sift through the envelopes.

"Sleep notes," I said, a little nervous, not sure how they were being received.

He said a quiet "thank you" and continued sifting through, careful to keep them in the proper order, by date, as I'd arranged, when I noticed his eyes starting to well up. It was the most emotional I'd ever seen him, and the kiss he gave me turned into a long embrace. It would be many months before he told me that in that moment, he knew: I was the one.

Actually, his internal monologue apparently went something like this: *Shit. She's the one. Now I have to marry her.*

Not everyone aspires to be married. There are any number of reasons—financial, emotional—why someone might choose to delay making it "official," or to forgo the tradition entirely. In Taylor Mapp's case, a previous failed marriage had soured her on the idea of ever getting hitched again; her long-term boyfriend, Henry, wasn't interested, either. But after nearly a decade together, and after deciding to try for a child, they were starting to reconsider, or to at least contemplate an engagement.

"Henry felt strongly that in order to marry someone—from what he'd seen in other people's relationships, and what he'd heard," Taylor explained, "you have to go through a 'shit-your-pants moment.' And then you decide, are you all in or not?'"

"What do you consider a shit-your-pants moment?" I asked. I assumed it was a metaphor for some arduous trial you endure together, or some magical moment where you realize that your partner is indeed "the one," as the Brit had in Stowe.

"Oh, no. I mean that literally," she said with a chuckle. "Here's why it's called a shit-your-pants moment. Henry has a friend who was on his second date with a woman, and the girl has celiac disease. And she'd inadvertently eaten some gluten or—something happened. And they're driving, they get stuck in a traffic jam, and the girl very calmly says, 'I need to get out of the car. I need to go to the bathroom on the side of the road. And I need your underwear.'"

I was already dying laughing. "Oh, *nooooo.*"

Taylor was cracking up now, too. "And the guy's like, 'What?' She says, 'Can you take off . . . ?' I mean, this was a real disaster. A true shit-your-pants moment. The poor guy—"

She was really cackling now.

"What happened?" I asked.

"So Henry later asked him, 'What were you thinking in that moment?' And the guy said he realized, right then, that he was either going to be with her forever, or he'd have a really funny story to tell for the rest of his life. And ultimately he decided, *I really like her. This is it. I'm in. I'm going to give her my underwear.*"

Taylor paused for a moment to catch her breath.

"Henry had heard that story, and then *we* started telling other people, and it turns out a lot of people have those examples. Like, someone is in the hospital, and the other one realizes, *I could just leave.* Or, *This is the person I'm going to spend the rest of my life with.*"

"Did you have one?" I asked. "A shit-your-pants moment?"

"We'd always talked about it, and it got to the point where my friends were starting to get annoyed, because Henry kept hemming and hawing. Everyone was telling him, 'Henry, you guys have been together for a decade. Are you trying to act like you're not sure, like you're not going to be with her? Stop it. There is no shit-your-pants moment.' And then we went to Southeast Asia."

I braced myself. "Uh-huh."

"And it had become a joke, because Henry is thinking that something is going to happen to me while we're over there, or he's going to be washed over with this feeling of: *The heavens have aligned, I'm going to be with her forever.* So we're in Southeast Asia, and we're on a boat—but not a nice boat. It's like a people mover with a wooden bench, a daylong excursion. And Henry gets as sick as a person can get. He has terrible diarrhea, and the toilet is just a hole—"

"I can't," I said, laughing through tears. "This is the *worst* place to have a shit-your-pants moment."

"Yeah, he's thinking that if he slams his head into the door hard enough, it will kill him—or at least knock him out. He's like, *I can't do this.* It's an eight-hour excursion. We asked, and there's nowhere to disembark. It's a full day. It's a thousand degrees. He's so miserable, so sick. So finally, in the afternoon, we get somewhere where people are able to go snorkeling, and I say, 'Why don't you just jump in the ocean?' When he gets back on the boat, I'm like, 'Will you marry me?'"

I couldn't believe this story had taken a turn to the sentimental. Somehow, I heard myself saying, "Aw."

"And he says, 'What?' He's so sick, he's not really registering what I'm saying. And I explain, 'Well, you were waiting for a shit-your-pants moment.'"

Several years after their trip to Asia—after a second, more official proposal, the birth of their son, the search for a house, and COVID-related delays—Taylor and Henry were indeed married. And in the course of my own research, I discovered that such moments are pretty widespread, just as Taylor had told me. Like, for example, with Cameron Fowler, an LA-based entrepreneur.

"She actually shared this story when she said her wedding vows," he said of his wife, Daphne. "It was Valentine's Day—we had our first date on December sixth, so it wasn't very long after that. We had already said 'I love you.' We just felt that so strongly. And I must have been working or had plans, because usually she would come over to my place right after work. But for some reason we had decided to meet up later. And she told me, 'It's a really good thing that happened.' Because half an hour from home, well, her bowels opened up. She shat herself, in leather pants, and had to, like, sit in it for thirty minutes—which is gross."

Here we go again, I thought. "Nooooo."

"Yeah, but the way she talked about it afterward? When she told me?" Cameron said, with what I can only describe as the most adorable look of adoration and awe. "Just a complete lack of shame. She was able to laugh at herself, and it made me love her so much more, instantly. On the spot. To the point where a lot of people know that story—because I tell it a lot."

"It's a great story," I conceded.

"It's also so indicative of who she is. Daph is a stunningly beautiful, curvy woman. As a society, we tend to think women like that might be aloof, or people will say that she's intimidating? But I'm like, 'Have you heard the poop story?' Because I assure you, she's human.'"

As admittedly (and weirdly?) charmed as I was, I have to admit: I was sort of grateful that the Brit and I didn't have . . . you know, *a poop story*. And I figure that if you're trying to decide if your partner is the person you want to spend the rest of your life with, you can certainly wait for a shit-your-pants moment (ready-made wedding toast!) or you could go with the slightly less scatological option: R&P.

R&P QUESTION #188 **Do you have any doubts about the future of our relationship?**

I was chatting with Abby Matthews, a human resources manager, when she started raising some red flags—just not about *her* relationship.

"My fiancé and I have been dating for five years now," she told me. "And I had a friend who got engaged one week before me—and it was a little annoying, to be honest. They had been dating for nine months. And they had an elaborate engagement. I did not have an elaborate engagement. Everything about this annoyed me. And I asked her—I was being nice—I asked her, 'Were you so surprised? Were you expecting it?' Because *I* wasn't surprised. My fiancé and I had been talking about getting engaged. He proposed when we were on a week of PTO, so it was the perfect time. I was, like, handing it to him on a silver platter. But she said, 'I had no idea.' And I thought, *This is a recipe for disaster*. I had a friend who once said, 'If you don't know you're getting engaged, you're not in a healthy relationship.' I mean, if you're shell-shocked, that's probably not a good sign. And, of course, they ended up breaking up, because they never talked about certain things."

"What kinds of things?" I asked. "Do you remember?"

"There was a big issue with his mother; like, his mom was very involved," Abby said. "There was a lot of family drama. But I kept saying,

'This is crazy,' because she owned a home and was independently wealthy. She inherited a lot of money from her grandfather. So she wanted a prenup to protect her assets, and he wouldn't sign one. My fiancé is a former finance guy, and he was like, 'This is so stupid. She should just put it in a trust.' But that isn't the problem! I mean, sure, you could call her and tell her how to hide this money. But that's not solving the problem of this distrust. I would never get engaged to someone who didn't respect my wish for a prenup to protect my family's assets."

Ah, the prenup. Once considered the exclusive province of the ultra-rich, or a de rigueur aspect of (notoriously short) Hollywood marriages, pre-nuptial agreements have always been more than a little controversial. Many consider them to be deeply *un*romantic, and fear that merely contemplating a future separation might in and of itself hasten divorce. Fun fact: until the mid-1980s, prenups were not regularly enforced by the American court system for exactly that reason. But in the interven-ing years, they've become decidedly more popular. Though statistics are hard to come by—as prenups are private documents—recent reporting in *The New Yorker* (and a small poll conducted by Harris Interactive) sug-gests that as many as 40 percent of couples between the ages of eighteen and thirty-four have signed one—to protect assets, as a buffer against lost income when staying home to raise children, and increasingly, to shield a partner from debt.

"I'm a big believer in prenups," Gabrielle Hartley, divorce attorney and mediator, author of *The Secret to Getting Along* and cochair of the American Bar Association Mediation Committee told me. "Here's the thing about a prenup, though. What I have seen happen very often is the non-moneyed spouse is so worried about being seen as a gold digger or money-grabber that they give away too much. They give away so much that they're in this adverse position. I mean, you marry someone when you're young, and neither of you has anything. You think, *If we get divorced, I'll have savings by then. I'll be working. I won't have to pay support.* But now you're fifty-five years old, and the reality is, you stayed at home and your spouse has a business that's now worth, I don't know, in the millions. And you have no rights to it, because you waived them. So you have to be really careful with prenups."

Despite their growing popularity, prenups aren't a fail-safe. Rules and requirements—like, say, the stipulation that each partner must have his or her own attorney—can vary significantly from state to state. Not all terms or clauses you might wish to include are enforceable. (Generally speaking, prenups cannot include anything related to future child custody or child support.) For couples with similar or with few to no assets, they may add up to little more than an unnecessary expense. But the biggest potential pitfall might be in the negotiation of a prenuptial agreement—which presents an opportunity to be fully transparent with your partner, to grapple with the concepts of joint versus separate property, and to plan for the future together. Or, conversely, it's an opportunity for coercion, or hurt feelings, or setting up an "us versus them" dynamic that could taint the entire marriage. (It's no wonder Gabrielle told me that she hates to write prenups but loves to mediate them.) Even more important than a partner's blanket willingness to sign one, is whether or not the two of you can honestly and effectively talk about it.

"A prenup is really essential if you have money going into a marriage," Gabrielle said, "but it doesn't mean you have to leave your soon-to-be-spouse nothing, and it doesn't mean you're being negative. It just means you want things to be simpler, so that you don't spend years of your life arguing. You want to set up a prenup in such a way that if your marriage should unravel, you know what's expected. If you don't set it up right, if you're fighting and emotions get in the way, then the only people who will make money are the lawyers, right?"

For the record, those with substantial assets but no desire or intention to wed can still protect themselves in the context of long-term partnerships. "If you're buying property," Gabrielle advised, "you should have a buy-sell agreement, a process for unraveling, because you're not going to have jurisdiction in a court that hears divorces or family law cases. If you're not married, don't assume that you have rights to anything except child support."

Finally, and because Gabrielle is an expert in mediation, I asked what couples might do long before facing the prospect of divorce. Did she have any advice for staying together?

"Oh, my gosh! There's so many things! Shelving is so important," she said, by which she meant a willingness to briefly shelve heated conversations, to take a time-out in order to de-escalate. "It's really important to understand *why* we're arguing, what our interests and motivations are, because we get really stuck in the *what*, and then we have these destructive tendencies that keep us in these intractable loops. So we blow things up that don't need to be blown up. We stir the pot. We deflect. We all do all of these things—no judgment. We all do them to a greater or lesser degree, but catching yourself when you're doing them is magical in terms of scaling back. Because the number one reason that people divorce? Poor communication."

I couldn't help but smile—where had I heard that before?

"And did you know that only 18 percent of couples ever seek help before getting divorced?" she continued. "So don't be afraid to get a therapist."

R&P QUESTION #194 **If you want to wear a wedding or commitment ring, what would it look like? How much money should we spend on them?**

One of the best parts of writing a book about relationships is getting to hear so many different love stories—all those juicy details about first dates and first kisses, the first time someone said "I love you," the moment someone realized their partner was "the one." I spent hours and hours chatting about all aspects of weddings and engagements, too, and when it came to engagement rings, turns out a lot of people got right down to business.

One woman presented her soon-to-be-husband with an entire spreadsheet explaining her wishes regarding size and clarity. Another gave her fiancé a twelve-page guide—with pictures—and when that didn't cut it, sent him an invoice. A husband I spoke to explained that he was happy to propose with the exact ring his then-girlfriend wanted—so long as she could acknowledge that diamond engagement rings were not always the ubiquitous symbol of love and partnership they are today. ("The DeBeers marketing campaign was incredibly effective," he told me. "Most people have no idea about it. She was totally like, woke, but also able to say, '*I* still want it.'") A soon-to-be-wife made clear to her partner that she was not only willing to help pay for her engagement ring, but practically insisted she contribute financially. ("I didn't want to take anything away from him, but I looked at this as an investment for both of us. I think it's stupid that there's all this pressure on guys to pay for the diamond on their own.")

"It's funny—the practicality piece actually comes in a lot more these days," said Stephanie Gottlieb, founder and creative director of her eponymous jewelry line, Stephanie Gottlieb Fine Jewelry, whom I called up not only in light of her gemstone expertise but for her thoughts on the ritual of engagement. "At this stage, people know what kind of rings they like—the four Cs [cut, color, clarity, and carat] are just factors of budget. So gone are the days where a partner is coming to the store to pick out a ring that he thinks his future fiancé will love, and buying it and surprising her—that isn't how the world works anymore. Everything is far too tangible. We can access everything online and see what we like and create our Pinterest boards and share those with a partner."

Or our spreadsheets, I thought to myself.

"What we more often see now is a couple coming in together and making decisions about how much they want to spend, how comfortable they are with a certain budget, whether they're leaning toward a lab-grown or natural stone, whether other family members are going to be involved—there actually are a lot of practicalities involved with the process. And more and more, I find the romance comes in once those big decisions have been made, when someone starts to think through little details that maybe their partner hasn't yet thought about. So, is their favorite color pink? Or is their birthstone an amethyst? Do they want to incorporate that, or to engrave a funny or silly message that's going to surprise them? It's in those little unexpected details that we see the romance."

"What about when a couple can't seem to agree?" I asked, thinking of a friend whose fiancé was partial to a round stone, which he thought of as classic, while she was more interested in an emerald cut. They'd eventually come to an agreement after she'd reminded him, repeatedly, that *she* was the one who'd be wearing the thing every day.

"Well, I think that's so telling, right?" Stephanie said. "If this is a decision that you're not willing to budge on—as the person buying the ring—then that's probably indicative of a bigger power struggle in your relationship. I have seen that play out, someone not wanting to budge because they have a set idea of what the ring should be quote-unquote worth."

"Are there ever times when someone leaves a consultation, and you have a feeling the relationship isn't going to work out?"

"Not always, but we definitely have couples come in who are arguing during the appointment, or she may come in by herself preemptively, and we have a sense that he doesn't know this is happening, or it may not be on his radar. I don't think there are any true tells, unless it's obvious that someone just got dragged there. What I think is important is making sure that the couple is on the same page. What I would want to see is mutual agreement."

"What else do you like to see? Or, any sort of red flags?"

"Sometimes it's a question of maturity, not being able to make a decision for themselves—do they need to have their mom with them? And that could be a whole other issue in the relationship. Do they not want to take the time to understand what it is they're buying, and where the value is? That to me is a red flag. I couldn't marry someone who didn't care about something they're spending that much money on, that they're using as sort of a tool to commit to me for the rest of my life. I would want someone to be thoughtful about that process. So anyone who's really flippant, that's sort of a turnoff. It's not my role to judge or to play therapist, but it tells me a little about that person."

"Do you ever feel like you're playing therapist a little bit, though?" I asked.

"Totally," Stephanie said, laughing. "Because this is usually the first big purchase a couple is going to make together. And it's just the beginning—forget about *wedding planning*."

"Always Ask the Tough Questions": A Conversation with Colin Cowie

For the better part of three decades, Zambian-born wedding and events planner Colin Cowie has been regarded as the best in the business. With a client list including Oprah, Jennifer Aniston, Nicole Kidman, and Jennifer Lopez, Cowie is a mainstay on *Vogue*'s list of best wedding planners; maintains offices in New York, Los Angeles, San Francisco, Las Vegas, and Miami; and employs a full-time staff of twenty—I was humbled that he shared some of his (very valuable) time to give me a peek behind the scenes.

R&P QUESTION #182

Do you have a vision for your dream wedding?

I feel like you can really shed some light on the things couples should talk about before attempting to plan an event that costs such a significant amount of time, emotional energy, and money, so they don't fall victim to certain traps or pitfalls . . .

Colin: I think alignment is probably the biggest thing. It doesn't matter whether it's a wedding or an anniversary—or any party. It's just very evident in the first meeting whether a couple is aligned or not.

Why? What sorts of things do you see?

Colin: Well, different opinions, different points of view. She might want to do a much bigger production. He might want something more low-key. And then we kind of find ourselves in the middle of it, having to navigate our way through a minefield—because we wear many hats. At that stage, you're wearing the hat of the event planner, the producer, the designer—

The therapist—

Colin: Best friend, arbiter, *and* chief psychologist, right? I actually find that more and more couples are aligned today. Twenty years ago, the bride and groom would come in, and the groom would say, "Just tell me where to show up and at what time." Now he has a very strong opinion. He's involved, he has a point of view—which I think is kind of nice, because it puts you on the fast track to how life is going to be.

An endless series of decisions.

Colin: And if you're not aligned, each decision coming down the line is the potential for a problem. Listen, I've been doing this for a very long time, and you can see when a couple is madly in love and they make decisions jointly. But when a couple is fighting during the tasting, fighting during the creative presentation . . . it invariably means they haven't figured it out yet. That's very different from the couple who was aligned beforehand and came out the other side unscathed.

How do you help couples keep their feet on the ground—no matter how extravagant (or not) the affair—while maintaining focus on celebrating their partnership?

Colin: Two things: The first is to establish a budget. One of the biggest arguments in our business is always over money, right? And then, *dream.* It costs nothing to dream, and you want that "big picture" in mind. It'll help you make every other creative decision that you have to make along the way, because everything will be in service to that big picture. Then you just value-engineer it according to the budget. If it's not Dom Pérignon, it's prosecco. If it's not prosecco, it's an Aperol spritz bar. If it's not the seventeen-piece band, it's a saxophone player and a percussionist, or it's a DJ. There are many ways to celebrate. There are many ways to get from A to B without feeling like you're missing out on anything. I always say to the bride and groom, "If we have to give up something because of the budget, the only people who will know about it are us."

It's such an intimate, interesting time for a couple—it sort of forces you to look at the person you're choosing and think, *This is how we're going to make decisions together, this is how we're going to live our lives.*

Colin: Yes, absolutely. You know, money, alcohol, and weddings are the ultimate truth serums. They bring out the best and worst in everyone.

● ● ●

Not quite a year after the Brit and I went to Stowe, I was back in New York, basking in the glow of another trip, which I'd come to think of as our first "proper" vacation: a whirlwind through the Golden Triangle in India, the popular tourist circuit comprising the towns of Agra, Delhi, and Jaipur. We'd chosen India for the simple fact that neither of us had ever been. (Well, the Brit had been to Delhi for business, but never for pleasure.) I had anticipated the beauty of the Taj Mahal, but hadn't been prepared for the absolute onslaught of tastes and smells and colors, the markets and food stalls, the spices and textiles. We were in Jaipur—the "gemstone capital of the world"—when I spotted a stunning pair of sapphire studs. To my surprise, the Brit insisted we also get the matching tennis bracelet.

"Honestly, I just came looking for earrings," I'd said. "These are beautiful."

"*You're* beautiful. And we aren't likely coming back to Jaipur anytime soon," he'd replied, before turning to the shopkeeper. "So yes, please. We'll take the bracelet, too."

While we waited for the jeweler to resize it, I kissed him. I was deeply in love—with my man, the earrings, the experience we were having, the people we were meeting, and the ease between us, our ability to travel a foreign country without so much as an argument, that deep-in-the-gut knowledge that, at long last, I had found my person. Feeling whimsical that evening, like there was nowhere else for the conversation to really go, I brought up the subject of our future lives together.

It wasn't one of our better talks. I was hoping for a timeline, and the Brit wouldn't commit to one. He was committed to *me*, but he wasn't ready to make it official, to put something on the calendar. And so I had taken a deep breath (or two), kept my emotions in check, and reminded myself that the journey had always been about the man—our love and our partnership—and never "the ring."

Which is why I was so surprised when mere weeks later, as we were sitting on my sofa, deciding which show to watch, the Brit started talking about the logistics of it all—of getting engaged and planning a wedding. He wanted to know if I *also* didn't want to get married in winter, if I *also* didn't want to wait a whole year to say "I do." I realized he was being true to himself, the person I knew and had fallen in love with—the logical guy, the maths guy, the ruminator, not ready to make a move until he had the timing right.

It took every ounce of strength I had not to hop up and down on the couch and shout from the rooftops, *Yes! Dear God, yes!!*

"That means we really only have about six months to plan and execute a dream wedding. Hypothetically speaking," he said with a wink.

"Uh-huh, for a summer or fall wedding." *Oh, look at me. So casual. So chill.*

"Be right back," he said, and I sat there, confused, until he returned, held out his hand, and opened his palm. In it was a ring of blue sapphires—the sapphires that had been removed when the shopkeeper made my bracelet smaller.

"I wasn't sure when I would give this to you," he said. "But now seems like the perfect time, so we can begin planning our special day . . ."

There are as many ways to propose to someone as there are couples—from the middle-of-the-game, your-picture-suddenly-on-the-jumbotron very public moment to the utterly private, just-the-two-of-you-in-bed early morning declaration. I couldn't have planned our moment any better, only knew that it somehow felt entirely and perfectly true to *us*.

". . . Until your engagement ring arrives," he continued, the corners of his mouth turning up into a cheeky grin.

And just like that, I started to dream.

11

Religion, Spirituality & Politics

If you want to avoid heated arguments, never
discuss religion, politics, or whether the
toilet paper roll should go over or under.
—*Al Yankovic*

It was 2008, and my roommate and I were headed to a Super Bowl party at a mutual friend's apartment. Beth had just moved in with her boyfriend, and they were entertaining as a couple for the first time: Giants versus Patriots. We brought with us a large pie from Joanne's Pizza and absolutely zero desire to watch the actual game, just the halftime show.

The real show, however, turned out not to be Tom Petty—it was a political argument between my roommate and another guest, Ajay, whom we'd just met that evening. To this day, both still insist that what they had was merely a "heated discussion." But trust me, it was explosive. Back and forth they went about health care and voting rights, the military-industrial complex and the national debt. Those of us watching were deeply uncomfortable—including Ajay's wife, who tried to step in multiple times, but the fight kept raging.

"Ajay and I weren't uncomfortable," my friend and former room-mate Natalie told me recently. "*You all* may have been, but *we* were the ones having the conversation. We actually found it really interesting. And clearly, it all worked out."

That's the best part of the story: everyone else may have thought those two were on the verge of killing each other, but Ajay suddenly pivoted and said, "I like you. If you're single, can I set you up with one of my best friends?"

Natalie and Ajay's friend, Richard, have been married for more than a decade now and have three gorgeous children. But it doesn't al-ways work out that way. Religion, politics—these are potentially some of the diciest issues to discuss, and for many people form core aspects of their worldview and beliefs. And more and more, it seems, those beliefs may be intractable.

R&P QUESTION #205   **Would you convert religions at the request of your partner? Why or why not?**

"I've learned to lead with the Jewish thing," Allison Grinberg-Funes told me.

In the hope of speaking to as wide a swath of people as possible, I had reached out to everyone I could think of, tapped my networks in the UK, the United States, and beyond, and posted in an array of Facebook and WhatsApp groups. In Allison's case, I came across an article she'd written for HuffPost about an unexpected breakup she experienced—and I knew I had to talk to her.

"There's such a wide spectrum of observance," she continued, "and people feel very strongly one way or another about their Jewish iden-tity. I learned a long time ago that because my dad's Jewish—and not my mom—I don't 'count' as Jewish to some people. I don't pass the halakha, the law of the Torah. So I've been up-front about it, for that reason."

"And were you up-front with your ex?" I asked.

"I was. We met on OkCupid, and I had specified that my dad's Jewish, not my mom, that they had let us choose our own adventure. I'm also spiritual. I have, like, tarot cards and crystals. His profile opened up with: 'I'm Greek, my family is like *My Big Fat Greek Wedding*.' Immediately, I was obsessed. I loved that movie growing up, and I had just rewatched it before we connected. Then when we met in person, we talked about all the common points of Judaism and that culture, and Greek Orthodox and that culture. Like, the families are usually big. People are nosy. Things are really food oriented. Everyone's got an opinion. There are a lot of overlaps, right? So we were going back and forth, comparing and contrasting. But nowhere in this conversation did he say, 'By the way, if I marry someone someday, I'm going to ask them to convert.'"

Given that it was their first date, I don't know that even *I* would've expected him to be quite that direct—but I'd read Allison's article, and had a sense for what was coming. "All right," I said. "Tell me what happened next."

"It was about two months into our relationship, and I had been telling him about spending Thanksgiving with my sister and brother-in-law. And he asked, 'Well, how do you feel about having two feasts in one weekend? Do you want to come to my family's Thanksgiving?' Which I knew would be a lot. This wouldn't be a four-people-around-the-table kind of meal. But he gave me the rundown of who was going to be there, and I started referring to it as 'My Big Fat Greek Thanksgiving.' And it actually was like the movie! We walked in, and he shouted, 'Everybody, this is my girlfriend, Allison.' And everyone was like, 'Allison!' Like, all together. Then his aunt kept apologizing to me, 'I'm so sorry. We're so loud.' And I kept saying, 'You don't understand. My family in Argentina and Miami are the exact same.' I felt like I was with my extended family, because the cultures were super similar. Also, their sense of humor was so great. I sat down at the table, and his dad said, 'So, Allison, do you like lamb?' Because that's a big thing in the movie. I had a great time, loved meeting everybody."

"What changed?

Allison wrinkled her nose ever so slightly and took a deep breath. "In typical Greek guy fashion, he lived very near his parents—and by nearby, I mean they had a duplex. He had the upstairs apartment, and they had the downstairs. Shortly after Thanksgiving, I was at his place, his mom came up to say hi, and she was talking about their Christmas plans. She said, 'You're invited, by the way. We want you to come.' I realized that *he* hadn't asked me. But I mentioned it to him later, and he said he was fine with me coming. Later on, I was trying to get the rundown of what to expect, because he'd given me the download before Thanksgiving. I asked, 'Do you go to Mass?' I've been to plenty of Mass ceremonies. I find them very aerobic—stand, kneel, sit, stand, kneel—but I'm used to it. And he said that they go the night before Christmas, and they go all night. I joked, 'Well, I don't have to go all night, right?' Like, I'll go. But I don't want to be there all night, like some kind of Christian high school lock-in. And he said, 'Oh, actually you wouldn't be allowed.' That's when I was like, 'Wait, what? *Why?*'"

"And what did he say?" I asked. "What was his answer?"

"He said, 'Uhhh, because you're Jewish.' And I could see him hesitating."

"Wait," I interjected. "Was he saying the church wouldn't allow you in the doors? Or he wouldn't? Or his family wouldn't? Who's doing the not allowing?"

"That's the thing," Allison said, shaking her head. "How would they even know I'm Jewish? But he said his entire family would be there, and they knew, and if word got to the priest, he would most likely ask me to step out. And I was like, *First of all—wow.*"

I couldn't help but feel a little suspicious at that point. "Places of worship are generally welcoming places. I don't believe they turn people away?"

"Right. And I kind of checked. I asked around. *Is this legit a Greek thing?* Then I asked him about it, and he started to explain the difference between new calendar Greek Orthodox and the much more conservative Old Calendarists. His family are old calendar people. At that point, I was dumbfounded."

That uncomfortable revelation led to a series of tough chats for Allison and her now-ex. He admitted that he one day planned to marry in the Greek Orthodox church, which could only happen if Allison (or any non–Greek Orthodox partner) agreed to convert. For Allison, who'd already told him that she "felt Jewish in her soul" and hoped to incorporate Jewish elements in her wedding, that wasn't an option. There was no other recourse for the young couple than to split up. But some lingering questions remained—his family had known Allison, and liked her. What had they been thinking? Why had he been so willing to meet her family? Why hadn't this come up before? Why hadn't she and her boyfriend really *talked* about their nonnegotiables?

"You mentioned in your article that you knew politics and children were important to discuss, as they can make or break a relationship," I said. "But before this experience, you couldn't have imagined ending a relationship because of faith. Why?"

"I think it had to do, in part, with the circles in which I was dating," Allison said. "Having lived in Boston and New York City before that, I tended to date people who were not very religious. They're secular. It's like, 'Yeah, we're gonna do an Easter egg hunt.' Not like people who answer the phone, 'He is risen. Happy Easter.' Based on the pool of people that I've been fishing in, it just hadn't been that big a deal. Until now."

That's the thing about religion, or any complicated topic; it's why conversations like these can't stay surface-level: Despite all the chatting about their backgrounds, all the similarities she thought she saw, only in hindsight was it clear that she'd missed some big differences. The Jewish traditions Allison cherishes are largely cultural. When her ex had sinus surgery and casually mentioned that he'd stopped by the church to light a candle first, the fact that he might've been much more religious than she'd realized didn't register.

"I'm dating again," Allison said when I asked her, "and the religious/cultural thing is so important to me now. For example, I'm not necessarily opposed to somebody who has 'atheist' in their profile—but I always ask about it. Because in my experience, people seem to think that spirituality and intellectualism are mutually exclusive. For me, I was raised by scientists; my parents are in medicine. I'm also into the woo-woo stuff. So something that I would ask is, 'Hey, I see you're an atheist. What does that mean to you?' For some people, it means they're agnostic. Others might say, 'I'm an atheist, and I think anybody who isn't is stupid,' and then it's like, *Well you just wrote yourself off.* Same goes if someone writes 'moderate' in their profile. I'd say, 'Hey, I see that you describe your politics as moderate,' and I'd ask about their views on some hot-button issues. Things like that."

In light of Allison's story, and while contemplating the religion section of R&P, I couldn't help but hear the start of that old joke in my head: *A priest, a minister, and a rabbi walk into a bar . . .* All are people of God, of course, but each has a different interpretation of faith. Given the very real challenges of interreligious coupledom, and the profundity of religion to so many people, I thought it was important to reach out to the clergy.

Specifically, I called up a rabbi and a priest.

Reverend Chris Lee, vicar of St. Saviour's Wendell Park in West London, has built a massive online following—ITV dubbed him "the internet's favourite vicar"—thanks in part to his youth (early forties), his delightfully upbeat and easy-to-digest "60-second sermons," and his decidedly modern take on evangelism. And yet weddings are a centuries-old rite. As a cleric in the Church of England, he explained that one of his duties is to help couples plan for their "banns of marriage."

"It's a really awkward, antiquated system," he told me, "but it comes from the idea that years back, you know, Joe wants to marry Jane, and they're from different parishes." On three different Sundays in the three months before the ceremony, a couple's intention to wed had to be announced in their respective churches—because presumably, if Joe or Jane was a drunkard, thief, floozy, or already married to someone, people in the parish would know and could lodge an objection. "With social media, it's not really necessary anymore. But the premise is a good one. Community and family and friends around you are vital. And if your community is saying you shouldn't get married—you don't know this person—it's important to take that on board."

Something that came up repeatedly in my interviews and my research was the widespread religious tradition of *mandating* premarital counseling. In the Catholic church, the practice is known as Pre-Cana (in reference to the biblical wedding at Cana); while neither Protestant nor Jewish premarital coursework has a formal name, it's likewise common that a minister or rabbi will require it before officiating a ceremony or lending their place of worship for a service. There isn't really a secular analogue, but it's not that hard to understand why. The "church" isn't as central to society as it once was. And as my friend Jo Piazza, who spent time in twenty different countries to research her travelogue *How to Be Married*, observed, "the idea that it takes a village not just to raise children but to nurture a marriage has kind of gotten lost in American culture."

That's a shame. Because despite the obvious religious bent, "marriage prep" with a cleric or pastor tends to be surprisingly practical. "In my own kind of journey, when I was thinking of marrying my wife, Jenny," Rev. Chris said, "I asked myself three questions. The first one was: Do I fancy her—am I attracted to this person? As you know, attraction—there's a physicality there that I would think is important, is helpful. The second was: If I had daughters, would I want them to be like her? The third was: Am I the best version of myself with her? Those are just three things I tend to ask—and that you can ask of yourself. I think if you don't have them, you're probably set-tling. You know, my wife always says it's better to be single than to be in a bad relationship."

I also spoke with Rabbi Hayley Siegel, currently the Rabbi in Residence at Temple Israel in the City of New York, who offers pre-marital counseling and officiating services for those planning to wed in the Jewish faith. "Planning a wedding is a really important time of transition—I call it *developing your family voice*," she said. "A lot of couples come in, and they have very close and beautiful relationships with their families, and a wedding is sort of the first time they have to make these really big, adult decisions, and take ownership over those choices, and realize that there is an assembling of a unit separate from their families. You know, in the book of Genesis, right after Adam and Eve are created, it says that therefore a man should leave his mother and father and cling to his wife, that they should be one flesh. That doesn't mean you have to abandon or totally disconnect, but it means you have to leave that status to create something new—and the Jewish wedding is such a beautiful illustration of that tension. We have the chuppah, the canopy that's open on all four sides, harkening back to the tents of Abraham and Sarah, who welcomed travelers from every place. But immediately after the ceremony, we do something called yichud, which is when the bride and groom—or the groom and groom, or whoever the pairing is—go into a room by themselves. Now, in the ancient period that may have been for conjugal reasons—"

I couldn't help but laugh at the idea of having a quickie right be-fore the reception—you're in the dress, all made up. "Like, that is *not* happening."

"No, definitely not." She laughed. "But it's a very powerful state-ment, because before you go out to meet your family and friends, you take a moment to pause, a moment for just the two of you. There's a world contained within both of you. So in the Jewish tradition, we really play with this openness, but also boundaries, because both are really healthy and important in a relationship."

Both Reverend Chris and Rabbi Hayley spoke beautifully of the sanctity of marriage, the rich traditions and customs of their faiths, the biblical symbolism associated with weddings—but given their positions as counselors, as leaders, I wanted to know: Did they have any advice for couples who are interfaith?

"Just using a personal example," Reverend Chris said, "my mother's a Christian. My dad wasn't when they got married. He thought religion was a crutch, he thought it was foolish. Now he sees the wealth of it; he does pray, and he has faith. But my mum—while she meant well, she didn't help by trying to make him a Christian. I helped, by him seeing the change in me. It wasn't banging on the door: *You have to become a Christian!* There wasn't any of that. It was him seeing the change in me that made him think: *Maybe there's something to this?* So, it's hard. In those relationships, you have to be confident in your identity, in why you believe what you believe. But you also need humility. If you start to impose your beliefs too much, you might actually push someone away, and you're not really—you're loving the idea of them, rather than them. So I would say, be strong in your identity, confident in your faith, do your practices—and know *why* you do them and love them. I think that is really a key thing."

For her part, Rabbi Hayley hit on something I've always tried to warn couples about: just because you think you know the answers doesn't mean you shouldn't ask the questions.

"I think it's really important to recognize that we all come in with an operating system, right? That's sort of programmed into us, from all the experiences that have shaped us, the moments that have made us who we are. And when we join with someone else, it's almost like you're mingling two kinds of music. One person might be more classical, one might be more jazz—where do you find that synchronicity *within* the melody? You know, you can be from the same religion but still have different family traditions. That's important to explore, too. There might be beautiful customs that your partner brings in, that you didn't have growing up and that would enhance the lives of your family—it could be a tradition, a recipe, something special that they do. Just because somebody practices the same faith doesn't necessarily mean they had the same experience."

•   •   •

As for the Brit and me, I have to admit that we didn't *entirely* take our own advice. After all that time and all those questions—after an engagement, and a marriage even—we still hadn't answered a crucial question in the religion section of R&P.

That's not to say we hadn't discussed our respective faiths at all. The Brit met my parents for the first time during Passover, when he'd come to visit the Long Island home where I'd grown up. Though it's a no-yeast holiday, it collided with Easter that year, so I made sure to have hot cross buns on our table in addition to the matzoh.

When planning our wedding, we sought out an officiant who was excited to help us build a ceremony from the ground up, incorporating rituals and customs from both our faiths. My husband-to-be wanted to incorporate the Celtic tradition of handfasting and was drawn to the symbolism of lighting a unity candle, which we'd slowly burn throughout our lives. (These days, the three-foot pillar sits outside the front door to our home protected by a large hurricane vase—you have to pass it to enter.) When it came to breaking the glass, meanwhile, he needed no encouragement; he was delighted to conclude by hearing the most precious people in our lives shout in unison, "Mazel tov!" Another Jewish tradition I'd always loved was the Seven Blessings, traditionally read in Hebrew. Together, we rewrote them in English, adapting the sentiments to feel truer to us.

Being with him had only deepened the understanding of my faith—after all, it's hard to ask someone to light a menorah or hang tinsel or have a bris or a baptism or abstain from pork (not me, I'm a sucker for bacon) if you can't even articulate why *you* want to do it. And whereas I had once feared that we were two of too many things, I'd grown to believe that we were stronger because of the ways in which we'd approached and even embraced our differences.

A little less than a year after our wedding, there was really just one thing left to discuss. And in fact, I didn't fully confront it until I was ten weeks pregnant.

I was boarding a flight from Heathrow to New York when I got the call: the results of my blood work had just come in, and if we wanted, my doctor was prepared to reveal the sex of our baby. In the final moments before the cabin doors closed, I furiously conferenced in the Brit so we could hear the news together: *boy.*

We said a quick goodbye; I clicked my belt and touched my belly, now growing the child we'd once talked of in theory, back when we were still getting to know each other, strolling past Little Leaguers and stopping for ice cream.

During our chat, Rabbi Hayley had told me that when her son was young, he used to stare up at her ketubah, the Jewish marriage contract, which is beautifully framed and hangs in her home. "When he started being able to read," she said, "he would ask, 'Mommy, where's my name? Why am I not on your *tuba*,' as he called it. And I would say to him, 'You weren't there yet, but your soul was pending.' I always think a wedding is such a special occasion because it's this sort of crossroads in life. You have the past, all the people who stood before you and shaped who you are through their lineage. The present, obviously. And the future, because for the people standing under that marriage canopy, the seeds of their future life are being planted in that moment, all the souls that are pending and yet to be."

How wild to know that *our* son's soul was no longer just pending.

But later, when I was thirty thousand feet in the air, I made the very silly decision to watch *Lion,* the 2016 film starring Dev Patel and Nicole Kidman, about a boy separated from his family and miles from home. Between the film, the pregnancy hormones, the gravity of our news—and anxiety about the conversation I now knew was coming—I bawled my eyes raw. As a doctor I'd once consulted on the matter joked, 'You can't *half* circumsize.' The Brit and I had a big decision to make, and there was only one way forward: to take things step by step, to talk it through, to get practical.

Granted, we could have made a decision sooner—but the goal of R&P actually isn't to effectively navigate every single question and resolve every issue and check every box before you commit. It's about building a foundation you can rely on for the duration of your journey. By then, based on the strength of our partnership, I knew the Brit and I would work through it together, and that we'd be okay.

R&P QUESTION #219   **What do you think happens to us after we die?**

"My husband grew up in a house where they never talked about death. My in-laws think they're going to live forever. But my parents were the opposite."

In addition to her acid wit, writer-actress Jill Kargman is also famously macabre. As a child she was constantly compared to Wednesday Addams; her (surprisingly upbeat) memoir is titled *Sprinkle Glitter on My Grave.* "They were touring cemeteries the way people tour colleges," she continued. "They were on Pinterest picking out tombstone fonts. And I think in that way, the morbid side of my family has made me the happiest person. It's like, let's eat the dessert and turn on music! I don't know why people put their heads in the sand about it. My dad always said, 'If a gargoyle falls off a building and takes me out tomorrow, I know I've left everything perfectly.' He always said shit like that. It still makes me laugh. I think about it that way, too."

It's probably safe to say that Jill's perspective is not the norm—she's built an entire career off subversive humor. In fact, death is maybe the one subject that almost no one wants or knows how to talk about. And, of course, that's precisely why I sought out David Kessler, one of the world's foremost experts on grief and loss, author of a slew of books on the subject (including two with Elisabeth Kübler Ross, of "the five stages of grief" fame).

"Let's start with the practical," I said. "Personally, I'm terrified of death. A lot of people are. I do know where I would like to be buried, and if something were to happen to me, how I'd like to live out my final days—is it important for people to know that about themselves, and have a preference about that?"

David flashed me a kind smile and shook his head. "No. Listen, I would say we are a mixture of our feelings, our parents' feelings, and fears. Death is an area where we often don't even sort out what's *ours,* what we really think about it. So when you say that to me—that you're terrified—I would want to know: What is it about death that you fear? Is it a fear of pain? Is it a fear of the unknown? Is it a fear of losing control? Is it a fear of saying goodbye? All those things?"

"Well, as a parent," I conceded, "it's changed. I think now it's that I want to be there for my children as long as possible. I don't want to leave them with the pain of not having me. I don't want to miss seeing them grow up. So it's not about fearing the act of it. It's the fear of what happens when."

"I run an online grief group called Tender Hearts," he said with a nod. "It's people all over the world. We gather four times a week. And a man came on yesterday and talked about his father, whom he loved dearly. And I spoke to him about a parent's final lesson, which is about loss. It's about teaching your children how to be ready and independent in the world. As parents, we think, *I have to teach him how to safely cross the street. I have to make sure they get into a good school.* But you also have to make sure they know how to deal with loss. Because they're going to experience loss. One of the most consistent and constant challenges of life."

As he was speaking, I flashed back to a moment a year or two earlier. I'd been in the kitchen with the Brit and our children, and on a whim queued up an on-demand episode of *Mister Rogers' Neighborhood*, which my brother and I loved as kids. I'd selected an episode at random, and it turned out to be about a fish dying. "It was not at all the way I would approach death with my kids," I explained. "It was such a darkly serious, morbid way of looking at it, and I turned it off immediately, because I didn't want my kids to see it. *I* want to bring that to them."

"Yeah. When it comes to kids, sometimes a parent will tell me that 'the goldfish died, but we didn't want the kids to know.'"

"So we got another one," I said.

"Or we flushed it down the toilet. We told them it swam to the river. I'll ask, 'Why did you do that?' And they'll say, 'Well, we didn't want them to have any sadness.' But that's a missed opportunity. Parents always want to know: *When* do we teach our children about loss? And I'll tell them, 'When the goldfish dies. When the pet dies. When the neighbor dies. That's when you teach them.'"

"How might this apply to talking about death with someone you're in a partnership—or a potential partnership—with?"

"The talk about, you know, what are your beliefs around this, what are your fears, will tell us so much about the other person," David said. "If someone's been taught that we come to earth, live a whole life, and at some point it's time to say goodbye, that when that sunset comes, we want to feel like we've done everything in life—actually, I don't know anyone who's really been taught that. I've never met *that* healthy a person. Most people in those moments are going to share their anxieties, their fears, some of their old wounds. And those are the same anxieties that are often going to show up in relationships."

"How do you mean?" I asked. "Can you explain?"

"My mother died when I was thirteen," he said. "Very young. So I had huge abandonment issues. Every relationship I had in my twenties, if someone said, 'I'm not sure I want to commit,' I'd say, 'Great. Do you want to go on a date with me?' In other words, I made sure to choose anyone who was likely to abandon me. I kept setting that up. That's how our wounds work—we're going to find people who are going to play out those primary roles. And hopefully, as we heal, we choose people who are more healed."

What he was describing was exactly the dynamic I'd always hoped to encourage with R&P. "If you can look at a list of questions, a list of things you should know about *yourself*—even before committing to someone else—I think that's a step in the right direction," I said.

"Yes, as a start. But here's the thing: trauma, grief, we're all learning that those can't be healed in isolation. We actually need another person. That person that we've connected with is there for our healing. And we're there for theirs. So yes, it's one more chance to abandon each other or treat each other poorly. It's also a chance to say, 'Oh, that happened to you? Let's do it differently. You were abandoned? I'm going to try to be a person who, whenever I leave, makes sure to tell you that I'm coming back. Oh, you were cut off and minimized and not allowed to speak? I'm going to let you know how important your voice is.' Through those wounds we can actually learn what the other person needs. And how we approach death—are we living in fear? do we let our fears run our lives? are we overcautious?—is often a clue to how we approach life."

● ● ●

Claire and Finn, the couple who'd whiteboarded their finances—who'd bonded over their shared financial histories—also shared the same faith. They'd met while attending the local all-boys' and all-girls' Catholic schools.

"Going through Pre-Cana," Claire said, holding Finn's hand now, "there were some topics that made us think, *Damn, that never came up.* Like, if someone falls ill . . ."

"It's morbid"—Finn nodded—"but fuck, man. If I'm on the hose, just pull it. Don't spend the money—"

"It was contract versus commitment," Claire continued, shooting a playful glance at her fiancé. "That was the big thing. They kept saying, this is a commitment. Not a contract."

"Sorry, what's the difference?" I asked. "I don't understand."

"Basically, the Catholic view is that you are *committing* to each other. Whereas if we had a contract, there would be a very specific set of things we were signing up for. In a relationship—a marriage—I'm not just signing up for Finn as healthy or, you know, all the idealistic things: dual income, kids. The commitment part of it comes in when you start to ask yourself, What if Finn gets sick in five years? What if he loses his job? What if we can't have kids? That's the difference. And it sounds obvious, but I liked that they said it, because you shouldn't feel like: *You broke the contract. Now this is not a marriage.* You're signing up for this living, breathing relationship. I'm not signing up for what I want Finn to be. I'm signing up for *Finn*: good, bad, ugly. Our priest told us that a lot of people who don't go through this process or don't have those conversations get down the line and a curveball gets thrown their way. And they're like, 'This isn't what I signed up for.' I didn't sign up for a mother-in-law living with us, or not being able to have children, or not being financially stable. He said, 'You are committing to working through that.' And to me, that was the biggest takeaway."

12

Routines, Rituals, Hobbies & Travel

Make a bucket list and fill it with
dreams that have no boundaries.
—*Annette White*

As the Brit and I settled into life together, without even really meaning to or talking about it, we adopted a number of pastimes and practices that became uniquely ours, little routines and rituals for just the two of us. He introduced me to the "Round on the Links" quiz in the UK's *Financial Times*, for example, which is a complicated, twofold quiz wherein you have to not only answer ten questions, but also figure out what links the ten answers together. I should point out that something like this is not my strong suit.

And in another country's paper? *Forget it.*

But we started making a point of doing it together. One of the Brit's best attributes is that he would never make me or anyone feel less than—no matter how off-the-wall some of my guesses may be—and as a result, I've seriously improved. (We also like giving the quiz a go when we're with our families, or sometimes we'll just FaceTime my dad, since he too has a seemingly unlimited amount of useless information at his disposal.) Every night, the Brit and I do the *New York Times* crossword puzzle while cuddled in bed—I guess we're suckers for all types of quizzes—and when *Love Island* is on, we snuggle up together on the sofa.

For the record, *he* got *me* into the show.

But until recently, I wouldn't have been able to articulate why something as silly as a crossword puzzle or a dating show seemed so important to our relationship—other than to say that it's the little things that make up the rhythm of our lives.

Then I checked in with Sam Garanzini and Alapaki Yee, both Gottman-certified therapists as well as cofounders of the Gay Couples Institute, through which they've counseled more than four thousand LGBTQ+ couples and individuals. They've also been a couple themselves for nearly twenty years. And it turns out I really had been onto something.

"Broadly speaking, routines and rituals are very important," Alapaki told me. "They've been very well researched in terms of helping couples stay together and feel closer, because they tell the 'story of us.' They're what make Sam and Alapaki, for example, *Sam and Alapaki*. So it could be crossword puzzles. It could be a summer trip. For us, it could be Gay Pride. All these little things you do daily, weekly, monthly, seasonally build your emotional bank account. Every time you do a crossword puzzle, that's a deposit in this savings account that you can use on a rainy day."

I had to laugh at the reference, because at that very moment I was standing in the pouring rain, barely managing to balance my umbrella and the phone. The eight-hour time difference between us meant that I suddenly had to carry forth with our interview on the go, having already been booted from my quiet spot in the public library—and yet I was so riveted by the conversation that it didn't matter.

"And there's going to be a day when your partner says, 'I'm so sorry, babe. I can't today,'" Alapaki continued. "Or 'I can't for three weeks.'"

That's going to sting way less than if you're working on a deficit, because when you've done these things more often than not, you can lean on that, and trust that."

I thought of all the people who'd shared with me (almost always without prompting) their own little personal routines. Like Todd and Avery, who after fourteen years together remain very intentional about kissing each other hello and goodbye—every single day—as well as before bed. Over time, that last kiss of the evening has turned into a bit of a game for them, a faux competition to see who's the first to remember to proffer the kiss and say the official "good night." Or Angela, who as a single woman hadn't yet adopted her own rituals with a partner but instead fondly remembers the 2 p.m. Sunday dinner she had each week with her Italian grandparents. Or Carey and Jim, who as I mentioned used to tune in each week to Suze Orman's old Sunday-night show, and who also told me that "the most important thing, maybe *the* most important thing for us is that we laugh a lot."

But something else occurred to me, too: how often, over the course of my research, I heard people lament the fact that we *don't* communicate with our partners regularly—from Jo Piazza, who mentioned that we mandate continuing education for virtually every professional trade but not for marriage; to Franchesca Ramsey, who wondered why we do our taxes every year or have annual performance reviews at work but don't make a point of evaluating the financial aspect of our romantic relationships; to Emily Morse's emphatic recommendation to talk about sex at least once a month. All those potential check-ins, I realized, are in and of themselves rituals.

Which is of course why, in the broadest sense, Sam and Alapaki recommended doing exactly that.

"There's a really interesting exercise the Gottmans created called the State of the Union," Alapaki said. "A weekly check-in to ask, 'How are we doing? How did last week go? What went well? What didn't go well? How do we set each other up for success next week?' It ensures that you don't go very long without connecting—but also that you don't relapse. We work with a ton of couples who feel very disconnected, lonely, bored. They'll tell us, 'We used to go on date night every Saturday. We haven't done that in two months.' The first reaction to that might be: 'Okay, set up a date night.' On the surface, that seems like sound advice. But the question under that is: Why aren't they doing that?"

And for new couples? I asked. What was their advice?

"Actually, we just did a podcast—what advice would you give couples in their first twelve months together?" Alapaki said. "And it's exactly what we've been talking about: build in rituals. New couples don't always realize or understand why rituals are building blocks, but it's because they're a way of paying attention to one another, which ultimately increases and accelerates connection and trust."

R&P QUESTION #230 **Would you say you're a very routinized sort of person? Do your days tend to look the same or follow the same patterns? Do you follow a strict schedule or are you more spontaneous and come-what-may?**

"The problem, I would argue," Dr. Michael Breus said, "is that now everything is sped up. There's very little courtship. And I know I sound like a really old guy when I say that. But when I was growing up, you had a girlfriend or a boyfriend—or whatever, doesn't matter the sex—but you had one person, and you were monogamous. And you didn't get very far with that person until a history was built. Nowadays, I know young people who are like, 'Yup, I'm getting laid tonight.' Just, *boom*. They know exactly what's about to happen. And I think that fast-forwards you into a whole new set of circumstances that maybe you're ready for, maybe you're not. But when you spend the night at somebody's house on a regular basis, you had better think about sleep."

Dr. Breus is a clinical psychologist, better known as the Sleep Doctor—and if it seems odd to talk to a sleep specialist for a book about relationship compatibility, I would've thought so too . . . until I heard him on a podcast (incidentally, on Emily Morse's *Sex with Emily* podcast) joking that he'd saved more marriages as a sleep expert than he ever would have as a marriage therapist.

Which, when you think about it, makes a whole lot of sense.

"Yeah, I use that line all the time," he told me. "But it is so the truth. Snoring is a big one. When one partner snores, it's like, *What do we do with that?* Insomnia. There are a lot of sleep disorders out there."

"And when one person has a sleep disorder," I ventured, "it's kind of like you both have it."

"Oh, it's both," he said. "Totally for both. Absolutely. And the thing with marital therapy—a lot of times there's some primary issue of distrust or disrespect. If you were to ask, 'What's the biggest issue in your marriage right now?' Eh, nobody's really too thrilled to talk about that. But if you were to ask, 'How are you sleeping?' It's, 'Oh my God, I sleep like shit'—you know? I'm easy to talk to at a cocktail party. And there are some very simple things people can think through to improve how they sleep."

Since he'd mentioned the sped-up pace at which partners tend to fall into bed these days, I figured we might start there. "It's kind of a perfect segue into one of the things I wanted to talk to you about," I said, "which is that period of time when you're newly dating, and you're just getting to know someone, and you think, *Am I staying over? Shit, I never sleep well in someone else's bed.* Can we talk about how you might address that, in the sense that it's such a fun time, but we all also need our sleep?"

"I would say, that first night, all bets are off. That's just pure passion. By the third time you spend the night, you're probably ready to have the conversation. And one of the big things you really want to think through is temperature," he said. "Some people sleep hot, some sleep cold—that's usually a genetic variant. It's just how people are.

But women sleep both hot and cold, depending on where they are in their menstrual cycle, where they are in their pregnancy, or pregnancy plans, or menopause. Women have all kinds of variability in their temperature, and guys don't really understand that. They just don't get it. So having a way to change the temperature fairly easily is going to be important."

I figured he'd start off with something more obvious—it hadn't occurred to me to take temperature into account, so already: *mind blown.*

"Also, the material your mattress is made from either sucks in heat or it doesn't," he continued, "and memory foam is kind of the worst. So, avoiding those beds—or if you and your partner are going to be moving in together, and he's got memory foam and you don't, you're probably in better shape selecting your bed rather than his. Another thing is schedules. I think schedules are really big, and a lot of people don't think about that at all."

"That's also something I wanted to talk to you about," I said. "If one person is a night owl, and the other's a morning person, what are some things you can do to avoid sleeping in separate beds, or *sometimes* sleeping in separate beds?"

"Actually, I think choice B is an option: sometimes sleep in separate beds. People call that a 'sleep divorce,' but I hate that term. It's just not a good term. A lot of people think that the strength of their relationship is a linear relationship with whether or not you sleep in bed together, but that is not the case. There's no data to suggest that whatsoever."

"I love hearing you say that as an expert," I said, feeling somehow relieved. "It's like, get your sleep whichever way you need to, so you can be a better partner. Right?"

"A hundred percent. At the end of the day, you're not only a better partner, you're a less depressed partner, you're a less anxious partner—I mean, sleep doesn't hurt anything. Literally everything you do, you do better with a good night's sleep. So I think that's really a biggie, and schedules are important. A lot of people don't realize it, but if you're dating a stockbroker who lives in New York and you live in LA, and then she moves to LA, the stock market still opens at the same time. She'll have to be up at four a.m. Are you down with that? Or shift work. For some people, the graveyard shift is the most valuable shift. You know, 'I make the most money there as a nurse,' or whatever. How does that play into a relationship? And it's complicated, right? So it's about understanding those variables."

And since we hadn't addressed it yet, I asked about seemingly the most disruptive—or at least the most obviously disruptive impediment to getting your z's.

"For snoring in particular, there's three or four things you want to do. First, a lot of these apps are actually pretty good now—SnoreLab is one of the decent ones. You stick it right next to your partner and let it analyze the snore. It'll tell you how many times they stopped breathing. If it's more than two times an hour, go to your doctor. If you hear that person stop breathing for more than two or three seconds, go to your doctor. If that person wakes up in the morning with a headache, or is tired during the daytime—and they snore—go to your doctor. And if you think your partner has sleep apnea, they now have at-home tests. You don't even have to go to the hospital anymore. They send it to your house, you put on a couple of electrodes, go to bed. It's super simple."

"Attractive when you're just getting to know someone and you show up with a snoring app," I teased.

"Well, yeah. But there's a way to couch it that might be easier to handle. You know, 'I'm starting to really care for you, and I know a lot about sleep apnea, and it *kills* people. So guess what?'"

"I want you to stay alive," I chimed in.

"Right. 'I'm down for you staying alive for a little while, so why don't we get you tested?'"

"And if it's not apnea?"

"If we're talking about plain old snoring, weight loss always helps. Another not-great topic to bring up on the second date."

I couldn't help but laugh, thinking about all the seemingly "not-great" topics you might discuss with a partner that, in fact, can lead to deep intimacy. Communication is horny, after all. "I think if you're comfortable with someone—and that's the whole thing about talking regularly, and getting comfortable talking—sleep, and what you like and what you need regarding sleep, can actually be a fun thing to talk about."

"Oh, absolutely," Dr. Breus said. "You can have as good a time with it as you want, or make it as difficult as you want. If you want to have a good time, start off talking about what you like to wear to sleep. Just boxers or briefs? Or do you like pajamas? Or ask, 'What would you prefer I wear to sleep?' And then you can take that anywhere."

Finally, I wondered about a purely hypothetical scenario wherein one partner needs absolute, total darkness to sleep. The kind of partner who, when visiting a hotel room, for example, pulls the blackout shades tightly closed and shoves a towel under the door even though it totally messes with *your* circadian rhythm and makes it difficult for *you* to wake up in the morning. Again, purely hypothetical.

Dr. Breus looked at me with a smile. "Get him a really good eye mask."

R&P QUESTION #235 — Are we satisfied with the quality and quantity of the friends we currently have? Would we like to be more involved socially? Are we overwhelmed socially, and should we cut back on such commitments?

When I first reached out to Dhru Purohit and his wife, Yasmin Nouri, both entrepreneurs and podcast hosts, I had no idea they'd ever struggled with sleep issues.

"Yasmin tended to be a late nighter," Dhru told me. "She was just starting her business at the time. Mine was a little more established, and I'm in the wellness space, right? I want to hit a certain amount of sleep. I also get very tired at night. So we started to create a wind-down ritual."

An hour or so before bed, Dhru explained, he goes around the house and starts dimming the lights. Nearer to bedtime, he flips on a red light (which stimulates the production of melatonin, the sleep-inducing hormone, so the theory goes). "And then we do this weird thing. During the week, I might come across interesting little videos, things that aren't overstimulating, but more educational, informative. On my own, I'd been watching a few videos before going to sleep."

"And he would laugh, and have a good time," Yasmin chimed in. "Meanwhile, I'm sending emails or doing stupid stuff on my phone, wondering, like, *What is he doing?*"

Soon enough, the couple started watching those videos together, and Dhru would save new ones with Yasmin in mind. "We'd watch a few, and sometimes have conversations about them. And we'd do that for twenty or thirty minutes and then go to bed, and have a great night of sleep. That's one thing we still do pretty much every night."

The routine shouldn't have surprised me.

I've known Dhru for fifteen years, and for very nearly that long have known just how thoughtful and intentional he is. (He's also deeply kind and empathetic, the sort of dear friend you can call with any question or problem, and suddenly you've been on the phone for an hour.) But in perhaps no aspect of his life was he more intentional than when it came to finding a life partner. How intentional? After only three or four dates, Dhru suggested to Yasmin that they might speak with a therapist. He thought of this as, essentially, pre-*pre*-marital counseling.

"I think we had both been in a place of feeling jaded," Dhru explained. "Maybe not *jaded.* But feeling like, *How am I going to connect with the right person?* I think women sometimes don't realize that a lot of guys are marriage minded. We go through this stuff, too. And we both happened to be in a similar place when we met. I'd been seeing somebody long-distance, but it didn't work out. I was taking a bit of a break. Yasmin had also been on a break from dating. Serendipitously, we got introduced at a dinner with mutual friends, and I realized very quickly that she was someone I could easily fall for. So it was about wanting to really get to know her and seeing if we were in alignment.

"Also, we didn't have your book at the time," he joked.

Speaking of serendipity, it just so happened that our chat took place on their second wedding anniversary. And it was clear why Dhru had indeed fallen for Yasmin—her energy and enthusiasm were infectious. She was warm and supportive and generous, a total doll.

"I'd been in relationships before, but I'd never really thought about marriage," she said. "I was career oriented. I'd dated guys who were wonderful, but an intentionality about the future was never really there. Then I broke up with someone, and I started to realize that I really wanted to find someone who I could build a life with. So when Dhru brought up this idea of, 'Let's go to counseling, let's do some work,' I was all over it. I wanted to get to know each other as fast as we could, because I didn't want to waste my time, you know?"

Certainly, you don't have to be *as* intentional as Dhru and Yasmin, but to me it seemed pretty undeniable that that intentionality—their commitment to the practical—has in all sorts of ways set them up for success.

"Another thing we do pretty religiously," Dhru said, "is every Sunday, we have a planning session." Part of that planning is fairly straightforward: they discuss their schedules and goals and various obligations, what's working and what's not. "What I think is maybe unique," he continued, "is that we ask questions like, 'Who are the people in our life that we maybe need to devote a little more time to?' Like, 'Hey, we haven't seen your mom much lately, let's carve out some time to do something special for her.' Or, 'Which are the weekends that my family's scheduled to be in town?' Or, 'What about our friends?' We regularly think about the ecosystem around us, and how we want to prioritize and nurture those relationships. We're very aware that it's not just about paying attention to each other."

That focus on their social ecosystem intrigued me, too. "One of the earliest things I wanted to know about Yasmin," Dhru responded, after

I'd asked him to elaborate, "was about her friends. And I asked her on maybe our first or second date, 'Who are your friends? How long have they been your friends?' Because if you've maintained friendships over the long haul, it shows me that you're good at keeping in touch. It shows me that, you know, you've probably gotten into fights, but you've been able to repair. It shows me that I don't have to be your everything, because I want to be so much for you, but I cannot be *everything*. I'd been in relationships with people who didn't have close friends, or there was a constant cycle of rotating friends every few years, and that was a bit of a red flag, because maybe this person doesn't have the patience or the emotional intelligence to maintain friendships? When Yasmin told me about her friends, and how she's maintained those friendships, I knew I was dealing with a sophisticated person, and someone who had quite a full life. The hope was that we could go on to create a full life together, that she wasn't expecting me to be or become her life."

And when they miss a weekly planning session, or haven't been as intentional about their schedules and the demands on their time?

"We really do not feel good," Dhru said. "Conflict tends to happen when we don't sleep well—not after just one night, but multiple nights out. You're feeling more irritable. Or you didn't work out that week. We talk about that, too. What do your workouts look like this week? What do you need this week? If we nail that, we're in a good place. Otherwise, we're hangry and tired and grumpy. And we fight about bullshit. The same bullshit as everybody else."

Finding Your Pace and Place:
A Conversation with Courtney Adamo

Courtney Adamo is a blogger and author in the parenting and lifestyle space, known (and loved) for her minimalist aesthetic and for documenting her family's stripped-down, screen-free, sun-kissed existence in Australia's Byron Bay—but I happen to know it wasn't always sand and surf. Courtney and I have known each other since college (shout-out to Northwestern!) and I phoned her up to hear more about why slowing down the pace of her life took a leap of faith.

Back in 2015, after twelve years in London, you and your husband, Michael, sold your home, your car, virtually all of your belongings, uprooted your four (now five!) kids, and embarked on an eighteen-month trek around the world. I just have to ask: What in the world were you thinking?

Courtney: [laughing] *I know.* When we started to sell everything, I had so many friends who were like, "Why would you do that? Why would you take your kids out of this school? Why would you sell the house you just renovated?" But I remember saying to Michael, "I just can't do another winter here." I wanted to go somewhere that was less busy and less stressful. I was working really hard. He was working really hard. And we couldn't really afford the life we were living. We had to take out an extra bank loan, twice, just to afford the school fees. We had a nanny to help watch the kids while I was working, and then the nanny was picking up the kids from school, and making the kids breakfast, and it was just such a contrast to the way I grew up. I realized, *Wait a second. This actually* isn't *the parenting mum life I had always envisioned.* But how do you scale back when you've gotten yourself so committed financially?

R&P
QUESTION
#239

What's on your
bucket list?

So how did you manage to scale back? And how did your desire for a less busy life manifest into traveling the globe with four kids? Because to me, that sounds pretty stressful!

Courtney: When I was nine years old, there was a family that lived next door to my grandma. They had three girls, one of whom was my age, and they went on a trip around the world. I remember when they said they were going to "travel around the world," I thought of an airplane literally going *around the world*. I didn't actually understand what it meant. And when they came back a year later, I remember seeing the photos. They would talk about places I had never even heard of, and the people in those places. The whole concept—I was just so intrigued. Ever since then, I've thought, *Someday, when I have kids, I want to do that*. It's something I'd talked about with Michael since we met. So he's always known. And then one day we were sitting in bed, talking about life and what we might change, where we might go, and he was like, "Why don't we just do this thing you've always talked about? Why don't we travel?" He said it was maybe the right time, that we only had a few years left before it wouldn't be logistically feasible. And I literally sat up in bed, and I looked at him, and I said, "Are you serious? Because if you're not serious, stop talking about it right now."

This was, like, the one thing he could not joke about.

Courtney: Right. And we put our house on the market one week later, and that was it.

So you cross this major item off your bucket list, this thing you'd always dreamed of doing. Talk to me a little about what you took from the trip, and if that influenced your decision to eventually settle in Australia.

Courtney: I remember we flew from Sri Lanka back to London for a few days. And that contrast from having been in Sri Lanka, and having traveled for eight months before, in terms of the pace of life and the people we'd met, was so stark. In London, you'd see people get out of their big Range Rovers, slam the door, and they just seemed so angry. I remember walking past this mum who was, like, dragging her child down the street after picking him up from school, because he was moving too slow. You'd see these people, and they didn't look happy, even though they had everything. That was such a message to me. You start to realize: this is the one life that we get. And the stuff we acquire is not important. I loved London. We had such a great life there. But I think sometimes when you live in these big cities—I had friends who put a lot of pressure on their kids to do really well in school so they could be successful. But it's a narrow kind of success. There were maybe a few different types of jobs their kids could get that would be the "right" jobs. None of them would have been happy being a surfing instructor in Chile, for example. So traveling, letting our kids meet people who were happy doing all sorts of different things, and living in all sorts of different places—yeah, it opened up this idea of how to live.

I know it isn't always easy, though, even in a place that's renowned for its slower pace.

Courtney: Definitely not. Michael and I actually fell into a bit of a rut last year. We weren't as social. We stopped surfing. We lost track of the reasons we'd picked this corner of the world in the first place. And I know these are minor problems to have. We're very lucky. But you still have to work at it. We still have to make an effort to maintain that balance. Getting back on track, making a point to surf more and to see our friends has given us new ideas, and new energy.

R&P QUESTION #237 Let's discuss our hobbies: those we enjoy separately and together. How can we best support each other's hobbies?

Before I let Sam and Alapaki go, there was one other aspect of routines and rituals I wanted to discuss: the need to carve out time for oneself, the importance of nurturing and maintaining the interests, hobbies, and practices that make you *you.*

For the first time in a while, Sam, the quieter half of the couple, piped up. "I just know that, for me personally, I am much more introverted," he said. "Every day I need some time to myself, to run an errand or get out of the house, just to feel like I did something of value—even if it was running to Walgreens or getting a haircut."

"I'm glad you mentioned that," I said. "Because I imagine some people might think, *Why don't you want me to go with you?* Or, *Why don't you want to come with me?*"

And in truth, I didn't have to imagine it. I'd already spoken with plenty of couples who'd dealt with this exact issue. Like Jeremy, of Jess and Jeremy, who happened to be an avid snowboarder. "Being a snowboarder who lives in New York City involves travel," he'd said. "I might be gone for a whole day, or a weekend, or even sometimes a week. Jess doesn't do any winter sports, so I'm always leaving. If she was like, 'Please stay home,' I'd say no. It's important to me."

Or Claire, of Claire and Finn, the couple who'd whiteboarded their finances before moving in together. "I really had to learn how not to overschedule us," she told me. "Finn needs downtime. Social interaction is draining for him, whereas it's very recharging for me."

"Did you ever have to say to Claire, 'I love you, but this is too much'?" I asked Finn.

"Oh, a hundred percent. She would go to the gym, go to work, friends would come over for drinks, and then somehow there was dinner and I was just like, 'This cannot happen all the time.' Like, this is absurd. I am an introvert at heart. And Claire is a full-blown extrovert. Sometimes I just want to watch the game or sit on the couch."

"He calls it nesting," Claire added, with a laugh. "He'll be like, 'I need a nesting day.'"

Or even the holistic psychologist Dr. LePera. "Lolly is hyperindependent," she said of her wife. "Loves alone time, wants to go do all these things, will lock herself away. And I'd be like, 'What about me?

Don't you love me? Is something wrong?' But all of us need solitude—even those of us who are codependent. We might not feel safe in that stillness, or we haven't learned to feel safe in that way, and again, that's about the nervous system. It does feel threatening, so we project all these meanings onto other people."

I asked Sam, "How do you address that, or broach that?"

"You have to keep in mind that along with picking a particular partner, you've also picked all of their needs," he said. "I've picked Alapaki's need to do things together, even though I'd sometimes prefer time alone. Those are the cards I inherited. And as Julie Gottman would tell you, *People's needs are their needs.* You can't really argue with them. That's ultimately what partnership is all about. You turn something that could be a win-lose scenario—you know, I go to Walgreens by myself, I *win*; I go with you, I *lose*—into a compromise. You figure out how to get both of your needs met. Because that's actually the responsibility of both of you."

Listening to Sam was a little like coming full circle: we were back where we'd started, in that it's not about getting a "right" answer, that it's not about winning, because in order for someone to win, somebody else has to lose.

"I guess what you're saying, too," I suggested, "is that by communicating your needs, you're helping your partner to meet your needs. Instead of leaving them to wonder, 'Why doesn't he ask me to run errands with him?' you're saying, 'This is something I need to do to clear my head. I love you, but I need this.' In other words, if you can make your needs known, then you can both win."

"Yeah, and it's easier said than done," Alapaki chimed in. "This balance between independence and togetherness is a thing we see new couples *and* couples who've been together for a long time grapple with. And I think you're spot-on: we need to ask for what we need as a way of setting our partner up for success, rather than watch them fail. Because people make a lot of assumptions. As an example, 'I do crossword puzzles with Lindsay all the time. Today I want to do crossword puzzles by myself'—or switch to Sudoku or whatever—'but I predict that Lindsay is going to be super disappointed. So I'm not going to say anything.' We don't articulate what we need in an attempt to prevent negative feelings—perceived or real—from coming up. Except we're *not* actually preventing the negativity, we're just delaying it. And the longer we delay, the more amplified it becomes, because now he's sulking for months or silently stewing or growing resentful—and then what happens? An explosion."

"You never let me do crosswords by myself!" I said.

"Exactly. And we're using the crossword puzzles as an example— but let's say it's something bigger than that, something that's very meaningful. So it can be difficult for people to ask for what they need and want, because they're afraid they're going to disappoint or hurt their partner."

I thought back to Claire and Finn, and the adjustment period they'd gone through after moving in together. Claire, the social butterfly, was used to having regular girls' nights and chatting late into the evening, seated on the patio with a gaggle of friends. Meanwhile, Finn, the introvert, is also a chef, which comes with long and odd work hours.

"She'd be on the porch with her friends till eleven, eleven thirty," he told me. "And I'd be thinking, *Yo, it's Wednesday. I gotta be up at four.* At first I felt like, *I don't want to rock the boat.* But then you get to a point where you realize, *If I don't say something* now, *this will be the norm. And then I'll look like the weirdo who all of a sudden just flipped the script.*"

"Yeah. I had to adjust, too," Claire said. "At first, when Finn wouldn't want to do certain things, it would hurt my feelings. But eventually, I was able to understand that he's on his feet all day. He needs downtime. So we came to a good understanding: he gets to hang out in my office—which is our second bedroom—and play video games when I have friends over. That way they can come earlier in the evening, but I don't have to miss out on a girls' night."

I thought of Dr. LePera, too, and how she adjusted to Lolly's need for independence. "I had to learn that solitude, even for myself, is needed. For some of us, that looks like errands on a Sunday morning. Others might want to go golfing on the weekend. Having time and space away, to replenish ourselves or tap into a curiosity or an interest, is an important part of any relationship. And figuring out how to honor each other's needs may require a bit of negotiation. You learn to accept that your partner's need isn't about you; in fact, they're actually going to replenish themselves so that they're more present and attentive when they get back, right? It's the process of depersonalizing it, not assuming that someone's need for time away means they don't love you. And, likewise, you communicate what's important to you. Maybe that's watching a movie together on Sunday nights. What are other moments throughout the day or week that you can get your need for connection met? That adjustment takes time. But now, many years later, I love my own solitude."

Epilogue

• • • • •

PRACTICALITIES & ACTUALITIES

> How you love yourself is
> how you teach others
> to love you.
> —*Rupi Kaur*

The Brit and I had driven to Montauk for the day—our first trip to-gether to the tip of the island. I took comfort in knowing that I was at the right place in my life, at the right time. The man with whom I was meant to be was in the passenger seat, our baby the size of an ear of corn in my belly. We passed Ocean Colony in Amagansett, where I have sand-castle-making memories, ate at the Lobster Roll (affec-tionately known to locals and visitors alike as LUNCH), which wasn't much more than a shack during my childhood, versus the institution it is now.

Life feels different when you're revisiting places from the past with your first child growing inside you. We walked along the beach. The tide was out, and our feet sank into a tide pool of warm water as we walked through it.

"I know we haven't decided on Nugget's name," the Brit said, using the nickname we'd adopted for our future son. "But I'd like his middle name to be Stowe."

Stowe. Where we'd fallen in love.

"It's perfect," I replied, agreeing instantly. "I love it. I love you."

We drove home that evening, riding not the waves but the Old Montauk Highway, which my brother and I had coined "the bumpy road" as kids because the hills made our stomachs flip-flop, like riding a roller coaster. We were convinced that my dad did something special to make it feel that way. Turns out, anyone driving can ride the bumps, and the Brit and I giggled as we flew over each one, our now family of three almost realized, but still pending.

● ● ●

As an adult, I've realized that there are a few periods in my life I wish I could redo. Not to change them, but to relive them without the uncertainty and fear that was once buried inside me.

I want to perform as the White Rabbit in my fourth-grade school play again, knowing I'll nail it.

I'd like to start sleepaway camp at six (instead of eight), having two extra summers in what is still one of my happiest places.

I'd revisit high school—which I loved—but without the stress of test scores and the pressures of college acceptance. Like, it wasn't *that* long ago, was it?

It was.

With a week back at Northwestern, I'd talk to the boys who I was hoping would come talk to me.

Most important, I want two weeks of being young and single in Manhattan again, to date with abandon, knowing everything would work out perfectly in the end. I was once so subsumed with finding "the guy," with finding my person, that I made myself smaller. I wasn't always as open or true to myself as I should've been. It took really understanding and embracing who I am, working hard to put up boundaries, to realize there wasn't actually anything wrong with me. There's freedom in that.

That's the kind of love I hope you'll find—or nurture and keep—after reading *Romances & Practicalities*, the kind of love where you don't have to run your texts by your friends, where you can share your intimacies because they inform you, not define you. Where you can be your truest, most authentic self. And I hope you'll remember that this isn't easy. It takes work, and patience, and perspective.

It takes being practical.

My life with the Brit has taken on a new shape as we've grown in our lives and careers, evolved as a couple, and had two children—but the conversations we started when creating R&P have remained a constant. We've learned to honor our communication styles—his need for space and my need to immediately engage. We review our finances regularly and talk—*really talk*—about money. We discuss intimacy and make real efforts to ensure the other is still physically satisfied—because, wow, when your bed is suddenly inhabited by two little monkeys sneaking in at night, sex can fall by the wayside.

Lately, and in the process of raising those two small monkeys, I've been focusing on something called "specific praise." In life, we're conditioned to acknowledge the efforts of others via phrases like "good job" or "that was great." *Specific* praise sounds more like, "You helped James clean up his room today; you're a great big brother," or, "I really liked how you listened and followed the directions to make that art project." I've realized that specific praise shouldn't be limited to our interactions with children—it goes miles with adults, too. Because what's better than being seen?

When the Brit is having a particularly brilliant parenting moment or handling something beautifully with our kids, I tell him.

A few evenings ago, as we were putting our boys to bed—amid the chaos of "night-night time" with a four- and six-year-old—my elder son insisted that he needed a cookie. He'd already eaten a full dinner, of course, brushed his teeth—we'd read three books together—and still was negotiating hard. I said no repeatedly to this very cute but now annoyingly persistent request.

The Brit, having successfully gotten our youngest to sleep, stopped outside the door, no doubt wondering how many more minutes I'd be before we could resume the latest series we were bingeing. When our son jumped out of bed and asked his dad for a cookie, the Brit smiled. "What did Mommy say?"

"She said no more cookies today," our son responded quietly, tucking his little hand into my husband's big one.

"Well, Mommy and I are on the same page. So if Mommy said no, I also say no. Now climb back into bed, Puppy. I love you, and I'll see you in the morning."

He gave our son a kiss, winked at me, and continued down the hall.

We still write sleep notes when one of us is away, and I'm still the only tea drinker in the family. But now it's our children who pose the questions we need to answer—together, not separately.

Oh, and by the way: the Brit's name is Gavin.

Romances & Practicalities

• • • • •

THE COMPLETE QUESTIONNAIRE

Animals & Pets

1. Did you have pets growing up? How does that color your perception about having pets now?

2. Do you have any fears of animals? If so, why and when did they start?

3. Do you want to be a pet owner? If so, how many and what kind?

4. What pet(s) would you be absolutely unwilling to own?

5. How do you feel about allowing pets in the bed?

6. If you had children and they wanted pets, would you indulge them even if you didn't want one?

7. How do you think children should interact with pets?

8. Would you take care of family or friends' pet(s) if they asked?

9. If we were to have a pet, what would the division of labor look like? Who would be responsible for walking/feeding/cleanup/vet visits, and so on?

Communication

10. How do you fight? How do I fight? How do we fight, and how does that feel?

11. If we haven't argued yet—why? Is that healthy? Are you not saying things you should?

12. How did your family members communicate, share, and argue growing up?

13. How did your family resolve conflict? Do you approve or disapprove of that method? What would you change or not change to resolve conflicts in your future family?

14. When you're upset or annoyed at someone, do you prefer to (1) remain silent, (2) say something as soon as those feelings arise, (3) wait a certain amount of time before raising the issue, or (4) do something else? If so, what?

15. How can I be better about communicating with you?

16. How would you communicate if you weren't satisfied sexually?

17. If we communicate about big things differently, how can we both make sure the other is satisfied and feels that their natural patterns and communication styles are being respected?

18. If you say you're going to do something but don't, what is the most effective way to bring this issue to your attention?

19. Do you feel you can communicate with me about any subject and under any circumstance?

20. What makes you not want to talk to me?

21. If we weren't in the same location, would you prefer to write your feelings? Speak on the phone? FaceTime?

22. Who, other than me, do you or would you confide in, and why?

23. Are you okay with me sharing with or getting advice from my friends or family?

24. Who should or shouldn't know about the arguments we have?

25. What about our lives is/isn't appropriate to share with friends or family?

Relationships, Sex & Sexuality

26. Who were your celebrity crushes growing up, and why?

27. What relationship(s)—romantic or otherwise—did you learn the most from or had the most impact on your growth as a partner? Why?

28. Is there something you've never had in a relationship or with a partner that you've always wanted and that we can strive to achieve or be?

29. Is trust automatic (until something occurs to take it away), or does it evolve over time?

30. Do you believe that love can pull you through anything?

31. How are we different? Could this be a source of future conflict? Do our differences complement each other?

32. How do you feel about masturbation, both alone and alongside a partner?

33. Do you enjoy vibrators, costumes, or sex toys? How would you feel if we used them together?

34. Is there a sexual act you've always wanted to try but haven't yet? Is there anything you absolutely do *not* want to try or that you consider to be off-limits?

35. How do you feel about pornography? Do you ever watch? Do you mind if I watch? Would you ever want to watch together?

36. Would you ever want to have sexual experiences with more than one person at a time?

37. Would you ever want to have sexual experiences with a partner whose sex or gender is different from mine?

38. Do we have good sex? Is there anything you'd like me to do differently?

39. How often should we have sex?

40. If we eliminated physical attraction from our relationship, what would be left?

41. What are your views on monogamy/infidelity/polyamory?

42. What do you want to know about my past relationships? Does anything about my former relationships concern you?

43. Could feelings of attraction or romance be revived if you ran into an ex-partner, even if you feel strongly committed to me?

44. What one thing would you change about our relationship?

45. What are your thoughts on couples therapy or marriage counseling?

46. How do you show love to others?

47. What makes you feel loved and appreciated? What are some loving things people have done for you?

48. How important are anniversaries to you? How would you like to celebrate them? How important is gift giving to you?

49. What is the best way for me to show that I love you?

50. What do you think is the best way to keep love alive in a long-term relationship?

51. If this is a rekindled romance, why didn't it work previously? What can (or should) we do differently this time around?

In-Laws & Families of Origin

52. What is your relationship like with your father (or father figure, if that's what you have)? With your mother (or mother figure)?

53. Do you want to emulate your parents' marriage or relationship? Why or why not?

54. Is there a couple other than your parents whose relationship you respect or whose relationship has served as a guide for you?

55. Was the way in which your nuclear family was perceived by outsiders—friends, neighbors, coworkers, extended family—an accurate presumption? Did your family portray itself one way in public but function differently at home?

56. How often do you speak with your family? How often do you visit?

57. How often would your family like to visit you/us? Is that okay?

58. If you don't live near family, how would you feel if they came to stay with you for an extended period of time?

59. Is there anything you prefer to keep from your family—aspects of your life you have chosen not to share?

60. What are the ideal roles of in-laws within a family? How involved should they be?

61. How do we stay aligned as a couple among our friends, in-laws, parents, and siblings?

62. If an issue arose between someone in your family and me, would you rather handle it with that person on my (or our) behalf or rather I handle it with them directly?

63. How do you feel about my siblings? How much time would you want to spend with them?

64. What if one of your family members disliked me? How would you handle that?

65. If your parents became ill, would you take them in?

66. How would you like to handle holiday family visits? Divvying up the holidays? Sharing holidays with extended family? Would you prefer to spend holidays alone?

Chores, Domestic Duties & Building a Home

67. Which would you choose: laundry or dishes?

68. Which would you choose: cooking or washing up?

69. Ordering in or preparing meals at home?

70. Toilet lid—open or shut?

71. Toilet paper—over or under?

72. How do you feel about having a TV in the bedroom?

73. Will you be angry if I leave my wet towels on the floor? How will you handle it?

74. What is the ideal division of domestic labor?

75. What was the division of labor like in your home growing up? Do you expect to emulate that?

76. How do you feel about employing someone to clean or help around the house?

77. What type of house or apartment do you prefer to live in? Urban or rural? City or suburbs?

78. What does your dream home look like?

79. If something breaks, would you prefer to fix it yourself or call a professional?

80. How do you feel about DIY renovations? Wallpapering? Painting? Furniture assembly?

81. What styles of décor do you prefer? What styles do you dislike?

82. How much money is appropriate to spend on things like furniture, art, and décor?

83. Would you be annoyed if I opened your mail?

84. Would you ever live abroad if the opportunity presented itself? If so, where?

Health & Medical

85. Have you ever broken any bones? Is there a good story to go along with it?

86. How do you like to be tended to/taken care of (or not) when you're ill with something like the common cold?

87. Do you smoke or vape? If so, how often? Habitually? Medicinally? When out drinking?

88. What are your thoughts on cigarettes, marijuana, and recreational drugs?

89. What are your medical fears and phobias?

90. What are your thoughts on going to the doctor? The dentist? Getting regular checkups or physicals? Would you want me to make those appointments for you?

91. What is your family medical history?

92. Do you have a family history of congenital diseases or genetic abnormalities?

93. Does anyone in your family have a history of neurological or mental health issues, ranging from ADHD to depression to addiction?

94. What are your thoughts about mental health treatment for either one of us? For our children, should we have them?

95. Do you want to know more about your genetics?

96. Do you want to know more about your future health?

97. If I had to change my diet for medical reasons, would you be willing to change yours?

98. How do you feel about exercise? Are you willing to exercise with me to improve our health?

99. How do you feel about cosmetic medical procedures (from Botox to surgery)?

100. How do you feel about holistic healthcare and functional medicine? Vitamins and supplements? Eastern versus Western medicine?

Children

101. How comfortable are you around children?

102. What values do you want to instill in your children?

103. How much say should children have within a family?

104. Would you like to have children? If so, how many?

105. Do you want or need to be married before having children?

106. When would you like to have children?

107. How far apart in age would you like your kids to be?

108. Would you be willing to work with a fertility specialist if we struggled to have kids the traditional way? What are your feelings on freezing eggs, embryos, or sperm? On pursuing IVF? On surrogacy? Adoption?

109. How would having a child change the way we live now? Would we take time off work or work a reduced schedule? For how long? Would we reevaluate our shared roles at home and our division of labor?

110. What aspects of our lives are very important for you to maintain after having children (e.g., regular date nights, weekend workouts, basketball practice one night a week, regular mani-pedi or self-care appointments, and so on).

111. If we have children, who will change the diapers, heat the bottles, prepare the meals, draw the baths, get up in the middle of the night, visit the pediatrician, purchase clothing, and so on?

112. What religion would our kids be?

113. Would our children be circumcised?

114. How do you feel about co-sleeping (i.e., babies or children sleeping in our bed)?

115. How important is breastfeeding to you?

116. Do you anticipate raising our children the same way you were raised, completely differently from the way you were raised, or a mixture of both?

117. Would you prefer one of us to be a stay-at-home parent or send our kids to daycare? How do you feel about employing a nanny?

118. What are your thoughts on homeschooling?

119. Would you prefer our children attend public or private school?

120. Beyond formal schooling, what types of education should our children receive? Religious? Foreign language? Where? How?

121. What activities or extracurriculars are important to expose your children to? Sports? Music? Which did you most enjoy growing up?

122. What sort of discipline would you implement to correct a child's or teenager's behavior? Were these practices you experienced or are they new techniques you've developed on your own? How were you disciplined growing up?

123. Do you believe it's okay to discipline your children in public?

124. How involved should grandparents be in our parenting? How often should they see the kids? What if they want to see them all the time?

125. Would you be opposed to our parents babysitting occasionally so we can spend time alone?

126. How will we handle parental decisions?

127. How would you respond if one of your children came out as homosexual or transgender, or wanted to use a specific pronoun?

128. What if our children didn't want to attend college?

129. How would you feel if our child wanted to join the military?

Careers

130. How important is your career in terms of your identity?

131. What are your career aspirations? Where do you hope to see yourself in five years? Ten? Fifteen?

132. What's a realistic or appropriate amount of time to spend at work—during the day? What about weeknights and weekends?

133. Why do you have the job or career that you do?

134. Who are your career role models?

135. How does your career lend itself to being in a relationship?

136. How does your career lend itself to starting a family?

137. If there was one other job or career path you could embark on, what would it be?

138. Do you have any passion projects that you're working on or want to create? If so, how would that work around your job? Our relationship?

139. If I wanted to move away from our families for work, would you support me?

140. What does balance mean to you regarding your job?

141. How can we best support each other in our respective jobs or businesses?

142. If we have children, how would that impact our careers?

143. At what age would you like to retire?

Money & Finances

144. How do you feel about debt?

145. Do you own or rent? Do you prefer to own or rent?

146. How do you feel about mortgages?

147. Do you pay your credit card bills on time/in full every month?

148. What would you eliminate from your life if you suddenly had to live on a tighter budget?

149. What's your salary or hourly wage?

150. Do you have any student loans?

151. Do you have any desire or intention to go back to school in the future? How would you hope to pay for tuition?

152. What's the maximum amount either of us may spend without consulting the other?

153. Who should handle paying the monthly bills? Are you comfortable with autopay?

154. Do your parents pay any of your bills currently (including your cell phone bill)? If so, will they continue to do so in the future?

155. How was money modeled for you growing up? How did you learn about spending and saving? Was money discussed in your childhood home, or was that considered a private or off-limits topic?

156. Would you want to maintain separate or shared bank accounts? For all of our money? Some of it?

157. How should we handle our long-term financial planning?

158. What are your thoughts on future investments we might make as a couple or family?

159. If we have children, will we put money away for them regularly if we can?

160. Is paying for our children's education important to you? What level of education—primary through university—would you like to pay for? How do you feel about public versus private school as relates to cost?

161. Would you accept financial help from your parents or elders if they offered it?

162. Would you seek financial counseling if we decided that we needed it?

163. Have you ever declared bankruptcy?

164. Would you be comfortable declaring bankruptcy if we found ourselves in a tight spot?

165. Do you owe money to anyone currently? Friends? Family members?

166. Would you help your parents/siblings/friends financially if they needed it? Would you expect them to pay you back?

167. How would you define or explain your spending habits?

168. How do you like to spend your "extra" money? Travel? Fashion or personal care? Dining out?

169. Do you prefer name-brand goods or generic?

170. Do you prefer paying for things with cash or credit?

171. Do you have money saved?

172. Do you try to save money each month? If so, what's your strategy?

173. Is saving for retirement important to you?

174. Do you have a retirement savings account or a 401(k)? Does your employer match contributions?

175. What would happen if one or both of us lost our jobs?

176. What would happen if we each wanted to purchase something extravagant but we couldn't afford both items?

177. Do you prefer to lease or own your cars? Should we own more than one vehicle?

178. Do you trust me with money?

Weddings & Marriage

179. What's the best thing about marriage?

180. What's the worst thing about marriage?

181. What's the best thing about a long-term partnership between couples who choose never to marry?

182. Do you have a vision for your dream wedding?

183. Do you think our lives would change if we got married? If yes, how?

184. Who comes first, your spouse or your children?

185. If we got married, what would our last name be? Who should or should not change their name, and why?

186. What are your expectations regarding marital roles? Who should be responsible for cooking, cleaning, paying the bills, raising the children, running the home?

187. What would you do if we fell out of love?

188. Do you have any doubts about the future of our relationship?

189. Would you ever consider having an "open" (i.e. non-monogamous) relationship?

190. What are your views on divorce/separation? Can couples amicably divorce or separate, or does it have to be contentious?

191. What is your biggest fear about marriage?

192. What excites you about getting married?

193. What do wedding rings mean to you?

194. If you want to wear a wedding or commitment ring, what would it look like? How much money should we spend on them?

195. What are your thoughts on prenups? Would you want us to have one?

196. What kind of aunt/uncle or grandparent would you like to be someday?

197. Suppose we were experiencing troubles in our marriage. From whom would you seek help or guidance? Your parents? Siblings? Friends? A marriage counselor? Church leader? A divorce lawyer? Me? Why?

198. Is there anything you feel you wouldn't be able to do or accomplish if you married me?

199. What does this relationship cost you? Would you have to give up anything to marry me or to be with me long term? If so, how do you feel about that?

Religion, Spirituality & Politics

200. Are you more spiritual, religious, or cultural?

201. What is your current religion?

202. What was your religious education or experience growing up?

203. In what religion would you ideally like to raise children?

204. Would you consider observing other religious or spiritual practices, or combining your current traditions with another religion or culture?

205. Would you convert religions at the request of your partner? Why or why not?

206. What does spirituality mean to you?

207. Do you or have you ever prayed?

208. What religious or cultural practices are important to you and why?

209. Are there practices from your religion or culture that you don't observe but would like to?

210. Are there practices from your religion or culture that you perform but don't fully understand why?

211. Would you like to continue certain religious traditions or celebrations but secularize them?

212. Would you prefer to send your children to a denominational school? What if the best school in your area was of a different culture or religion than yours?

213. What are your political beliefs and affiliations?

214. If we differ in our political beliefs, do you think that might be helpful, harmful, or wouldn't impact a partnership?

215. What are your thoughts on gun ownership and gun safety in the home?

216. What are your thoughts on abortion?

217. How often do you vote?

218. For whom did you vote in the last election?

219. What do you think happens to us after we die?

220. Would you prefer to be buried or cremated (or would you prefer an alternative burial method)? What traditions and customs having to do with death and mourning are important to you, if any?

221. Have you experienced a death that has strongly impacted you?

222. How do you feel about the concept of death and dying?

Routines, Rituals, Hobbies & Travel

223. Where is your "happy place" and why? Describe it physically.

224. What would the perfect weekday evening look like?

225. What would be the perfect weekend?

226. On average, how many nights a week do you go out? Are you more of a homebody or a social butterfly?

227. How important to you is spending time with friends?

228. What helps you de-stress?

229. What rituals, routines, and traditions did your family observe growing up? Daily prayer? Sunday dinner? Family game night? Yearly photos? Are they important to you now?

230. Would you say you're a very routinized sort of person? Do your days tend to look the same or follow the same patterns? Do you follow a strict schedule or are you more spontaneous and come-what-may?

231. What are your current rituals and routines?

232. Are there any important rituals you'd like me to maintain when we're together?

233. Is it okay if I participate in some of your rituals and routines—but not all?

234. What are our rituals and routines? Do your friends or family have any you admire or would like to try?

235. Are we satisfied with the quality and quantity of the friends we currently have? Would we like to be more involved socially? Are we overwhelmed socially, and should we cut back on such commitments?

236. How do you feel about friends coming to stay with us for a few days? A few weeks?

237. Let's discuss our hobbies: those we enjoy separately and together. How can we best support each other's hobbies?

238. Do you enjoy traveling? How often would you like to travel? Where would you like to go?

239. What's on your bucket list?

240. How much money are you comfortable spending on travel?

241. Rank the items on which you're most likely to splurge for a holiday: travel (i.e., first or business class versus coach); accommodations (hotel or rental property); food/dining out; shopping; activities and excursions; spa or self-care.

242. Do you prefer weekend getaways or longer trips?

243. How important to you is spending time alone—both generally and while traveling?

244. How would you feel if I traveled on my own—either frequently or infrequently—to (1) visit family, (2) earn income, (3) pursue a hobby, or (4) deal with stress?

245. Which would you prefer: vacationing in a warm or cold climate? Beach vacation or cultural excursion? Boutique hotel or big resort? Relaxed downtime or lots of scheduled activities? Self-led or tour-guided? How do you feel about cruises?

246. How do you feel about traveling with a group of friends versus just the two of us? With extended family?

247. If there were a global crisis—a pandemic, a war, a depression— how would we handle it?

248. If we had to make an escape plan—if we had to abandon our homes and head somewhere safe—where would that be?

249. If you were stuck on a desert island, what five things would you bring?

250. If we were stuck on that desert island together, what natural strengths would you bring to the table to help us survive and thrive?

Acknowledgments

For years I dreamed of turning R&P—the *questionnaire*—into something more than a list, but life always seemed to get in the way. Then COVID-19 hit, and something shifted: people became more intentional about how they interacted, and with whom, a trend that certainly trickled down to dating. The time felt right.

But even before I married my story with the system behind it, I found my very first beta testers: friends and friends of friends and even strangers who eagerly agreed (or in some cases, sweetly demanded!) to try a system that wasn't quite yet a system, that wasn't quite yet *a thing*. To them, I owe a debt of gratitude. Your willingness to dive in and report back, to discuss—at length—your struggles and triumphs, to evaluate the usefulness of each and every question, reinforced the belief that R&P worked and should be shared more broadly.

Yfat Reiss Gendell, the word *agent* isn't enough to describe your role in this project—or in my career. You believed in R&P (and in me) so very early on and have been my advocate every step of the way. I admire and respect you tremendously. AT YRGP, to Lisa Tilman; and to Ashley Michelle Napier: thank you for your guidance and encouragement, especially as a member of *R&P*'s target audience.

To my editor, Cassie Jones, who understood my vision and voice from day one, and who made what can be a tricky process especially fun: I was hoping to land in your capable hands from our very first

Zoom. Your notes, anecdotes, and general observations about life and love not only made the book better but also gave me the confidence and validation I needed to keep drafting. And *redrafting.* (Thanks for your patience!) To Jill Zimmerman, for your wise insights and exacting eye. To Liate Stehlik and everyone at William Morrow who made the publishing experience such a joy: Nicole Braun, Jeanie Lee, Andrew DiCecco, Mark Robinson, Nancy Singer, Kelly Dasta, Melissa Esner, Megan Wilson, and Ana Deboo. I'm incredibly lucky to have found a home with all of you.

Courtney Hargrave, without your expertise, this project wouldn't have been possible. Each chapter is better because of your input and meticulous attention to detail. For the rest of my life, whenever I see a meatball sandwich, I will lovingly think of you.

To Gail Gonzales, for your guidance and advice from proposal stage and beyond. How fitting that we met so many years ago—both still single and searching. Simply put, I adore you. This book would not have happened if not for you.

To Jaspre Guest, forever friend and trailblazing PR dynamo at Noise 784. It lifts me up to even be in your orbit. Your radiant positivity and boundless generosity are nothing short of inspiring. Thank you always for your support.

To the late, great Larry King, who taught me to always ask the hard questions, but to listen harder, and who once said to me, "Date with abandon—because I didn't date women, I just married them," I hope these 250 questions are working for you up in heaven, Larr.

My profound gratitude to the more than one hundred people who generously shared with me some of the most painful, inspiring, joyful, and intimate details of their lives, many of whom I met for the first time when they clicked into my Zoom meeting room. I am moved by your generosity and your openness; thank you for trusting me with your stories. Our conversations are the backbone of this book.

I'm also grateful to the renowned subject matter experts whose knowledge and wisdom made the R&P system richer, more meaningful, and—yes—even more practical. Thank you for the gift of your time, as well as your nuanced and thoughtful contributions, especially Courtney Adamo, Barbara Corcoran, Jill Kargman, Logan Levkoff, Suze Orman, Damona Hoffman, Eve Rodsky, and Alexandra Solomon, who said yes long before R&P was an official proposal, let alone an in-progress book. A special shout-out to Jacqueline Dion, Kelly Mullen, Julie Rashid, Dana Steere, and Claire Stephens, for helping to secure interviews, and to Amy Tischler, for your graphics expertise.

We are each the sum of our experiences, and I'm lucky to be surrounded by a vast network of people who have enriched my life *and* my work, and who supported my writing in various ways, including: Jessica Abo, Zain Asher, Emily Barnes, Chloe Coscarelli, Heather Dorak, Lindy du Plessis, Georgina Fitzpatrick, Shruti Ganguly, Elena Hernandez, Darren Hostler, Nicola Kraus, Ming Liu, Emma McLaughlin, Cele Pasternak, Chrysi Philalithes, Dhru Purohit, Marni Rothman Ellis, Jason Rovou, Danilo Sangaletti, Jackie Seaman, Cerine Shalak, Jodi Shapiro, Tali Shine, Mieke ter Poorten, and Deni Watts. And my UK Girl Gang: Sarah Auteri, Cathy Bowers, Juliet Hall, Christina Lemieux, Marisa Lorch, Emily Miller, and Julie McKee.

To the Coopers, Mandy, Jim, Chloe, and Noah—my New Jersey family—who each brought different but essential gifts to this project. To Dave Gaspar, who "yes-anded" his way into my heart and has a spot there forever; and Ed Riew, the hardest-working business partner and a true friend, whose taste and talent make me a better producer.

To the men who ghosted, bread-crumbed, cookie-jarred, and zombied me—terms that didn't exist when I was dating—thank you, too. Those experiences taught me to love myself first, and to do the big, scary thing of asking for what I need and trusting that the right partner would consider it an opportunity.

And then there are *those* girlfriends—the ones whom you want to write pages and pages about, but when you try, it comes out sounding like a high school yearbook tribute (*trust me, it did*). To the girlfriends who were there through slumber parties and summer camp, who helped me past heartaches and heartbreaks, who made me feel bigger than life when I'd been feeling small, who also offered radical candor when needed: Jill Bernard, Victoria Browne, Samantha Aaron Goodman, Pamela Goldman, Bridget Siegel Hazan, Lauren Lipson, and Trish Pashazadeh-Allen—I am blessed to have had each of you in my corner (in life and for every single story in this book). You are forever my family.

Meghan Sussex, *Meg*, to be sisters by choice, still thinking the same thing at the same time after all these years—no matter how many miles between us—is my favorite part of our unbreakable bond. There for each other always, sharing a deep loyalty and understanding—I could tell you anything, and it would be okay. I carry your heart (I carry it in my heart).

Rachel Gaspar, *Roobie*, I didn't know how comforting and nourishing a friendship could be until you (literally!) grabbed me by the arm and brought me into your world. You're more than a friend; you are a part of me, shayna maidel, and I love going through life by your side.

Amanda Davies, you will live in my heart forever.

And finally: Rosemary Jordan, Peter Jordan, and Tanya Jordan, I won the jackpot when I married into your family of Spurs, and so appreciate how warmly you took me in as your own. Your efforts to understand—and even try to enjoy—sweet potatoes with marshmallows on top, or a cheese plate at the *start* of a meal, have never been lost on me. All of these small and large moments make me love you all the more. Justin: to have such a special sibling bond is something I appreciate more than ever now that we've each become parents. Thanks to you and Cydney Roth, too, for giving my children such precious cousins, Lucy and Stella. Deepest love and gratitude to my parents, Cheryl and Andrew Roth, for their unwavering support, guidance, and encouragement: your love has been the foundation of my success. I never expected to have to love you from across an ocean, but you are with me always. Especially when words flying out of my mouth could've come straight from yours, Mom!

To Gavin Alexander Jordan, my "Brit": R&P would not exist without you. You are an incredible father to our beautiful children—attentive, loving, and ever present, no matter how bone-tired you might be. I wouldn't want to go through this crazy journey partnered with anyone else. Thank you for always supporting my dreams, my ambitions, for actively listening, and for making me laugh. I'm funny—*you're funnier*—but I am the luckiest.

Alexander Stowe and James Spencer Jordan: It is the honor of my life to be your mommy. My heart explodes just by looking at your tiny faces. I love you the most.